WESTERN STATES

"Will tell you how to get there, what to see, and what camping and recreational facilities are available. Like our national parks themselves, a bargain for motorhomers!"
—*Motorhome Life* magazine

"The Scotts did a lot of traveling, and their first-hand research has paid off."
—*Kliatt Paperback Book Guides*

"Offers excellent encouragement for leaving the beaten paths of overcrowded tourist areas and getting back to America's treasures."
—*Hudson Valley* magazine

"The information the authors pass on in their book will help many travelers prepare a wonderful vacation."
—*Camp-orama*

"The Scotts have a winner here. . . . good basic information."
—*Pike County* (PA) *Dispatch*

"This information will enable the travelers to make the best use of . . . these beautiful, but often out of the way, areas of the National Park Service."
—*American Reference Books Annual*, 1988, Volume 19

Guide to the National Park Areas:

WESTERN STATES

Third Edition

by
David L. Scott and Kay W. Scott

A Voyager Book

The Globe Pequot Press

Chester, Connecticut

Text photographs and Facilities and Activities Chart reprinted courtesy of the National Park Service.

Cover Photo: Denali National Park, Alaska (Charles Kebs/Allstock)

Library of Congress Cataloging-in-Publication Data

Scott, David Logan, 1942–
    Guide to the national park areas.   Western states / by David L.
Scott and Kay W. Scott. — 3rd ed.
      p.   cm.
    "A Voyager book."
    ISBN 0-87106-194-5
    1. National parks and reserves—West (U.S.)—Guide-bboks.   2. West
(U.S.)—Description and travel—1981- —Guide-books.   I. Scott, Kay
Woelfel.   II. Title
E160.S45   1992
917.804'33—dc20
91-30130
CIP

♻ This text is printed on recycled paper.
Manufactured in the United States of America
Third Edition/First Printing

Contents

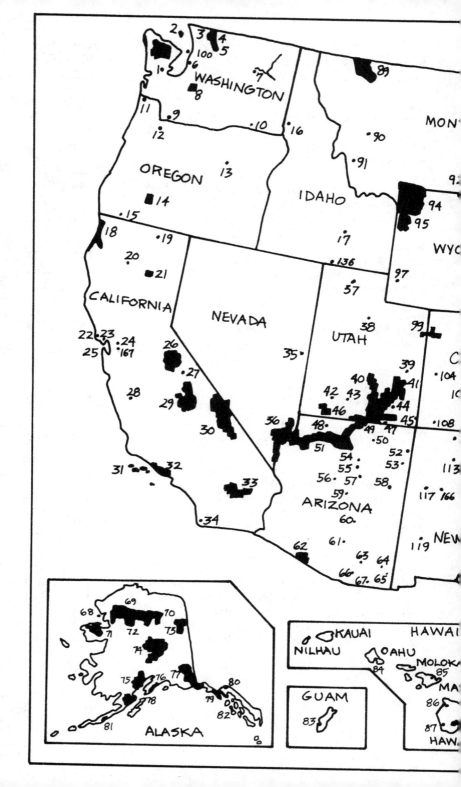

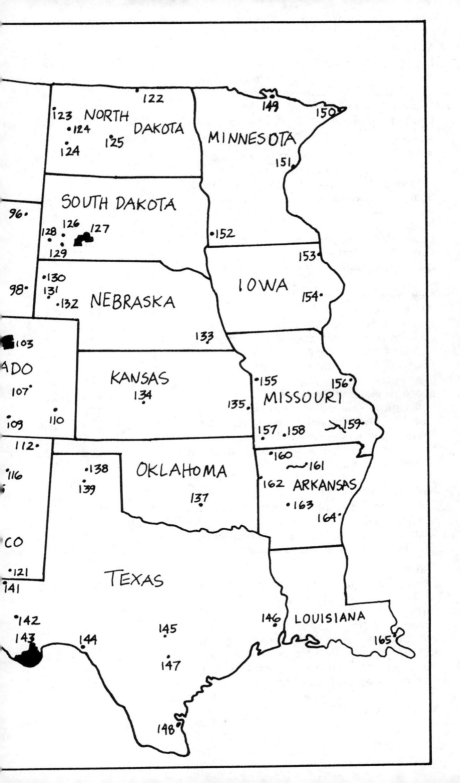

Introduction

As these books are written we have spent twenty summers touring the national parks. We have visited all the states and have seen nearly all of the parks and monuments administered by the National Park Service. We have spent a week hiking Canyonlands National Park and a day walking around Fort Laramie National Historic Site. We took a ferry to Klondike Gold Rush National Historical Park in Skagway, Alaska, and a plane to Hawaii Volcanoes National Park on the Big Island of Hawaii; and we drove the Alaska Highway to Denali National Park. We have seen the sights, walked the trails, talked with the park rangers, and visited with other campers. We have loved it all and in virtually every case would like to be able to go back and visit the same places again. In many instances that is exactly what we have done.

The idea for this series of books occurred to us about the fifth summer of our travels. Each time we headed in a new direction we found ourselves trying to decide which areas of the National Park Service to visit and, once there, attempting to determine which particular points of interest and activities held the most promise for our limited time. We discovered that we often delayed trips to areas we should have visited earlier and spent time driving to parks that were found to hold less interest for us. In addition, after arriving at a park we were often unsure of which campgrounds to use or what activities and facilities were available.

Our hope is that the contents of these books will assist others in avoiding these same pitfalls. We have tried to include enough information to allow readers to decide which parks to visit as well as how long to allow to adequately discover the major features of each park. For most areas we have tried to provide information on why the area was set aside, a summary of the history and/or geology of the area, activities for visitors, facilities such as availability of food service and overnight accommodations, campgrounds and their facilities, and possibilities for fishermen. In the limited space allotted to each area, we believe that this information is most useful to the majority of visitors.

For those who are new to visiting the national parks, a few introductory comments may be helpful. An increasing number of areas charge for entrance and nearly all areas charge for camping. Fees vary, and the most developed areas are typically the ones that charge the highest fees. These same developed areas are also generally the ones that are most crowded. If you plan to camp at Yosemite Valley, Bryce Canyon, or the South Rim of the Grand Canyon (among others), you had not only better take a little extra money, you also need to arrive early. In such cases it is often best to drive as close as possible the day before you intend to arrive. In the morning, rise with the sun and head for the campground of your choice. If you plan to visit a number of parks and monuments during the same calendar year, a Golden Eagle pass allows unlimited entries for a single fee. Free passes are available for senior citizens and the handicapped. All three passes are available to qualified individuals at any Park Service fee station.

For your own benefit, don't overlook the small park areas. Big, busy parks are out of necessity often set up to process visitors on a production-line basis, but many of the small, less frequently visited parks offer a real personal touch. We have been the only members on guided walks and experienced a wonderful campfire program with only six other visitors. These experiences frequently become the most memorable events of an entire trip.

The material in these books is believed to be accurate. However, the Park Service is constantly altering the areas under its jurisdiction, and no doubt there will be changes before you buy this book. Budget limitations have resulted in the closing of certain facilities as funds for maintenance and personnel have been cut or, at least, not kept up with visitation growth. In some cases, the closings are temporary; in other instances, they appear permanent. Regardless of the changes, we can assure you that you will enjoy yourself. The people are nice, the scenery is breathtaking, and the history is real.

We want to express our thanks to park personnel who took the time to read and correct the early drafts of this book. In addition, we appreciate the time that rangers have spent with us on our annual tours. We hope these books can help you have some of the wonderful times in our national parks that we have enjoyed.

David L. Scott
Kay W. Scott
Valdosta, Georgia

Alaska

The national parks of Alaska are immense. With a cumulative total of more than 50 million acres, or more than twenty times the area of Yellowstone, the fifteen Alaska parks include ten units authorized in 1978 that actually doubled the size of the National Park System. Many of the parks are so remote that it is necessary to charter transportation to reach them. Even for more developed and accessible parks such as Denali (formerly Mount McKinley), it is difficult to do much more than scratch the surface. Regardless, the parks of Alaska are superb, unspoiled areas and true national treasures.

Alaska may seem rather remote for most travelers, but transportation to the state is not difficult to arrange. For first-time visitors, tours involving air or a combination of air, bus, and ship are probably desirable, especially for those individuals with limited time. For visitors with more time who plan to drive, it is best to take the Alaska Marine Highway on one leg of the trip and drive the Alaska Highway on the other leg. The trip along the inland passage is spectacular. In addition, it is the only way to visit cities in the panhandle (as well as Sitka National Historical Park). Ferries leave Seattle, Washington, and Prince Rupert, British Columbia, regularly. For information on the ferry system, write Alaska Marine Highway, Pouch R, Juneau, AK 99811.

Another method of visiting Alaska is to drive the Alaska Highway from Dawson Creek, British Columbia, to Fairbanks, Alaska. Most of the highway is now paved, so the drive is not nearly as difficult and hard on a car or camper as it once was. In fact, any adventure-seeking traveler should try the drive at least one time. Anyone attempting the drive should pick up a copy of *Milepost* at a local bookstore (or write to Alaska Northwest Publishing Company, Box 4-EEE, Anchorage, AK 99509).

Because of the difficulty of reaching the ten parks brought into the system in 1978, we have allotted less space to each of these new undeveloped areas. Visitors contemplating a trip to one or more of these parks will need more information than we can hope to provide in a book such as this. Readers will find a brief description of each park

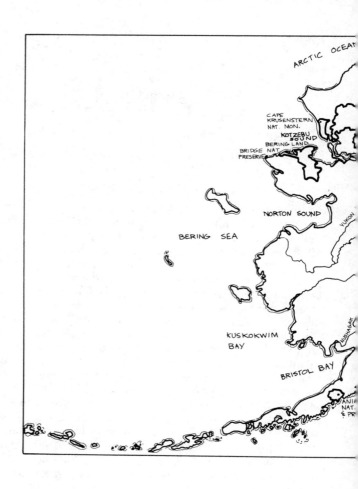

ARCTIC OCEAN

CAPE
KRUSENSTERN
NAT. MON.
KOTZEBUE
SOUND
BERING LAND
BRIDGE NAT.
PRESERVE

NORTON SOUND

YUKON

BERING SEA

KUSKOKWIM
BAY

NUSHAGAK

BRISTOL BAY

ANIA
NAT.
& PR

2 ALASKA

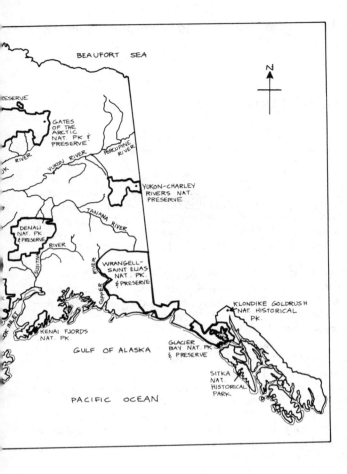

BEAUFORT SEA

RESERVE

GATES
OF THE
ARCTIC
NAT. PK &
PRESERVE

PORCUPINE RIVER

K RIVER

YUKON RIVER

YUKON-CHARLEY
RIVERS NAT.
PRESERVE

TANANA RIVER

DENALI
NAT. PK
& PRESERVE

RIVER

SUSITNA RIVER

WRANGELL-
SAINT ELIAS
NAT. PK.
& PRESERVE

COPPER RIVER

KLONDIKE GOLDRUSH
NAT. HISTORICAL
PK.

COOK INLET

KENAI FJORDS
NAT. PK.

GLACIER
BAY NAT. PK
& PRESERVE

GULF OF ALASKA

SITKA
NAT.
HISTORICAL
PARK

PACIFIC OCEAN

N

and an address to write to for more detailed information. Descriptions of the five older parks are more complete.

ANIAKCHAK NATIONAL MONUMENT AND PRESERVE
P.O. Box 7
King Salmon, AK 99613
(907) 246–3305

Aniakchak contains 615,000 acres, including the Aniakchak Caldera, which covers thirty square miles and is one of the great dry calderas of the world. The caldera, which remained undiscovered until 1922, has a floor of cinder cones, debris, and formations formed by volcanic activity, all surrounded by 2,000-foot walls. The volcano last erupted in 1933.

The Aniakchak National Wild River begins at Surprise Lake in the caldera, passes through The Gates in the caldera wall, and then flows 32 miles to Aniakchak Bay on the south coast of the peninsula. Over the first fifteen miles, the river drops sixty feet per mile as it runs through the tundra- and shrub-covered foothills. This rock-strewn section contains class 2 through class 4 whitewater. The final 17 miles are a much more gentle class 1. It is not uncommon for river runners to see brown bears, caribou, bald eagles, and, on the coast, sea otters.

Access to the park is difficult and expensive. Inclement weather often makes it impossible. Reeve Aleutian Airways flies between Anchorage and Port Heiden. From Port Heiden, a very difficult 10-mile hike is necessary to reach the monument. Access is also possible by charter plane from King Salmon or one of the towns in the lower Alaska Peninsula. The nearest lodging is in King Salmon.

BERING LAND BRIDGE NATIONAL PRESERVE
P.O. Box 220
Nome, AK 99762
(907) 443–2522

Bering Land Bridge, on the Seward Peninsula of northwest Alaska, is a remnant of a land bridge that connected North America with Asia more than 13,000 years ago. The bridge was once a migration route for people, animals, and plants, but is now covered by the Chukchi and Bering seas.

Most visitors arrive during milder summer months (40 to 60 degrees Fahrenheit) when plants burst into color and wildlife becomes active. Unfortunately, insects are also bad during this period. Fishing for char, grayling, and salmon is excellent. It is also possible to observe Eskimos in their native habitat.

Access to the isolated preserve is difficult. Airplanes may be chartered at Nome and Kotzebue. Nearest lodging and meals are in the same two towns.

CAPE KRUSENSTERN NATIONAL MONUMENT
P.O. Box 287
Kotzebue, AK 99752
(907) 442–3890

Cape Krusenstern National Monument, located in northwest Alaska, contains 560,000 acres and has been the site of seasonal marine mammal hunting by Eskimo peoples for more than 5,000 years. Eskimos continue to hunt seals along Cape Krusenstern's outermost beach.

The monument has no facilities of any kind and visitors generally come only to camp and backpack in this very primitive area. Insect repellent is recommended for summer months. A variety of wildlife inhabits the monument, including black and grizzly bears, caribou, lynx, moose, musk ox, and wolves. Offshore, polar bears, seals, walrus, and whales may be seen on occasion.

Access to Cape Krusenstern is by chartered boat or plane from Kotzebue. The monument, at its nearest point, is approximately 10 miles from the town, where lodging is available. Kotzebue also has small stores. The best areas for visiting are along the monument's west coast and in the hills running north to south through the park.

DENALI NATIONAL PARK AND PRESERVE
P.O. Box 9
Denali National Park, AK 99755
(907) 683–2294

Denali (formerly Mount McKinley) National Park and Preserve contains 6 million acres of mountains, alpine glaciers, and rolling lowlands with wide rivers. The park can be reached via State Highway 3, which connects Fairbanks and Anchorage. This road is open all year. Denali may also be reached during the summer

from Paxson via the gravel Denali Highway. The Alaska Railroad provides daily service from late May to mid- September and two trains per week during the remainder of the year. The ride from Anchorage (234 miles) requires five hours; the ride from Fairbanks (122 miles), two and a half hours. For information write Alaska Railroad Corporation Passenger Services, P.O. Box 107500, Anchorage, AK 99510 (Continental U.S. and Hawaii 800–544–0552; Anchorage 907–265–2494; Fairbanks 907–465–4155). Several companies provide business service in summer including Alaska-Denali Transit (907–276–6443); Alaska Sightseeing Tours (Anchorage 907–276–1305, Fairbanks 907–452–8518); and Grey Line of Alaska/Westours (Anchorage 907–277–5581, Fairbanks 907–456–7741). A 3,000-foot airstrip is maintained at the park for light aircraft.

Most of Denali is covered with alpine tundra, rock, and ice. Wet tundra contains dense brush and shrubs, while dry tundra along slopes and hills is characterized by small plants and wildflowers. The park contains a wide variety of wildlife, including more than 157 species of birds. Caribou, Dall sheep, moose, and grizzly bear are commonly seen in open spaces around the park.

Detailed information on the park and its visitor activities is available at the Visitor Access Center near the park entrance. During summer months, park personnel conduct sled-dog demonstrations at park headquarters, evening slide talks and conservation movies at the Denali National Park Hotel, walks from Denali National Park Hotel and Eielson Visitor Center, and campfire programs at major campgrounds.

An eighty-seven-mile park road parallels the Alaska Range from the park entrance to Wonder Lake. Only the first fourteen miles are paved, and the road is generally open from early June until mid-September. Driving beyond Savage River (mile 14) is restricted. At the closest point, the 20,320-foot summit of Mount McKinley is 27 miles from the road. Buses run regularly from the Riley Creek Information Center to Eielson Visitor Center and Wonder Lake. Scheduled stops are at Teklanika River, Polychrome Pass, Toklat River, Eielson Visitor Center, and Wonder Lake. A wildlife scenic tour leaves in the early morning and mid-afternoon from the hotel and goes to the central area of the park. The driver interprets park features, and tickets are sold at Denali National Park Hotel (907–683–2215). The park shuttles are a little rougher riding but the scenery is the same and you can't beat the price. Air tours are available through Denali Air (907–683–2261).

Facilities: A service station, located near the park entrance, has gasoline and oil. Pay showers are nearby. Groceries and supplies are available at the adjacent store, but no vehicle or food services are available after leaving the headquarters area. (Check your gas.) Denali National Park Hotel provides lodging and dining. Reservations should be made early and may be obtained by writing ARA Denali Park Resorts, P.O. Box 87, Denali National Park, AK 99755 (907–683–2215 summer, 907–276–7234 winter). Other lodging is available outside the park.

Camping: Improved campgrounds with flush toilets, tap water, tables, and grills are available at Riley Creek (102 spaces, dump station), Savage River (thirty-four spaces), and Wonder Lake (twenty spaces, tents only). Campgrounds with pit toilets are located at Igloo Creek (seven spaces), Morino (sixty spaces, walk-in), Sanctuary River (seven spaces), and Teklanika River (fifty spaces). Only Riley Creek is open year round.

Fishing: Fishing is generally poor because rivers are silty and ponds are shallow. Arctic grayling are caught in a few mountain streams, and lake trout are in Wonder Lake.

GATES OF THE ARCTIC NATIONAL PARK AND PRESERVE
P.O. Box 74680
Fairbanks, AK 99707
(907) 456–0281

Gates of the Arctic contains 8.5 million acres, including the heart of the spectacular Brooks Range. The entire park lies north of the Arctic Circle, where shrubs and tundra but few trees are found. Visitors will find long, magnificent valleys, rivers, lakes, and a few glaciers. Black bears, caribou, Dall sheep, eagles, grizzlies, marmot, moose, wolverines, and wolves are found in the park.

Most visitors to the park backpack the valleys or float the rivers. Rock and mountain climbing are available in the Arrigetch Peaks and Mt. Igikpak areas. Fishing resources include grayling, lake trout, and char.

Access to Gates of the Arctic is via scheduled airline from Fairbanks to Bettles or Anaktuvuk Pass. Charters are available from Bettles and Fairbanks. The nearest facilities are a general store in Bettles and Anaktuvuk Pass and a lodge in Bettles.

GLACIER BAY NATIONAL PARK AND PRESERVE
Gustavus, AK 99826
(907) 697–2231

Glacier Bay was established as a national monument in 1925 (changed to a national park in 1980) and contains nearly 3.3 million acres including some of the world's most impressive examples of tidewater glaciers. The park is located in southeastern Alaska, approximately 65 miles northwest of Juneau. No roads lead to the monument and entrance must be gained by either plane or boat. A small airport is located about 9 miles from park headquarters on Bartlett Cove.

Much of the snow that falls in the mountains around Glacier Bay does not completely melt away. As it grows deeper, it first changes into small grains of ice and gradually fuses into solid ice. When an icefield becomes sufficiently heavy, it begins flowing down the side of a mountain. The glacier's terminus in the lower and warmer region is where the rate of melting is equal to the rate of accumulation. Glaciers advance and retreat as an area's climate is altered.

The glaciers that can be seen in the monument today are the remains of what was formed during the "little ice age" about 4,000 years ago. The glaciers reached maximum size around 1750 before a milder climate brought about a general melting. When Captain George Vancouver sailed through Icy Strait in 1794, Glacier Bay was little more than a huge wall of ice extending more than one hundred miles to the north. By 1916, the Grand Pacific Glacier was sixty-five miles from the mouth of Glacier Bay. Today glaciers continue to retreat on the bay's east and southwest sides. However, glaciers on the west side stabilized by 1929 and many are even growing again. The park includes sixteen tidewater glaciers (glaciers whose snouts reach tidal waters) including a dozen that calve icebergs into Glacier Bay.

Glacier Bay National Park is rich in both plant and animal life. Brown and black bears, mountain goats, seals, humpback whales, and porpoises are frequently seen. More than 200 species of birds are here.

Park rangers are in the park year round with headquarters at Bartlett Cove, 7 miles north of the mouth of Glacier Bay on the east shore. Naturalists lead hikes, and a concessioner-operated tour boat (eight to nine hours) leaves from the lodge. Overnight boat trips are also available at the lodge. The park is best seen by boat. A permit is required for entry into the park during the months of June, July, and August. Applications are available from the park superintendent. Navigating the bay presents special problems and appropriate precautions should be observed. One-day tours by boat are available from Glacier Bay Lodge at Bartlett Cove.

Facilities: Glacier Bay Lodge provides rooms and meals from May 23 to mid-September. For reservations write Glacier Bay Lodge, Gustavus, AK 99826 in summer and 520 Pike Street, Suite 1610, Seattle, WA 98101 in winter (800–622–2042 for reservations). Docking facilities, gasoline, and #2 diesel fuel are available at Bartlett Cove. No other public facilities for boats are located within the park.

Camping: A campground (thirty-five spaces) at Bartlett Cove has bearproof food caches, fire pits, and firewood. Camping supplies and food are available in Juneau.

Fishing: Silver and king salmon can be caught in the park. Halibut are found nearly anywhere in the park's salt water other than the upper part of the bay. Cutthroat and Dolly Varden trout are in lakes and streams in the lower bay. An Alaska fishing license is required.

KATMAI NATIONAL PARK AND PRESERVE
P.O. Box 7
King Salmon, AK 99613
(907) 246–3305

Katmai National Park and Preserve occupies 4.1 million acres of rugged wilderness on the Alaska Peninsula. The interior wilderness of forests and lakes is bounded on the east by one hundred miles of ocean bays, fjords, and lagoons. Katmai has no rail or road approaches and there is no commercial boat service to any part of the park. Scheduled jets fly to King Salmon Airport on the Bristol Bay side of the peninsula. Daily commercial flights connect King Salmon and Brooks Lodge from June through Labor Day. Private float planes can be chartered for flights to scenic lakes within Katmai.

In 1912, the area that is now contained within the park was the location of one of the greatest volcanic eruptions in history. Novarupta Volcano sent forth an explosion of pumice and white-hot ash. Within a few hours two and a half cubic miles of ash had flowed into the Ukak River valley and forty square miles of the valley floor were covered to depths as great as 700 feet. Hot gases and water vapor percolating up through the ash as it settled gave rise to the name Valley of Ten Thousand Smokes. At the same time or soon after Novarupta was erupting, Mount Katmai, six miles to the east, was collapsing. A conduit under Mount Katmai allowed a transfer of magma and resulted in the loss of support for the mountain's top.

Katmai National Park and Preserve contains a wide variety of plant and animal life. Woodlands of spruce, poplar, and birch are interspersed with alder thickets, marshes, and grassland on the southern and western parts of the mountains. At higher elevations only plants typical of the Arctic tundra can survive the cold, high winds, and short growing season. Brown bears and moose are fairly common, and bald eagles are seen frequently. The Steller sea lion and hair seal are commonly observed on rock outcroppings. Much of the wildlife in the park at any one time depends on the runs of migrating salmon.

Park rangers give illustrated evening talks at Brooks Camp, and guided nature walks are conducted from the same location. A ¾-mile trail leads to Brooks Falls, where there is an elevated platform from which visitors can, at certain times of the summer, watch brown bears try to catch salmon as the fish jump the falls. A concessioner-operated scenic bus tour (23 miles one way) to the Valley of Ten Thousand Smokes begins at the lodge. Good views of the valley and surrounding mountains may be enjoyed from the shelter located at the end of the trip. In addition, a short trail from the Brooks River Ranger Station leads to the site of a prehistoric dwelling. A pit house built around A.D. 1300 has been excavated and restored for public inspection.

Facilities: A concessioner provides accommodations and services at four points in the park. Brooks Camp has modern cabins with plumbing and family-type meals. Fishing equipment and canoes may be rented, and limited camping and food supplies are sold. Guide service is available. Overnight packages are also available for Grosvernor Camp, Kulik Lodge, and Nonvianuk Camp. A privately owned lodge is operated at Enchanted Lake. In addition, there are a number of lodges outside of the park that cater to park visitors. Information may be obtained by writing to park headquarters.

Camping: A single campground (twenty-one spaces) at Brooks River is open year round. Piped-in treated water is provided from early June through early September. The camp contains pit toilets, weather shelters, and elevated food caches. It is a park regulation that campers' food must be stored in the elevated caches to secure it from the bears. Meals and showers can be purchased at Brooks Lodge. Visitors may camp anywhere in the park and preserve upon receiving a backcountry permit from a park ranger.

Fishing: Rainbow and lake trout, Dolly Varden, grayling, northern pike, and sockeye salmon are plentiful. An Alaska fishing license is required, and fishing in any way other than with hook and line (with rod or line held in hand) is not allowed. Coho, chinook, and pink salmon are occasionally seen in the streams, and one of the most magnificent sights is that of the sockeye salmon fighting upstream to their spawning ground. Brooks River is a fly-fishing-only river (catch-and-release for rainbow trout). Any salmon spawning stream is likely to have a number of brown bears in attendance. Park rangers can provide information on how to minimize conflicts with bears while fishing.

KENAI FJORDS NATIONAL PARK
P.O. Box 1727
Seward, AK 99664
(907) 224–3175

Kenai Fjords' 650,000 acres on the Kenai Peninsula include the 300-square-mile Harding Icefield, a remnant of a mass that once covered half of Alaska and currently radiates thirty-six named glacial arms. In addition to long glaciated valleys and mountain peaks, the peninsulas support rain forests. Wildlife includes bald eagles, sea lions, seals, whales, sea otters, porpoises, and puffins.

Park headquarters and a visitor center are in Seward, which can be reached by car from Anchorage. Commercial air and bus services are available between Anchorage and Seward. Just north of Seward is Exit Glacier, the most accessible section of the park, which is reached by a gravel road and short walk. Ranger-conducted activities take place here during the summer. Boat and air charters to the fjords are available.

KLONDIKE GOLD RUSH NATIONAL HISTORICAL PARK
P.O. Box 517
Skagway, AK 99840
(907) 983–2921

Klondike Gold Rush National Historical Park contains more than 13,000 acres and was established in 1976 to commemorate the 1898 Klondike gold rush. The park's main unit is located in the Skagway area of the Alaska panhandle. Access is via the Alaska Marine Highway from Bellingham, Washington or Prince Rupert, or by driving south approximately 100 miles on State Highways 2 and 8 from the Alaska Highway. A second unit of this park is in Seattle, and is listed under the Washington section of this book.

The Klondike gold rush went into high gear after the Seattle arrival of the steamer Portland with two tons of gold aboard. The event that started this flood of people into the wilderness area of Canada's Yukon River was a large gold strike in August 1896 on Rabbit Creek by two Indians and a white man. When other prospectors saw the gold these three brought to the settlement of Fortymile, they headed into the same area to make their own claims. It was this group that arrived in Seattle during the summer of 1897. Later that year the infusion of people created the town of Dawson at the confluence of the Yukon and Klondike rivers.

As word of the riches spread, people began a mass migration to the area. One entry to Dawson was by way of the White Pass route through the Coastal Range. Here, the city of Skagway quickly grew to a population of 10,000. A second route was to sail to Dyea and then use the less-swampy Chilkoot Pass. This popular route included three aerial tramways that helped Dyea's permanent residents number 3,500 in the summer of 1898. About this same time, construction of a narrow-gauge railroad began over the White Pass route. This route eventually captured most of the traffic, so that Dyea soon turned into a ghost town. The two other routes to Dawson were by ship to St. Michael, then by steamboat up the Yukon River; and the all-Canadian overland route from Edmonton. The first of these was very expensive and the second was backbreaking.

A visitor center in the old White Pass and Yukon Railway depot at Broadway and Second Avenue contains displays and artifacts from the gold rush. The Park Service provides a short slide presentation and a film, talks, and guided walks through the town. The historical district with boardwalks and false-front buildings retains much of the flavor of the gold-rush days.

Dyea, the gateway to Chilkoot Pass, is about nine miles from Skagway via a dirt road. The drive is beautiful. Most of the Dyea buildings were torn down for use as firewood or as materials for buildings in Skagway. All that remains now are scattered remains of foundations and a half-mile row of piling stubs from the old dock. The town fell into disuse after an 1898 avalanche and the completion of the railroad from Skagway in February 1899. Visitors may hike the old thirty-three-mile Chilkoot Trail (three to five days) to Lake Bennett. The trail offers historic ruins and artifacts along the way.

Facilities: Lodging and food services are not provided by the Park Service, but both are available in downtown Skagway. No facilities are found in Dyea.
Camping: A Park Service campground with tables and pit toilets (no water) is located in Dyea, and a city campground is in Skagway. The Dyea site is much nicer.
Fishing: Fishing is available at both Skagway and Dyea.

KOBUK VALLEY NATIONAL PARK
P.O. Box 287
Kotzebue, AK 99752
(907) 442–3890

Kobuk Valley National Park contains approximately 1.75 million acres in northwestern Alaska above the Arctic Circle. The park lies along the valley surrounding the Kobuk River, and includes a boreal forest, sand dunes, and archeological sites from 10,000 years of human occupation. Wildlife includes caribou, grizzly and black bears, lynx, moose, and wolves. Fishermen will find arctic char, grayling, salmon, and sheepfish.

Access to the park is via chartered aircraft from Ambler, Kiana, and Kotzebue or by chartered boat from Ambler or Kiana. A few visitors backpack in from these two villages. There are no facilities within the park. Lodging is available in Kiana and Kotzebue. Ambler, Kiana, and Kotzebue have small stores with staples.

LAKE CLARK NATIONAL PARK AND PRESERVE
4230 University Drive, Suite 331
Anchorage, AK 99508
(907) 271–3751

Lake Clark National Park and Preserve contains more than 4.5 million acres in the heart of the Chigmit Mountains, where the Alaska and Aleutian ranges join. The park lies along the western shore of Cook Inlet and contains mountain peaks, glaciers, two active volcanoes, and more than twenty glacially carved lakes. Three wild rivers are located here. Activities center around backpacking, river running, and fishing. Rainbow trout, northern pike, arctic grayling, Dolly Varden, and five species of salmon inhabit streams in the park.

Access to Lake Clark National Park is by chartered aircraft from Anchorage, Kenai, or Homer. The trip takes approximately one to two hours.

NOATAK NATIONAL PRESERVE
P.O. Box 287
Kotzebue, AK 99752
(907) 442–3890

Noatak National Preserve contains more than 6.5 million acres, including the largest untouched river basin in the United States. The Noatak River flows more than 425 miles carrying Mount Igikpak's glacial melt to Kotzebue Sound through boreal forest and treeless tundra.

There are no Park Service facilities within the preserve. Most visitors enter to canoe or kayak the Noatak or to backpack in the foothills. A variety of wildlife including bears, caribou, and wolves inhabit the park. Fish include arctic char, grayling, whitefish, and several species of salmon.

Access is by chartered plane or boat from Kotzebue or by air charter from Bettles. Kotzebue may be reached by commercial flights from either Anchorage or Fairbanks.

SITKA NATIONAL HISTORICAL PARK
P.O. Box 738
Sitka, AK 99835
(907) 747–6281

Sitka National Historical Park contains 107 acres. It was set aside as a federal reserve in 1890 and designated a national monument in 1910 to commemorate the site of the last major Tlingit Indian resistance to Russian colonization. The park is located in the town of Sitka in Alaska's southeastern panhandle. Sitka is reached by scheduled airline or by boat. The town is a stop on the Alaska Marine Highway, but the park is 7 miles from the ferry terminal.

An 1804 battle between the Russians and the Tlingit Indians resulted in an important "victory" for the Russians (the Tlingit claim the Russians won by default because of a Tlingit withdrawal caused by a lack of ammunition), who strengthened their hold on the northwest coast of the American continent. The Russians were able to continue using the area as an important source for furs and established Sitka as the busiest port in the North Pacific. Although the Tlingit lost the battle and their homes and culture, they returned after several years and settled just outside the Russian stockade. In 1806, Sitka became the capital of

Russian America. In 1867, the Russians sold their overseas empire for $7.2 million, and Alaska became an American possession.

The park's visitor center includes exhibits, native craft workshops, and an audio-visual room for slide presentations and movies. Exhibits include displays of Tlingit history and culture. A self-guiding trail begins behind the visitor center and leads into an Alaskan forest to the 1804 battleground and fort site. Twenty-seven totem poles are located in the park. The visitor center can supply visitors with a map of a walking tour of Sitka. The town is especially interesting and the tour is a must.

A second section of the park, the 1842 Russian Bishop's house, is one-quarter mile from the visitor center on Lincoln Street. The Park Service completed a restoration of this historically important building in 1988. The first floor contains exhibits about Russian America, the Russian American Company, and the efforts of the Russian Orthodox Church in Alaska. The second floor is refurnished to its 1842–53 appearance.

Facilities: A picnic area with tables and a shelter is located near the impressive visitor center. Restrooms and drinking water are available inside the building. The park is within walking distance of the town of Sitka where complete facilities are available.

Camping: No camping is available at the park, but a free U.S. Forest Service campground with tables and pit toilets is a short distance north of the ferry terminal on Halibut Point Road.

Fishing: The park is surrounded by Indian River and Sitka Sound where saltwater fishing is available with an Alaska license.

WRANGELL–ST. ELIAS NATIONAL PARK AND PRESERVE
P.O. Box 29
Glenallen, AK 99588
(907) 822–5234

Wrangell–St. Elias is the largest park area in the National Park System, with 13 million acres of mountains, remote valleys, wild rivers, and coastal beaches. The park has America's second-highest mountain, 18,000-foot Mt. St. Elias, and North America's largest collection of peaks above 16,000 feet in an area where three mountain ranges converge. More than one hundred glaciers exist in a landscape dominated by mountains and snowfields.

Visitors to the park engage in backpacking, camping, cross-country skiing, mountain climbing, and river running. Summers are often cloudy with rain although clear, relatively hot days occur in July.

Rustic overnight accommodations, many without electricity and plumbing, are available in Chisana, Kennecott, McCarthy, Ptarmigan Lake Lodge, Solo Creek, and Sportsman's Paradise Lodge. Major fish camps and guide cabins are on Copper Lake in the north and Ptarmigan Lake in the northeast. Modern motels and cabins are in Glenallen and along the Richardson Highway and Tok cutoff.

Wrangell–St. Elias is one of the few new Alaska parks with road access. A 61-mile road follows an old railroad route from the community of Chitina to McCarthy. In the northern section of the park, a secondary road extends from Slana to the privately owned mining community of Nabesna.

YUKON–CHARLEY RIVERS NATIONAL PRESERVE
Box 167
Eagle, AK 99738
(907) 547–2233

Yukon–Charley contains 2.5 million acres along the Canadian border in central Alaska. The park incorporates all of the eighty- eight-mile Charley River and 115 miles of the 1,800-mile Yukon River, including old cabins and relics of the gold rush.

The primary activity in the preserve is floating the rivers. The Yukon, with its swift current, is the most popular. It takes approximately a week to float between Eagle, at the preserve's upper end, and Circle, at the lower end. The Charley is more difficult and requires significant skill. Eagle and Circle both provide interesting sights for visitors. Fishing for grayling, northern pike, and whitefish is available.

Access to the preserve is by way of Eagle and Circle. Both are served by scheduled air taxis and both may be reached via a gravel road from the Alaska Highway. There are no roads within the park. Both Eagle and Circle offer food service, gas, groceries, campgrounds, and limited lodging. The preserve maintains an information center in Eagle to assist visitors.

Arizona

CANYON DE CHELLY NATIONAL MONUMENT
P.O. Box 588
Chinle, AZ 86503
(602) 674–5436

Canyon de Chelly (pronounced "d' Shay") National Monument contains 83,000 acres. It was authorized as part of the National Park System in 1931 to preserve ruins of Indian villages built in steep-walled canyons between A.D. 350 and 1300. The monument is located in northeastern Arizona, approximately 85 miles northwest of Gallup, New Mexico, near Chinle, Arizona. Monument headquarters is 2 miles east of U.S. 191. Highway 7, connecting South Rim Drive with Fort Defiance, is dirt between the monument boundary and the town of Sawmill. It is virtually impassable during bad weather. See the area map under Hubbell Trading Post National Historic Site.

Following an uplift of the Defiance Formation, Rio de Chelly cut through sandstone and has left canyon walls in Canyon de Chelly thirty to 1,000 feet high. Typically, the streams of this region are dry except during the rainy seasons and during the spring thaw of mountain snow.

The canyons contain the ruins of several hundred prehistoric Anasazi villages, most of which were built between A.D. 350 and 1300. The earliest known Indians lived in pithouses, grew crops of maize and squash, and made intricate baskets. Centuries later, the Anasazi began making pottery and constructed rectangular houses of stone masonry above the canyon walls. Subsequent to A.D. 700, the canyon dwellers (now known as Pueblos) built most of the large cliff houses between A.D. 1100 and 1300.

During the 1200s, a long drought forced occupants of the Four Corners region to abandon their homes and scatter throughout the

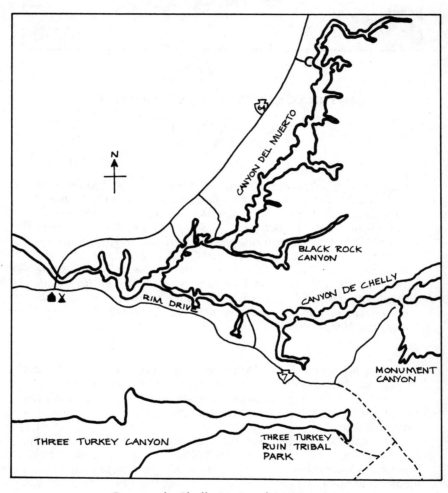

Canyon de Chelly National Monument

Southwest. In later years, the canyons of the Rio de Chelly were occupied sporadically by the Hopi, a Pueblo group culturally related to the Anasazi, and later, the Navajo, who continue to inhabit Canyon de Chelly today. The aggressive Navajo began to move into this area around 1700. Over the next 150 years, they battled the Spanish, and later, the U.S. Army. Over 8,000 Navajos were forced to resettle in eastern New Mexico, but the experiment failed and they returned to their homeland after only four years.

Except for a trail to White House Ruin, travel in the canyons is permitted only with a park ranger or other authorized guide. The park ranger on duty at the visitor center will help to arrange guides for those interested in hikes or four-wheel-drive vehicle trips. Horseback-riding tours are also available. Thunderbird Lodge near monument headquarters offers group trips to the canyon floors.

The first order of business upon entering the monument should be to stop at the visitor center, where exhibits help explain the history of the canyon and the cultures of its inhabitants. A Navajo silversmith is sometimes in the center demonstrating crafts. Here you may also obtain guide books for driving both the north and south rims. These books are quite helpful in interpreting the drives. From Memorial Day through Labor Day talks are presented at the visitor center and guided walks begin at various places around the monument. During the summer season, nightly campfire programs are provided in the National Park Service campground.

Twenty-two-mile Rim Drive, along the south rim of Canyon de Chelly, provides access to seven scenic overlook points and the trailhead of White House Trail. Even though the 500-foot climb back up the trail from White House Ruin (2½ miles, one and a half to two hours, round trip) will leave you breathless, the hike is worthwhile. Not only does it afford a close viewpoint of the impressive ruin and some pictographs, but unless you take a guided trip this will be your only chance to see this beautiful canyon from its floor. Spider Rock, an 800-foot sandstone spire, can be viewed from an overlook at the junction of Canyon de Chelly and Monument Canyon. Mummy Cave Ruin, in Canyon del Muerto, is one of the larger ruins and includes a three-story tower house. Pictographs may be seen at many places in the canyons with some dating from Prehistoric Basketmaker and Pueblo periods.

Facilities: Food, lodging, gifts, and tours are available at the Thunderbird Lodge near the monument entrance. Reservations and information may be obtained by writing Thunderbird Lodge, Box 548, Chinle, AZ 86503 (602–674–5841). Three miles away in Chinle, visitors will find a motel, a grocery, and a cafe.

Camping: Cottonwood Campground (104 spaces), set in a grove of cottonwood trees, is located near the park entrance. The campground is open year round and contains grills, tables, and, during the summer season, water and flush toilets. Three group camps are available by reservation only. Recreational vehicles and trailers are not permitted in the group camping sites. There is no camping fee at Cottonwood. No camping is permitted in the canyons.

Fishing: No fishing is available in Canyon de Chelly National Monument. Fishing for trout is permitted in Wheatfields Lake near where the North Rim Drive intersects Highway 12. A tribal license is required.

CASA GRANDE RUINS NATIONAL MONUMENT
P.O. Box 518
Coolidge, AZ 85228
(602) 723–3172

Casa Grande Ruins National Monument contains 472 acres. It was designated a national monument in 1892 to preserve ruins of a massive three-story building constructed by Indian farmers more than 600 years ago. The monument is about midway between Phoenix and Tucson, 1 mile north of the town of Coolidge on Arizona Highway 87.

Hohokam Indians began farming the Gila Valley more than 2,000 years ago by use of more than 600 miles of irrigation canals. Crops of cotton, corn, beans, and squash were grown with the use of canals measuring from two to four feet wide and two feet deep.

Approximately 600 years ago Indian farmers in the valley constructed the three-story Casa Grande. The building was given its Spanish name (meaning "Big House") by the Jesuit priest Father Kino when he discovered it in 1694. The Casa Grande is similar to structures found in Mexico and is unlike most Hohokam buildings. The purpose of the structure is uncertain, but recent research indicates it may have been used as a ceremonial building. Casa Grande was probably built around the mid-1300s and used for a relatively short period. This type of village in the Gila Valley had generally been abandoned by the mid-1400s.

The monument is open from 7:00 A.M. to 6:00 P.M. throughout the year although summer temperatures are very hot. The visitor center contains a collection of artifacts made and used by the Hohokam. Park rangers in the visitor center answer questions and conduct periodic tours. In addition, a self-guiding trail leads visitors through the ruins. Heaviest visitation occurs between Thanksgiving and Easter.

Facilities: Lodging and food service are not available in the monument but several restaurants and motels are located in Coolidge. A picnic area with tables, water, and shade is available at the monument. Flush toilets and drinking water are located in the visitor center.

Camping: No camping is permitted at the monument. Two mobile home parks in Coolidge accept overnighters.

Fishing: No fishing is available at Casa Grande Ruins National Monument.

CHIRICAHUA NATIONAL MONUMENT
Dos Cabezas Route
Box 6500
Willcox, AZ 85643
(602) 824–3560

Chiricahua National Monument contains 11,985 acres (including 10,290 acres of wilderness) and was established in 1924 in order to preserve varied rock formations created by volcanic activity millions of years ago. The monument is located in southeastern Arizona, 36 miles southeast of Willcox, Arizona, off State Highway 186.

An area of pinnacles and balanced rocks, Chiricahua stands out from the surrounding dry grasslands. The monument's range in elevation of 5,160 to 7,825 feet results in many species of shrubs and trees. The shady glens are alive with various types of birds. Arizona white-tailed deer are frequently seen and dense vegetation grows in the shaded canyon bottoms and on the north slopes at higher elevations. Temperatures are generally moderate with a January mean of 40 degrees Fahrenheit and a July mean of 74 degrees Fahrenheit. Annual precipitation is eighteen inches and falls mostly in July and August. Light snows fall during winter months.

The area's present geological features began forming millions of years ago when the region was subject to extensive volcanic activity. Explosions covered the area with many layers of volcanic ash. Later, the earth's crust was slowly lifted, and cracks developed in the land. These gradually grew larger as water and winds used the openings to work at erosion.

A visitor center is two miles inside the park's west entrance. It contains exhibits describing the area's history and geography. Rangers are present to answer visitors' questions. A single six-mile paved road

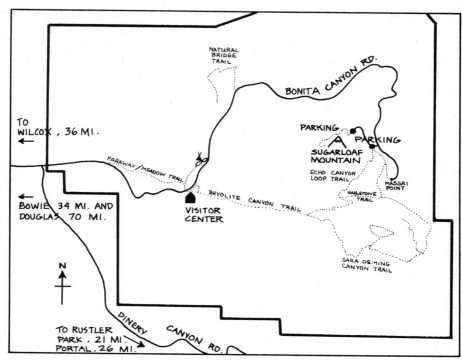

Chiricahua National Monument

winds through the monument, ending at Massai Point. The turn at the road's end provides an excellent view of the monument.

More than seventeen miles of trails are provided for hikers. A self-guided loop trail, located at Massai Point, takes about thirty minutes to walk. Features along the trail include a balanced rock and a lookout point with view finder. One of the highest points in the monument can be reached via the one-mile Sugarloaf Trail, which begins at the end of a side road. Round-trip walking time is one and one-third hours. Rhyolite Canyon Nature Trail is a self-guided loop that begins at the visitor center parking area. Walking time is approximately twenty minutes. One of the most scenic hikes is a three-and-a-half-mile loop trail through Echo Canyon and Echo Park. Round-trip time is two hours. A longer hike (four to five hours round trip) leads to Big Balanced Rock and Punch and Judy.

Facilities: No overnight accommodations or food services are available within the monument. Motels, restaurants, groceries, and gasoline are available at Willcox. Modern restrooms and drinking water are located at the visitor center and the campground. Picnic facilities are also available in the campground.

Camping: A single campground (twenty-six spaces) is located one- half mile from monument headquarters in Bonita Canyon. Flush toilets, drinking water, tables, and grills are available, and the campground is open all year. The monument is nearly surrounded by Coronado National Forest, where a dozen U.S. Forest Service campgrounds are located.

Fishing: No fishing is available within the monument. At the south end of the Chiricahua Mountains, 35 miles south of the monument, Rucker Lake offers fishing with a Forest Service campground nearby.

CORONADO NATIONAL MEMORIAL
Route 2, Box 126
Hereford, AZ 85613
(602) 366–5515

Coronado National Memorial contains 4,674 acres. It was established as a national memorial in 1952 to commemorate the Hispanic heritage and initial European exploration of the American Southwest. The memorial is located in southeastern Arizona on the Mexican border. It is 30 miles west of Bisbee, Arizona, and 22 miles south of Sierra Vista, Arizona, on State Highway 92.

Coronado National Memorial overlooks the valley through which Francisco Vasquez de Coronado first entered the present United States. The Coronado expedition was viewed as a failure at the time it was completed because no riches were discovered. Perhaps more important, however, the explorers brought back information about both the land and the people, and opened the way for subsequent Spanish explorations and colonization.

The Coronado expedition began from Compostela, Mexico, in February 1540, with a party of approximately 1,100 Spanish soldiers and Mexican-Indian allies. The expedition moved north and east before crossing New Mexico through present-day Albuquerque. By spring 1541, the group had crossed through northern Texas, the Oklahoma panhandle, and into central Kansas. Disillusioned with the discoveries, Coronado returned to Mexico in the spring of 1542.

Memorial headquarters contains a visitor center and museum, and is located near the east entrance, 5 miles west of Arizona 92. It is open daily from 8:00 A.M. to 5:00 P.M. Montezuma Pass, a 3-mile scenic road, provides access to viewpoints and to the beginning of a

Coronado National Memorial

foot trail that leads to Coronado Peak. From this point the visitor has a panoramic view of the country through which Coronado and his party marched. The 3-mile Joe's Canyon Trail leads from the Coronado Peak Trail to the headquarters and picnic area. The park's climate is relatively warm (high 80s) and rainy during summer months, and mild during winter (low 30s).

Facilities: No food service or lodging is available in the memorial. The nearest places for meals and overnight accommodations are Bisbee, thirty miles to the east, and Sierra Vista, twenty-two miles north. A picnic area near the visitor center contains tables and grills. Restrooms and water are also available at the visitor center.

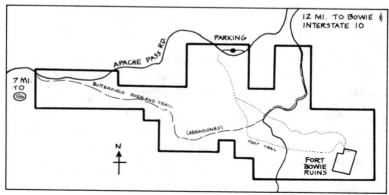

Fort Bowie National Historic Site

Camping: No camping is available within the park. A U.S. Forest Service campground is located at Parker Canyon Lake, eighteen miles west of the memorial. In addition, open camping is permitted in Coronado National Forest, which surrounds the memorial to the north and west.

Fishing: No fishing is available at Coronado National Memorial.

FORT BOWIE NATIONAL HISTORIC SITE
P.O. Box 158
Bowie, AZ 85605
(602) 847–2500

Fort Bowie National Historic Site was authorized by Congress in 1964 to preserve the Apache Pass Stage Station, Apache Spring, the Fort Bowie complex, and a portion of the Butterfield Overland Mail Route. The 1,000-acre park is 12 miles south of Interstate 10 at Bowie on a graded dirt road. From Willcox, also on Interstate 10, Fort Bowie is 22 miles southeast on Arizona Highway 186 and then east on a graded dirt road to Apache Pass. The major portion of the historic site can be reached only by a 1½-mile foot trail that begins at a parking area on Apache Pass Road.

The spring located at Apache Pass has drawn a procession of Indians, emigrants, prospectors, and soldiers. Apaches made this their home-land sometime around the sixteenth century but were unable to protect it during the westward expansion of the nineteenth century. In 1857, the Postmaster-General awarded an overland mail contract to John Butterfield, and the Apache Pass Station was constructed in 1858 as a stop along the St. Louis to San Francisco route.

After years of relative peace between Apaches and the white man, the early 1860s saw sporadic fighting between the Indians and the settlers and military. In 1862, Fort Bowie was built in order to keep Apache Pass open to white travelers. Peace was made by Cochise and his people in 1872. The Apaches were given a reservation of about 3,000 square miles, but two years later Cochise died, and soon hostilities resumed under the leadership of Geronimo and other war leaders. After years of intense fighting, a final surrender in 1886 resulted in the remaining Indians being shipped to forts in Florida and later, Alabama. Fort Bowie was officially abandoned on October 17, 1894.

A moderately strenuous, 1.5-mile foot trail to the fort ruins begins at the parking lot. The trail passes a number of historic features, and trail guide booklets are available just beyond the trailhead. Access to the fort ruins is by the trail only. Handicap access is available by appointment, by phone or mail. A park ranger is normally on duty at the small ranger station-museum.

Facilities: There are no lodging or eating facilities within the park. Overnight accommodations and food are available in either Willcox or Bowie. Drinking water and restrooms are located at the ranger station near the ruins of the fort.

Camping: No camping is permitted within the park, but a campground is located at Chiricahua National Monument, twenty-five miles southwest of Fort Bowie. Private campgrounds are in Bowie and Willcox.

Fishing: No fishing is available at Fort Bowie National Historic Site.

GLEN CANYON NATIONAL RECREATION AREA
P.O. Box 1507
Page, AZ 86040
(602) 645–2471

Glen Canyon National Recreation Area contains 1.25 million acres (most of which are in Utah). It is the result of the Glen Canyon Dam built by the Bureau of Reclamation between 1956 and 1964. Lake Powell, formed from the Colorado River in back of the dam, is 186 miles long with nearly 2,000 miles of shoreline. The southern portion of the park—the most accessible part—is intersected by U.S. 89 through Page, Arizona. Page is 129 miles east of Zion National Park and 132 miles north of Flagstaff. The park also may be crossed at Hite Crossing via Utah Highway 95, and via Utah Highway 276, which is connected by a ferry (cars and people), that runs from Halls Crossing to Bullfrog and back six times per day during the summer season and four times per day during the winter.

The name Glen Canyon was given to a long stretch of the Colorado River by John Wesley Powell, who led exploration trips through the canyons in 1869 and 1871. Around 1900, the area attracted prospectors looking for gold, but the particles were too fine to be economically recovered. The Navajo Reservation borders to the south of Glen Canyon. Navajos were latecomers to the area, arriving in the 1860s.

Prior to that time, prehistoric Anasazi Indians lived in the region. Ruins of these Indians exist throughout the park.

The canyons themselves are the result of a general uplifting of the region that occurred about 60 million years ago. As the uplift progressed, streams of the ancient, low-lying Colorado Basin ran faster, cutting the deep scars that remain today.

Most of the activities at Glen Canyon National Recreation Area are water-related. These include boating, fishing, and water skiing. A self-guided tour through the dam and visitor center is available from 8:00 A.M. to 4:00 P.M. daily in winter months, and from 7:00 A.M. to

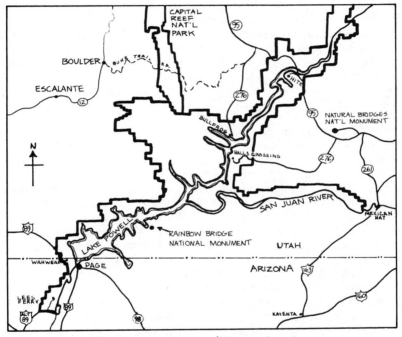

Glen Canyon National Recreation Area

6:00 P.M. in the summer months. Below the dam, U.S. Highway 89A leads to Lees Ferry, roadside exhibits, and relics of the gold mining days. U.S. 89 north leads to Kanab, Utah, where many western movies have been filmed. Numerous locations, including the beach at Wahweap, are good for swimming.

Facilities: All concession facilities listed are available through ARA Lake Powell Resorts and Marinas, 2916 North 35th Avenue, Suite 8, Phoenix, AZ 85017 (800–528–6154; 602–278–8888 in Phoenix).

Bullfrog: Ranger station, launching ramp, campground, and picnic area. Concessioner-operated lodging, service station, restaurant, camp store, marina, and trailer village with hookups. Write Bullfrog Resort and Marina, P.O. Box 4055, Bullfrog, Lake Powell, UT 84533 (801–684–2233).

Dangling Rope Floating Marina: Ranger station, restrooms, emergency communications. Concessioner-operated boat fuel service and camp supplies. Reached only by boat.

Halls Crossing: Ranger station, launching ramp and campground with ranger on duty. Concessioner-operated lodging, boat rental, marina, boat excursions, boating and camping supplies, and trailer village with hookups. Write Halls Crossing Marina, P.O. Box 5101-Halls, Lake Powell, UT 84533 (801–684–2261).

Hite: Ranger station, concessioner-operated boat rental, marina, camp store, service station, and small primitive camping facilities. Write Hite Marina, Inc., Box 1, Hanksville, UT 84734 (800–528–6154 outside Arizona; 602–278–8888 in Arizona).

Lees Ferry: Ranger station, launching ramp, and campground. A store, motel, restaurant, and service station are 3½ miles away at Marble Canyon.

Page: Motels, restaurants, and stores. Scenic flights are available from Page airport. Write Chamber of Commerce, Box 727, Page, AZ 86040.

Wahweap: Ranger station, campground (see camping section), picnic shelters, and launching ramp. Concessioner-operated boat rental, boat tours, boating supplies and repairs, marina, restaurant, motel, trailer village with hookups, and service station. Write Wahweap Lodge and Marina, P.O. Box 1597, Page, AZ 86040 (602–645–2433).

Camping: The major camping area is at Wahweap, seven miles northwest of Page. A National Park Service campground (178 spaces) offers water, a dump station, flush toilets, tables, and grills, but no hookups. A concessioner-operated trailer park (123 spaces) has hookups and pay showers. Campgrounds are also located at Hite (six spaces with pit toilets), Lees Ferry (fifty-eight spaces and flush toilets), Halls Crossing (sixty-five spaces with flush toilets), and Bullfrog (eighty-six spaces with flush toilets). Concessioner-operated trailer parks are at the latter two locations as well as at Wahweap.

Fishing: Striped bass, largemouth bass, and black crappie have been planted in Lake Powell. Catches of striped bass frequently include specimens of up to ten pounds. Native catfish are also plentiful. Below the dam, the clear cold river makes Lees Ferry famous for trout fishing. An appropriate state fishing license (Arizona or Utah) is required.

GRAND CANYON NATIONAL PARK
P.O. Box 129
Grand Canyon, AZ 86023
(602) 638–7888

Grand Canyon National Park contains nearly 1.22 million acres of land where the forces of erosion have unveiled a variety of spectacular formations that illustrate vast periods of geological history. The park is located in northwestern Arizona. The South Rim is approached from Flagstaff via U.S. 180 (82 miles to Grand Canyon Village) or by U.S. 89 and Arizona Highway 64 (108 miles). The North Rim is 45 miles south of Jacob Lake via Arizona Highway 67.

About 1,700 million years ago large mountains were pushed upward in the area of today's Grand Canyon. After the mountains were eventually eroded away, movements within the earth created a basin in which sediments and volcanic rocks collected. About 800 million years ago, these layers were pushed upward to form a new range of mountains that, in turn, eroded away. Between 225 and 570 million years ago, the region was a basin similar to today's Gulf of Mexico. The sandstones, shales, and limestones that collected in the basin make up today's upper three-fourths of the canyon walls. About 65 million years ago the region began to rise above sea level, and moisture falling on the newly created Rocky Mountains created the Colorado River that began cutting the canyon.

The park is divided into two separate sections—the North Rim and the South Rim—with the inner canyon accessible from either side. There are twenty concessioners licensed by the National Park Service offering three- to eighteen-day trips along the Colorado River. Information may be obtained at the South Rim Visitor Center or by mail from the park superintendent.

Although only ten miles separate the developed areas of the North and South Rims, the distance by road is 214 miles. By foot, the Kaibab Trail (20.8 miles) leads from Yaki Point on the South Rim down to the river, across to Phantom Ranch, and then up to the North Rim, ending two miles from Grand Canyon Lodge. Campgrounds in the canyon require reservations. Phantom Ranch, north of the river on Kaibab Trail, offers meals and accommodations. Reservations are required.

North Rim

The road to the less-developed North Rim winds through forests of pine, spruce, and aspen on the Kaibab Plateau. This area of the park is

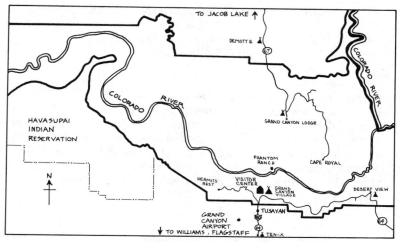

Grand Canyon National Park

at elevations of 7,800 to 8,800 feet and has a cooler and wetter climate than the South Rim. The North Rim is closed by heavy snowfall from mid-November to mid-May. Facilities close by mid- to late October.

The main information station is located in Grand Canyon Lodge at Bright Angel Point. Park rangers are available to answer questions, and publications concerning the park are for sale. An entrance station is located thirteen miles north of Bright Angel Point. A U.S. Forest Service information station is at Jacob Lake, 32 miles north of the North Rim Entrance Station.

A twenty-two-mile paved road connects Grand Canyon Lodge to Cape Royal. This latter point provides an eastward view of the canyon toward the Painted Desert. Point Imperial, on a 3-mile spur off the Cape Royal Road, offers the best eastward view across the canyon. Point Sublime is seventeen miles south of the park entrance via a seventeen-mile, four-wheel-drive, dirt road beginning ¾ of a mile south of the entrance station. Commercial buses leave the lodge every afternoon during summer months on tours of Point Imperial and Cape Royal.

Various ranger-guided walks are scheduled during summer months. Bright Angel Point Trail is a ⅓-mile self-guided nature trail that begins near the lodge. Transept Canyon Trail (1.5 miles) provides a leisurely walk along the canyon rim from Grand Canyon Lodge to North Rim Inn and campground. Uncle Jim Trail (2.5 miles) starts at the Kaibab trailhead and winds through the forest, ending at a point overlooking the canyon. Cape Royal Trail is a ⅓-mile self-guided nature trail from the Cape Royal parking lot. The inner canyon is reached via the North Kaibab Trail (9 miles round trip to Roaring Springs) by foot or mule. Information on mule trips may be obtained by writing Grand Canyon Trail Rides, P.O. Box 1638, Cedar City, UT 84720.

Facilities: Meals and lodging are available from mid-May to mid-October at Grand Canyon Lodge. For information write TW Services, 451 North Main, P.O. Box TWA Reservations, Cedar City, UT 84720 (801–586–7686). A general store, service station, post office, showers, and laundry are also located at Bright Angel Point. Additional food services and accommodations are located at Kaibab Lodge (five miles north of the entrance station) and at Jacob Lake.

Camping: North Rim Campground (eighty-two spaces) provides tables, grills, water, flush toilets, and a dump station. It is located at Bright Angel Point, 13 miles south of the entrance station. Reservations may be made by writing Ticketron, P.O. Box 617516, Chicago, IL 60661 (800–452–1111). De Motte Campground (5 miles north of the entrance station) and Jacob Lake Campground (32 miles north of the entrance station) are operated by the U.S. Forest Service and provide water and restrooms.

Fishing: Access to fishing is very difficult and catches are generally poor. Brown and rainbow trout live in the bottom of the canyon in Bright Angel Creek near Phantom Ranch. Channel catfish are taken from the nearby Colorado River and rainbows from Thunder River and Tapeats Creek. An Arizona license is required.

South Rim

The South Rim is open year round and temperatures during summer months range from the mid-forties at night to the mid-eighties in daytime. The visitor center is located in Grand Canyon Village, 3.5 miles north of the South Entrance Station. Rangers are available to answer questions, and a schedule of activities is posted. The visitor center museum contains exhibits explaining the historical and natural history of the park. Additional museums are the Yavapai Museum (0.5 mile east of the visitor center) with geological exhibits and Tusayan Museum (3 miles west of Desert View) with displays describing prehistoric inhabitants of the area.

From Memorial Day through September a shuttle bus provides free transportation throughout Grand Canyon Village. In addition, it goes to ranger activities, visitor facilities, and along West Rim Drive. This latter road (7.5 miles) offers several scenic viewpoints of the canyon on the way from Grand Canyon Village to Hermits Rest. East Rim Drive to Desert View (25 miles) offers an excellent view of the canyon at Lipan Point. The Watchtower at Desert View overlooks the canyon and the Painted Desert.

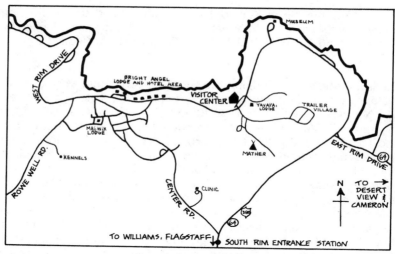

Grand Canyon Village

A number of self-guided nature trails, paths, and undeveloped trails lie along the rim between Yavapai Museum and Hermits Rest. Canyon Rim Nature Trail (1.5 miles) leads from the hotel to the visitor center and Yavapai Museum. Ranger-guided walks are presented on a scheduled basis at Grand Canyon Village throughout the year and at Desert View and Tusayan Ruins in summer.

Facilities: Nearly anything the heart desires can be found in Grand Canyon Village. This includes a bank, general store, post office, service station, laundry, showers, pet kennel, and lost and found facility. Lodging includes cabins, motel units, and a hotel. Information and reservations may be obtained by writing Reservations Dept., Grand Canyon National Park Lodges, P.O. Box 699, Grand Canyon, AZ 86023 (602–638–2631). Private lodging is available south of the entrance station. A general store, snack bar, and service station are located at Desert View.

Camping: The park's most developed campground is Mather Campground (310 spaces and seven group camps) at Grand Canyon Village. It provides tables, grills, water, flush toilets, pay showers, laundry facilities, and a dump station. Reservations for Mather are available by writing Ticketron, P.O. Box 617516, Chicago, IL 60661 (800–452–1111). Nearby, Trailer Village (eighty-two spaces) is operated by Grand Canyon National Park Lodges and provides hookups. Write Trailer Village, P.O. Box 699, Grand Canyon, AZ 86023 (602–638–2631). Desert View Campground (fifty spaces) is located ½ mile west of the east entrance station and has tables, grills, water, and flush toilets. Ten X Campground (seventy sites, pit toilets), operated by the U.S. Forest Service, is located ten miles south of Grand Canyon Village outside the park. Ten X is a pleasant campground with lots of shade. **Fishing:** Access to fishing is difficult and catches are generally poor. See fishing section under the North Rim section for details.

HUBBELL TRADING POST NATIONAL HISTORIC SITE
P.O. Box 150
Ganado, AZ 86505
(602) 755–3475

Hubbell Trading Post was authorized as a national historic site in 1965 to preserve an active Navajo trading post. The site is on the Navajo Indian Reservation, 1 mile west of Ganado, Arizona, and 55 miles from Gallup, New Mexico.

Hubbell Trading Post is the oldest continually operating trading post on the Navajo reservation. The post was established in 1878, when the founder, John Lorenzo Hubbell, purchased another post in the area. Hubbell eventually established a network of trading posts, a wholesale house in Winslow, and a stage and freight line. A personal friend of men such as Theodore Roosevelt and General Lew Wallace, Hubbell was instrumental in early Arizona history and statehood. His death in 1930 was mourned by the Navajos, and his body lies overlooking the trading post on Hubbell Hill. The Hubbell family operated the post for eighty-nine years until it became a national historic site.

Visitors may participate in the experience of a living, active post. Here, members of the Navajo, Hopi, Zuni, and other tribes still come to sell and trade such crafts as hand-woven rugs, jewelry, baskets, and pottery. Rangers offer guided tours of the trading post compound and the Hubbell home. Hubbell's home reflects his life and contains one of the most extensive collections of Southwest Indian arts and life on the western frontier. Weaving and silversmithing demonstrations are offered in the visitor center. Conducted tours of the Hubbell home are offered on the hour and a booklet for a self-guided tour of the area may be borrowed at the visitor center.

The site is open daily except Christmas, New Year's Day, and Thanksgiving. Hours are 8:00 A.M. to 5:00 P.M. October through April, and 8:00 A.M. to 6:00 P.M. the rest of the year. Daylight savings time is observed.

Facilities: The trading post continues in operation under direction of the Southwest Parks and Monuments Association, a non-profit organization operating the post for the National Park Service. Many fine Navajo, Hopi, Zuni, Apache, and other Indian arts are offered for sale in the trading post. Groceries and snacks may also be purchased here. Two gas stations are directly outside the park entrance. One mile east in the town of Ganado, visitors will find a cafe, gas station, and market. Restrooms and drinking water are available in the visitor center.

Camping: No camping is allowed at the site. Canyon de Chelly National Monument, 40 miles north on Highway 63, offers 104 sites at Cottonwood Campground (flush toilets).

Fishing: No fishing is available at Hubbell Trading Post National Historic Site.

MONTEZUMA CASTLE NATIONAL MONUMENT
P.O. Box 219
Camp Verde, AZ 86322
(602) 567–3322

Montezuma Castle National Monument was established in 1906. It contains one of the best-preserved prehistoric cliff dwellings in the Southwest. The five-story, twenty-room castle is 90 percent intact. The monument is located in central Arizona, just off Interstate 17, 55 miles south of Flagstaff and 4 miles northeast of the town of Camp Verde. The monument is approximately 90 miles north of Phoenix.

Several million years ago the Verde River was dammed by lava, forming a lake 35 miles long and eighteen miles wide. Later, after tributaries had deposited large quantities of limy mud in the lake, overflows wore down the lava dam and the lake drained. The Verde River and its tributaries then cut deep channels through the sediments, and further erosion caused a broadening of the valleys.

Although there is little evidence of the earliest inhabitants of the Verde Valley, Indians are known to have lived in the Southwest for several thousand years. About A.D. 700, the Hohokam Indians came into the valley from the south. About 350 years later, these farming Indians moved north to the fertile lands created by the eruption of Sunset Crater in 1065. Around 1100, a group of dryfarming Indians entered the valley from the north. About 1250, they began erecting large dwellings on hilltops or in cliffs. The limestone cliff along the north bank of Beaver Creek was an ideal place to build house clusters,

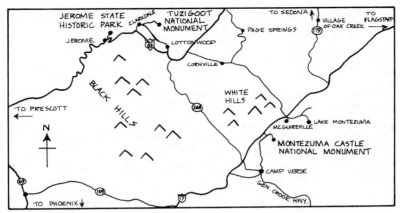

Montezuma Castle National Monument

because it had good cropland on the creek terrace nearby. Two of the clusters (including Montezuma Castle) eventually became five-story apartment houses that were occupied for about two centuries. By about 1450, Montezuma Castle appears to have been abandoned.

The visitor center is in the Montezuma Castle section of the park. It contains exhibits describing the culture of the people who lived here. Examples of weaving, basketry, jewelry, and pottery-making tools are on display.

Additional prehistoric Indian work can be seen at Montezuma Well, eleven miles northeast of Montezuma Castle. This part of the monument contains a limestone sink 470 feet in diameter with water fifty-five feet deep. Indians diverted the well water into irrigation ditches that are still visible today. This section also contains the remains of a Hohokam pithouse and Sinagua dwellings.

Facilities: No food or lodging is available within the monument's boundaries but both can be found nearby. Limited picnic facilities are located in each of the two sections of the park. Drinking water and modern restrooms are available in the visitor center. There is easy handicapped access to restrooms, the visitor center, and the trail at the Montezuma Castle section.
Camping: No camping is permitted in the monument. Forest service campgrounds are located in Coconino National Forest, and other private campgrounds are located nearby.
Fishing: No fishing is available in the monument, but the nearby Verde River offers fishing with an Arizona license.

NAVAJO NATIONAL MONUMENT
HC–71 Box 3
Tonalea, AZ 86044
(602) 672–2366

Navajo National Monument contains 360 acres. It was established in 1909 to preserve three spectacular cliff dwellings of Indian farmers living in this canyon country over 700 years ago. Park headquarters in northeastern Arizona can be reached by following U.S. 160 northeast 50 miles from Tuba City or southwest 19 miles from Kayenta. From here a 9-mile paved road runs from the highway to the monument.

For about 1,300 years the San Juan Basin of the Four Corners region was occupied by Indians called the Anasazi ("the ancient ones"). These Indians were originally hunters and gatherers, but by A.D. 400 agriculture had become an important part of the economy. Gradually, three cultural divisions emerged: Mesa Verde in southwestern Colorado, Chaco Canyon in northwestern New Mexico, and Kayenta in northeastern Arizona.

In the twelfth and thirteenth centuries, the small hamlets began to combine into a few relatively large villages. During this period household crafts reached a peak of artistic expression and the three great cliff dwellings of this monument mark the culmination of Anasazi culture in the Kayenta area. By 1300, probably due to drought and soil erosion, the Anasazi had migrated south and abandoned all three

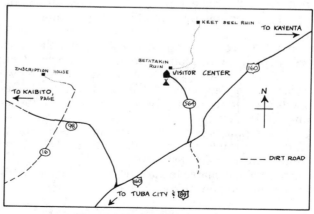

Navajo National Monument

centers. The Kayenta district is now inhabited by Navajos, not related to the Anasazi, who have lived here for over one hundred years.

Of the three prehistoric dwellings, Keet Seel is the largest with over 160 rooms. An 8-mile (one-way) primitive trail leads to the ruin. Keet Seel is open during summer months only, on weekends. Visits to the ruin are limited to twenty individuals per day when open, and though reservations can be made for backcountry permits up to two months ahead of the date, demand for these spaces is high. Hikers may camp overnight near the ruins with a permit. Riders must allow one day for horse trips with a permit. Call monument headquarters for details and reservations.

Betatakin, with 135 rooms, is the most accessible ruin. A walk from the visitor center to the end of Sandal Trail (one hour round trip) provides a viewpoint from which to see the ruin. Visits to the ruin may be made only when accompanied by a park ranger. Scheduled tours (a strenuous hike) are conducted in late spring and summer and require about five or six hours.

Inscription House consists of seventy-five rooms, including one Kiva. This ruin has been closed to the public since 1968.

The visitor center contains exhibits, a slide program, and a movie to describe the ways of the Anasazi and to show examples of their arts and crafts. Indian crafts are sold here.

Facilities: No food or lodging is available within the monument's boundaries, but both can be found nearby. Modern restrooms and water are available at monument headquarters and at the campground. A picnic area is located near the campground.

Camping: A campground (thirty spaces plus group camps) is open from mid-April until mid-October. Stays are limited to seven days and tables, grills, flush toilets, and a dump station are provided. A walk-in campground is at Keet Seel. A permit is required and no water is available.

Fishing: No fishing is available at Navajo National Monument.

ORGAN PIPE CACTUS NATIONAL MONUMENT
Route 1, Box 100
Ajo, AZ 85321
(602) 387–6849

Organ Pipe Cactus contains 330,689 acres. This park was established as a national monument in 1937 to preserve and protect unique Sonoran Desert plants and animals, including the rare cactus for which the park is named. The monument is located in southwestern Arizona on the Mexican border, 140 miles south of

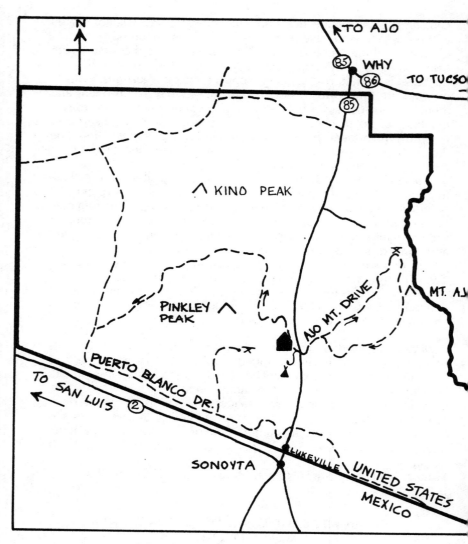

Organ Pipe Cactus National Monument

Phoenix and 142 miles west of Tucson. From Phoenix it is reached via U.S. 80 to Gila Bend and then Arizona 85. From Tucson, take Arizona 86 west and then Arizona 85 south.

Organ Pipe Cactus National Monument was designated to protect the natural features and life contained in this segment of the Sonoran Desert. The stark and rough landscape of the monument includes mountains, plains, canyons, and dry washes. Summer days can be quite warm—temperatures of 95 to 105 degrees Fahrenheit. are most common. Of the eight and one-half inches of annual rainfall, nearly one-half results from summer thunderstorms. Winter weather is generally mild with sunny days. Occasional chilly winds can be accompanied by sub-freezing nighttime temperatures during December, January, and February.

A visitor center containing exhibits explaining the monument and desert is located 17 miles south of the northern entrance. Evening campfire programs are presented in the campground amphitheater during the busy winter months of December through March.

A single paved road (Arizona 85) through the park connects Why, Arizona, with Sonoyta, Mexico. Two graded loop drives through remote areas begin at the visitor center, where guide booklets are available. Puerto Blanco Drive is 53 miles long and takes approximately one-half day to drive. This route circles the Puerto Blanco Mountains and parallels the Mexican border. Side roads lead to a stand of senita cactus at Senita Basin and to a manmade oasis at Quitobaquito Springs. Ajo Mountain Drive is a 21-mile road that provides outstanding views of the desert. Various species of cactus can be seen as the road circles the Ajo Mountains.

A number of trails are located in the park. A 1⅓-mile trail connects the campground and visitor center, and a one-mile self-guided Desert View Nature Trail leads from the campground to a nearby ridge overlooking the desert. Victoria Mine Trail (4½ miles round trip) leads to what was once one of the area's most productive silver and gold mines.

Facilities: Lodging and food service are not available within the monument. A motel, post office, grocery store, cafe, and service station are located in Lukeville, five miles south of the visitor center. Motels and restaurants are in Ajo, Gila Bend, and Sonoyta. A cafe, grocery store, motel, and service stations are in Why near the park's northern entrance. Modern restrooms and drinking water are available at both the visitor center and campground.

Camping: A single campground (208 spaces) is open all year and is located 1½ miles southwest of the visitor center. The campground contains tables, grills, flush toilets, and a dump station. There is a thirty-five-foot limit on trailers and motorhomes.

Fishing: No fishing is available in Organ Pipe Cactus National Monument.

PETRIFIED FOREST NATIONAL PARK
Petrified Forest National Park, AZ 86028
(602) 524–6228

Petrified Forest National Park was proclaimed a national monument in 1906 (changed to a national park in 1962) to protect 93,533 acres of Indian ruins and petroglyphs (writings or drawings on rocks), portions of the Painted Desert, and trees that petrified and changed to multicolored stone. The park is located in northeast Arizona, 46 miles from the New Mexico border on Interstate 40. It is 119 miles east of Flagstaff.

The Painted Desert of northern Arizona is a landscape of various colors and shapes. Within the badly eroded badlands, the visitor will find thousands of logs brilliant with jasper and agate scattered about. These logs were used by prehistoric Indians to build homes in this area, and ruins of the dwellings, along with prehistoric petroglyphs, can still be seen.

This region was crossed by many streams as part of a vast flood plain 225 million years ago. On drained areas of land, pinelike trees grew near the stream's headwaters. As some of these trees fell and were buried by mud, sand, and volcanic ash carried by the flooding streams, a scarcity of oxygen slowed the process of rot and decay. Eventually chemicals in the streams allowed mineral silica to dissolve and penetrate the logs' wood cells and holes. As the water evaporated, only the silica remained in the cell interiors and the holes. This silica eventually turned to quartz. (The surrounding deposits hardened into sandstones and shales of the Chinle Formation.)

The Painted Desert Visitor Center (near Interstate 40) contains information about the park. A movie about the geological history of the area is presented every half hour. At the park's south entrance (near U.S. 180), the Rainbow Forest Museum contains specimens of polished petrified wood, fossils, minerals, and diagrams explaining how badlands are formed and how wood becomes petrified. A short paved trail behind the museum provides close viewpoints of some excellent petrified specimens. A 27-mile paved road connecting these two locations contains wayside exhibits at points of interest. Park rangers are at some of these points to help interpret the features. Guided walks

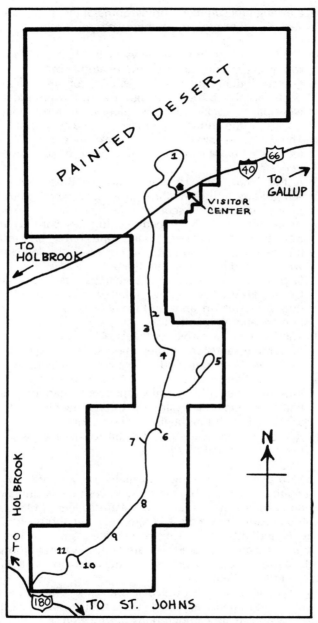

Petrified Forest National Park

take place throughout summer months. Some of the major points (with numbers keyed to those found on the map) are:

1. Eight overlooks provide views of the Painted Desert. Restrooms and picnic facilities are located here.
2. Puerco Indian Ruins—The remains of an Indian village occupied about 700 years ago. Restrooms are located here.
3. Newspaper Rock—Some excellent prehistoric Indian petroglyphs on the surface of a massive sandstone block.
4. The Teepees—Small colorful peaks that resemble colorful teepees or haystacks show the erosion of soft, layered clay deposits.
5. A three-mile loop road leads to the Blue Mesa where a self-guiding trail leads through an area where petrified logs play a major role in sculpting the landscape.
6. Agate Bridge—A huge petrified log lies partially exposed. Both ends are encased in sandstone, but a forty-foot ravine has been carved beneath the center of the log. Restrooms with flush toilets are located here.
7. Jasper Forest—Masses of log sections litter the valley floor.
8. Crystal Forest—Fossil logs filled with clear and amethyst quartz crystals in an area that was devastated by souvenir hunters and gem collectors.
9. The Flattops—Massive remnants of a once continuous layer of durable sandstone protecting a series of layered deposits that have been removed by erosion elsewhere in the park.
10. Long Logs and Agate House—An area of exceptionally long logs that are only partially uncovered can be seen on a half-mile loop trail. A partially restored pueblo is at the end of a half-mile trail that begins at the parking lot.
11. Rainbow Forest Museum—Exhibits of petrified wood and of the area's natural and human history.

Facilities: No overnight lodging is available in the park, but accommodations are in nearby communities. Refreshments, lunches, gifts, and gasoline can be obtained all year at Painted Desert Oasis near the north entrance. Rainbow Forest Lodge near the south entrance has refreshments and gifts. Picnicking is permitted only at Chinde Point and in Rainbow Forest, where there are tables, water, and restrooms. The park is open year round during daylight hours. It is closed Christmas and New Year's Day.

Camping: No camping is permitted in the park. The nearest public campgrounds are in national forests to the southeast and west, nearly 100 miles away. Private campgrounds are located at both Holbrook and Navajo. A county park near Joseph City has limited camping.

Fishing: No fishing is available in Petrified Forest National Park.

PIPE SPRING NATIONAL MONUMENT
Moccasin, AZ 86022
(604) 634–5505

Pipe Spring National Monument contains forty acres. It was established in 1923 to preserve a historic fort and other structures built by Mormon pioneers. Pipe Spring is located in northwestern Arizona near the Utah border. The monument is 15 miles southwest of Fredonia, Arizona, on Arizona Highway 389. It is located 66 miles from Zion National Park, 89 miles from the north rim of the Grand Canyon, and 45 miles from Hurricane, Utah.

Mormon missionaries to the Indians were the first white discoverers of Pipe Spring. A group en route to visit the Hopi Indians camped at the spring in 1858. The name of Pipe Spring supposedly originated when William Hamlin shot the bottom out of a smoking pipe to demonstrate his marksmanship.

James Whitmore established a claim at Pipe Spring in 1863 after following trails pioneered by the missionaries. Because of the abundant forage, in 1865 he built a dugout, fenced an area, and started a livestock ranch. At the same time that Mormons were migrating into the region, the U.S. Army was waging a war with the Navajos south of the Colorado River. Bands of Navajos crossed the river and inflicted casualties among the settlers. James Whitmore was killed in 1866 by Navajo cattle rustlers, and Pipe Spring was abandoned. Afterward, however, the area was used by the Utah Territorial Militia as a base of operations against the Navajos.

In 1870, Brigham Young and his advisors decided to establish a ranch to supply meat and dairy products to nearby settlements. The fort was built to protect the families and workers at Pipe Spring, and it was never attacked. It served as a ranchhouse until 1923.

The climate at Pipe Spring is fairly temperate because the area is nearly 1 mile above sea level. Plant and animal life are typical for a semidesert area. Small rodents live among the cactus and sagebrush, and coyotes are occasionally seen. Water from the spring provides a perfect habitat for the flora and fauna of this oasis. Birds are abundant in this monument.

National Park Service personnel provide guide service from 8:00 A.M. until 4:30 P.M. daily. Living history programs showing pioneer cooking, quilt making, rag-rug loom work, and cattle branding are also presented. In addition to a tour of the fort, visitors will find bunkhouses, work sheds, and corrals typical of nineteenth-century ranches.

Facilities: No lodging or food service is available at the monument. An area is designated for picnics. The nearest town with food and accommodations is Fredonia, 15 miles to the northeast. Similar facilities are also available in Hurricane.

Camping: No camping is permitted at Pipe Spring. A campground operated by the Kaibab-Paiute Indian tribe is located one quarter of a mile north of the monument. Hot showers, laundromat, dump station, electrical hook-ups, and tent sites are available. Zion National Park (66 miles) and Utah's Coral Pink Sand Dune State Park (45 miles) both have complete camping facilities.

Fishing: No fishing is available in the monument.

SAGUARO NATIONAL MONUMENT
Old Spanish Trail
Route 8, Box 695
Tucson, AZ 85730
(602) 298–2036

Saguaro National Monument contains 84,000 acres in two sections near Tucson, Arizona. It was established as a national monument in 1933 to preserve giant saguaro cacti. The park's largest part, Saguaro East, is about 5 miles east of the Tucson city limits on Old Spanish Trail. A smaller part, Saguaro West, is approximately 7 miles west of the city limits. This part can be reached by driving west to Kinney Road on either Gates Pass Road or on Ajo Way.

Saguaro National Monument was named after a large cactus in the Sonoran Desert that averages a height of thirty feet and lives up to 150 years. The seed of the saguaro sprouts and survives in the shade of another desert plant. After five years it grows only a few inches, and at thirty years is only a few feet tall. At seventy-five years the plant may reach fifteen or twenty feet and begin developing its first branch.

The saguaro is well suited to the dry climate. The root system is widespread and lies just below the ground surface so as to absorb as much of the infrequent rain as possible. A mature plant weighing six to ten tons may absorb as much as a ton of water. During long dry periods, the saguaro consumes its stored moisture and shrinks in girth. During May and early June clusters of white flowers appear on the saguaro's branch ends. These are Arizona's state flower.

Variations in elevation from 2,800 to 8,700 feet within the monument make it the home of numerous types of plant and animal life. The saguaro cactus itself serves as home for several species of

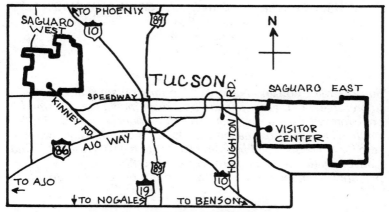

Saguaro National Monument

birds. Woodpeckers and flickers drill holes that are later used by owls, martins, and flycatchers.

A visitor center, located at the west entrance of the Saguaro East, contains exhibits describing the history and geology of this area of the country. Ranger-guided walks are conducted from here during winter months. An 8-mile paved road that begins near the visitor center takes the motorist on a scenic drive through the stands of large, old saguaros found in the eastern section of the monument. Pullouts are located along the drive so visitors can walk along some short trails.

Saguaro West contains stands of young saguaros. The main road through this section leads to hiking trails and scenic overlooks. Ranger-guided hikes are also conducted here during winter months. An information station is located at the south entrance, and the nearby Arizona-Sonora Desert Museum contains exhibits of living plants and animals of the Sonora Desert. Mild temperatures from fall through spring turn uncomfortably hot (over 100 degrees Fahrenheit) during summer months.

Facilities: Modern restrooms and drinking water are available at the visitor centers of both the East and West units. Four picnic areas with tables, shelters, and restrooms (but no water) are located in Saguaro West. Two picnic areas are also located on Cactus Forest Drive in Saguaro East. Other facilities can be found in nearby Tucson.
Camping: Other than walk-in camps along back-country trails, no camping is available in Saguaro National Monument. Camping is by permit only.
Fishing: No fishing is available in Saguaro National Monument.

SUNSET CRATER VOLCANO NATIONAL MONUMENT
Route 3, Box 149
Flagstaff, AZ 86001
(602) 527–7042

Sunset Crater Volcano National Monument was created in 1930 to preserve 3,040 acres containing a magnificent volcanic cinder cone formed around A.D. 1100. The monument is located 15 miles north of Flagstaff, Arizona, off U.S. 89 on FS 545. It is a convenient stop for motorists traveling from Flagstaff to the south rim of Grand Canyon National Park (approximately two hours away). Wupatki National Monument is a short drive north of Sunset Crater.

North-central Arizona is covered with cinder cones, volcanic peaks, and lava flows representing about ten million years of volcanic activity. The 200-year eruptive phase that started in A.D. 1064–65 resulted in the symmetrical cinder cone and black lava and cinder area of Sunset Crater. Lava, cinders, and ash were blown from a volcanic vent creating a 1,000 foot high cone-shaped volcano. Prevailing southwesterly winds caused most of the material to fall on the northeast side. As eruptions slackened, lava outpourings occurred from vents near the cinder cone's base. Later, hot springs and vapors seeped out from fumaroles near the vent. Minerals from these vapors stained the cinders and make the summit seem to glow with the hues of a perpetual sunset.

A visitor center is located along the 35-mile Sunset Crater-Wupatki Loop Road two miles east of Highway 89. The center contains exhibits and other information concerning the monument and should be your initial stop. Rangers are on duty on a year round basis to answer questions. During summer months a variety of activities are available, including evening programs (in the campground) and guided walks.

Lava Flow Nature Trail begins 1½ miles east of the Sunset Crater Visitor Center. This leisurely forty- to fifty-minute walk wanders across some of the lava flow, around part of the crater base, and by an ice cave. The hike is made more enjoyable by trail markers along the way.

Roads are kept open year round, although the summer tourist season is most popular. Daytime temperatures are generally pleasant and evenings can be quite cool, because the monument is located at an elevation of 7,000 feet. July and August can also be quite damp.

Facilities: No facilities are available within the monument. Drinking water and modern restrooms are located at the visitor center. Gas stations, motels, and food service are located along Highway 89 toward Flagstaff.

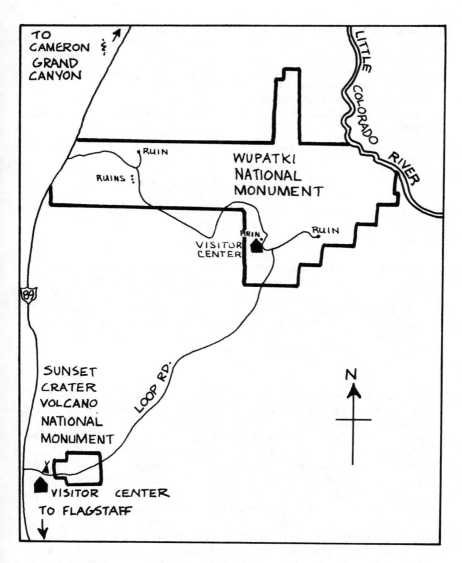

Sunset Crater Volcano National Monument and Wupatki
National Monument

Camping: The U.S. Forest Service's Bonito Campground (forty-four spaces) is across from the visitor center. Grills, tables, water, and flush toilets are available during the camping season of May until September. Campsites are widely spaced on a field of volcanic cinders, with scattered pine trees providing some shade. The extensive curbing must set a world record for campgrounds.

Fishing: No fishing is available within Sunset Crater Volcano National Monument.

TONTO NATIONAL MONUMENT
P.O. Box 707
Roosevelt, AZ 85545
(602) 467–2241

Tonto National Monument contains 1,120 acres. It was established in 1907 to preserve three cliff dwellings of the Salado Indians. The monument is located just off Arizona 88, 28 miles from Globe and 2 miles from Roosevelt. From Phoenix (two and a half hours), take U.S. 60/70 to Apache Junction; turn left on Arizona 88 and along scenic Apache Trail (25 miles of unpaved mountain road) toward Roosevelt.

The area occupied by Tonto National Monument was once the home of the Salado (Spanish for "salty") Indians. The newest archeology in the area suggests that the earliest identifiable Salado sites date from approximately 1100. The old theory about the Salado coming in from the Little Colorado is in disrepute. New theories suggest the Salado may have a largely Hohokam ancestry. The truth of the matter is that no one really knows for sure where the Salado came from. By 1100 they were just here. They lived in small villages along the river edges until the middle 1200s, when they began moving to defensible ridgetops. In the early 1300s, a move to caves commenced and three of the cliff dwellings built in natural caves remain preserved in the monument. The dwellings are now called the Upper Ruin (containing about forty rooms), Lower Ruin (nineteen rooms), and Lower Ruin Annex (twelve rooms). The villages are constructed of stone and mud and some sections are two stories high. As was the case with most Pueblo cultures in the Southwest, the Salado abandoned the Tonto Basin around A.D. 1450. Where they went and why they left is uncertain.

The monument's visitor center, one mile from the park turnoff, is open from 8:00 A.M. until 5:00 P.M. daily. The building contains items made and used by the Salado. A ranger is on duty to answer visitor questions. A self-guided trail to the Lower Ruin that begins at the visitor center closes each day at 4:00 P.M. Along the trail, the hiker will see many of the same species of desert plants that were used by the Salado—barrel cactus, saguaro, jojoba, sotol, cholla, yucca, and others. The strenuous three-mile, three- hour round-trip hike to the Upper Ruin must be arranged a minimum of twenty-four hours in advance.

Facilities: Picnic facilities, drinking water, and modern restrooms are available in the monument. Food and lodging are not provided in the park but both can be found in Roosevelt, at Roosevelt Lake Resort, and in the Globe–Miami area.

Camping: No camping is permitted in the monument but many campsites are available in nearby Tonto National Forest. Tortilla Flat Campground (seventy-seven spaces), located eighteen miles northeast of Apache Junction, and Lost Dutchman State Park (thirty-five spaces), six miles northeast of Apache Junction, are the only campgrounds with flush toilets and a dump station.

Fishing: No fishing is available in Tonto National Monument.

TUMACACORI NATIONAL HISTORICAL PARK
Box 67
Tumacacori, AZ 85640
(602) 398–2341

The seventeen-acre Tumacacori National Historical Park was established in 1908 to commemorate the introduction of European civilization into present-day Arizona. A typical frontier mission church illustrates Spanish colonial endeavor. The park is located in extreme south-central Arizona, just off U.S. 89/Interstate 19, approximately 45 miles directly south of Tucson.

More than 250 years ago, Spain sent soldiers and missionary priests into Central America and Mexico to bring Christian civilization to the Indian tribes of the frontier areas. Missions were built among friendly tribes, and military posts (presidios) were constructed in areas inhabited by hostile Indians. These missions served as both churches and centers of European culture. San Jose de Tumacacori was a northern outpost of a mission chain constructed by Franciscan priests in the late 1700s on sites previously established by Jesuits in what was then the Mexican province of Sonora. The Jesuits had been expelled from all Spanish dominions in 1767.

After Mexico won independence from Spain in 1821, most of the frontier missions were abandoned because the new government was unable to provide a defense against hostile Indians. In addition, Mexican law tended to weaken the power of the church, and missions were required to become parish churches. In 1844, Mexico sold the Tumacacori mission lands to a private citizen.

The park office and museum (open from 8:00 A.M. to 5:00 P.M.) are next to the parking area. Exhibits in the museum depict early Indian and Spanish history. Craft demonstrations take place on weekends. A self-guided walk leads through the church, and a park employee is on duty to help visitors. In addition to the church, which still stands, a cemetery and unfinished mortuary chapel are just north of the mission. A special all-day fiesta takes place on the first Sunday in December. Weather at the monument favors winter visits because of very high summer temperatures.

Facilities: No food service or accommodations are available in the park. Both can be found in nearby communities. Drinking water and restrooms are located at the museum, and picnic grounds are nearby.
Camping: No camping is permitted in the park, but private campgrounds are in close proximity on the Tucson-Nogales Highway. Patagonia Lake State Park provides over 200 camping sites (with flush toilets) fifteen miles northeast of Nogales on Highway 82. Coronado National Forest has campsites (pit toilets) thirteen miles off Interstate 19, approximately eighteen miles north of Tumacacori.
Fishing: No fishing is available in the park.

TUZIGOOT NATIONAL MONUMENT
P.O. Box 68
Clarkdale, AZ 86324
(602) 634–5564

Tuzigoot National Monument contains forty-seven acres and was established in 1939 to protect a prehistoric Indian town built between A.D. 1000 and 1400. Tuzigoot is located in north-central Arizona, 55 miles south of Flagstaff via U.S. 89A (an exceptionally beautiful drive). The monument is approximately 25 miles off Interstate 17 connecting Flagstaff and Phoenix. See the area map under Montezuma Castle National Monument in this section.

The Verde Valley's first permanent settlers were the Hohokam Indians, a farming people, who moved into this area around A.D. 600. The Hohokam, who used irrigation techniques to grow a variety of crops, were later joined by the Sinagua, who had inhabited and dry farmed the foothills and the plateau beyond the valley. The Sinagua borrowed the agricultural techniques of the Hohokam and began constructing above-ground masonry dwellings that eventually evolved into large pueblos constructed on hilltops and cliffs. By the early 1400s, the Sinagua had abandoned the Verde Valley. In the 1500s, Spanish soldiers entered the valley and found the pueblos, which then lay undisturbed for nearly four centuries.

Tuzigoot is a remnant of a Sinaguan village that began as a small cluster of rooms that were inhabited by about fifty persons. Over a century later, the village population expanded as farmers surrendered the drought-parched land and moved to the irrigated valley.

The monument and visitor center are open daily from 8:00 A.M. to 5:00 P.M. with a ranger on duty. The visitor center contains exhibits, and a short self-guided trail to the ruins begins near the center.

Facilities: There are no accommodations or food service available in the monument. Both can be found two miles away in either Clarkdale or Cottonwood. Water and restrooms are located at the visitor center.
Camping: No camping is permitted in the monument, but Dead Horse Ranch State Park (with flush toilets and showers) is located north of nearby Cottonwood.
Fishing: No fishing is available in the monument.

WALNUT CANYON NATIONAL MONUMENT
Route 1, Box 25
Flagstaff, AZ 86001
(602) 526–3367

Walnut Canyon is a 2,250-acre monument established in 1915 to protect the remains of Sinagua Indian cliff dwellings that were constructed nearly 800 years ago. The park is located at the end of a 3-mile paved road that begins 7.5 miles east of Flagstaff on Interstate 40 (take exit 204).

Nine hundred years ago the eruptions of what is now called Sunset Crater poured cinders and ash over an area of about 800 square miles. The resulting rich farmland drew farming Indian tribes from all over the region. Since the prime land was in an area lying no more than fifteen miles from the volcano, a population crush developed. As a result, the Sinagua moved south of the volcano to a canyon offering building sites and a means of livelihood.

At Walnut Canyon, the Sinagua used their masonry skills to build more than 300 small cliff rooms in the limestone walls. With a dependable source of water at the canyon floor and fertile farmland within two miles of both rims, the canyon offered a relatively secure environment. After living in Walnut Canyon for almost 150 years, the Sinagua abandoned their home for reasons that remain unknown. Some anthropologists believe that a number of the Sinagua's descendants live today among the Pueblo Indians. For 600 years the ruins were apparently untouched. The earliest known report of them was made in 1883.

The visitor center contains exhibits detailing the history of the Walnut Canyon area. Park employees are present to answer visitor questions. A paved foot path at the rear of the center leads to Island Trail, which provides a close view of twenty-five cliff dwelling rooms and allows observation of 100 others across the canyon. Interpretive signs are along the trail. The three-quarters of a mile round trip requires climbing that is fairly strenuous (309 descending steps and 240 ascending steps). Another walk along Rim Trail begins just outside the front of the visitor center. This ½-mile paved trail is relatively flat and provides views of cliff dwellings across the canyon. A cutoff from this trail to the parking lot takes visitors past some surface ruins.

Facilities: No accommodations or food services are available in the monument, but full facilities are a short distance away in Flagstaff. Water and modern restrooms are located at the visitor center. A shaded picnic area with restrooms and water is near the parking lot. Three smaller picnic areas with pit toilets but no water are on the entrance road.

Camping: No camping is permitted in the monument, but a number of private facilities are found near Flagstaff, and Forest Service campgrounds are south near Lake Mary and Sedona Canyon. Another Forest Service campground (with flush toilets) is located at Sunset Crater Volcano National Monument, fifteen miles north of Flagstaff and about twenty-one miles from Walnut Canyon.

Fishing: No fishing is permitted in the monument.

WUPATKI NATIONAL MONUMENT
H.C. 33 Box 444A
Flagstaff, AZ 86001
(602) 527–7040

Wupatki National Monument contains 35,000 acres. It was established in 1924 to preserve ruins of red sandstone pueblos built by farming Indians about A.D. 1065. The monument is located in north-central Arizona, approximately 35 miles north of Flagstaff via U.S. 89. It may also be reached by exiting U.S. 89 at

Sunset Crater Volcano National Monument (15 miles north of Flagstaff) and driving over a good 35-mile paved loop road. See the map of both areas under Sunset Crater in this section.

After the eruptions of Sunset Crater to the south of Wupatki ceased about 700 years ago, the land was covered with black ash. The improved farmland drew farming Indians into the area, which became a melting pot of Indian cultures as word of the rich farmland spread.

Of the villages that were established in the area, one of the longest inhabited is now called *Wupatki,* the Hopi word for "tall house." From its location near one of the region's few springs, Wupatki grew to three stories and contained one hundred rooms during the 1100s. Near the ruin are the remains of an open-air amphitheater and a stone-masonry ball court. By 1225, after a decade of drought, all of the Indians had left the area, perhaps because continuous farming and winds had stripped the land of volcanic ash.

The Wupatki visitor center, which contains exhibits of the area's cultures, is located near the south entrance to the monument, fourteen miles from U.S. 89 and eighteen miles north of Sunset Crater. Self-guided trails to Nalakihu-Citadel Ruins and to the Wupatki Ruin begin from the main road. The latter is just behind the visitor center. The Wupatki Ruin trail has guidebooks at the trailhead. Paved roads will take you to ruins at Wukoki and Lomaki. Wayside exhibits are on both the Citadel and the Lomaki trails. If time in the monument is limited, visitors should at least stop at the visitor center and walk through Wupatki Ruin.

Facilities: Restrooms and drinking water are available at the visitor center. Picnic areas are located about 5 miles north of the visitor center and on the road between Sunset Crater and Wupatki. All other facilities are available along U.S. 89 and in Flagstaff.

Camping: No camping is available at Wupatki. A U.S. Forest Service campground (with modern restrooms) is located near the visitor center at Sunset Crater Volcano National Monument. Contact the Peaks Ranger Station of the Coconino National Forest (602–526–0866) for more information.

Fishing: No fishing. Although the Little Colorado River borders the northeast corner of the monument, it is generally dry.

Arkansas

ARKANSAS POST NATIONAL MEMORIAL
Route 1, Box 16
Gillett, AR 72055
(501) 548–2432

Arkansas Post contains 389 acres that were incorporated into the National Park System in 1960 to commemorate the site of the first permanent French settlement in the Lower Mississippi Valley. The site is located in eastern Arkansas on the banks of the Arkansas River between Gillett and Dumas. It is on Arkansas Highway 169, 7 miles south of Gillett via U.S. 165 (Great River Road) and about 20 miles northeast of Dumas via U.S. 165.

While the French were the first white men to settle in this area in 1686, Arkansas Post passed through a number of hands as a strategic military and commercial center on the frontier. The reason for its importance is its location near the confluence of the Arkansas and Mississippi rivers. In 1763, France ceded Louisiana (which included the Arkansas Territory) to Spain following the British victory in the French and Indian War. The Spanish recognized the area's value in controlling British influence and Indian trade in the region.

Following the American Revolution, frontiersmen moved into the Mississippi Valley and settled on the rich river bottom land. In addition to provoking more Indian raids, this also caused Spain to strengthen the post. In 1800, the Spanish ceded Louisiana back to France after the French Revolution brought Napoleon Bonaparte to power. Pressed for money, Napoleon sold Louisiana to the United States in 1803.

As the first capital of the territorial government for Arkansas, Arkansas Post became a typical frontier village. In 1821, however, the capital was moved to Little Rock, and Arkansas Post began its downhill slide. The area was temporarily revived when Confederate forces constructed a fort here during the Civil War.

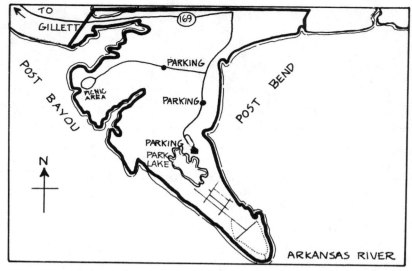

Arkansas Post National Memorial

Today, this post, which has contained at least five different forts and settlements, has few visible remains. Two miles of trails are in the park, including a ¾-mile trail near Park Lake that permits visitors to get a sense of the post's history. A visitor center is open daily (except Christmas) and offers exhibits and an audio-visual program to help explain the events that occurred here.

Facilities: No food or lodging is available in the park, but both can be found in nearby Gillett. Restrooms with flush toilets are in the visitor center and near the shaded picnic area, which has tables and grills. The visitor center, restrooms, and picnic facilities are accessible to wheelchairs.

Camping: No camping is permitted in the park. Moore Bayou, operated by the U.S. Army Corps of Engineers, is 1½ miles west of the park on Highway 169 and offers seven spaces with tables, grills, pit toilets, and water.

Fishing: Fishing is permitted with an Arkansas license. Catches are best in spring and fall and include largemouth bass, channel catfish, bream, crappie, and shad. No boat launching is allowed at the park, but a ramp is available at Moore Bayou, a short distance outside the Arkansas Post entrance.

BUFFALO NATIONAL RIVER
P.O. Box 1173
Harrison, AR 72601

The Buffalo River, which winds 134 miles through 95,700 acres, was authorized as a part of the National Park Service in 1972. It is one of the most scenic, unpolluted, and undeveloped free-flowing rivers remaining in the lower forty-eight states. The park is located in northwestern Arkansas across a three-county area. Lost Valley, on the west end of the park, is 25 miles southwest of Harrison via state highway 43. Buffalo Point, near the eastern edge, is approximately 18 miles southeast of Yellville on state highway 14.

The Buffalo National River flows eastward through forested hill country dominated by oaks and hickories. In the process, it has cut through rock, leaving stone cliffs of more than 500 feet. The area boasts a large variety of fish, plants, and wildlife along the river, which drops from a level of 2,300 feet in the Boston Mountains to only 400 feet at the point where the Buffalo joins the White River. A side canyon at Hemmed-in Hollow contains a 200-foot waterfall that is the highest of its kind between the Rockies and the southern Appalachians.

Two of the main visitation areas are on opposite ends of the park. On the east side, Buffalo Point is a mountainous area with hiking trails, a canoe launch area, a swimming beach, and a picnic area. Guided walks and campfire programs are conducted during summer months. On the west side, Lost Valley is a narrow gorge cut by Clark Creek. The creek winds between steep cliffs for nearly a mile before forming a waterfall from a cave. A trail follows the gorge to the falls. Interpretive programs are offered at both Buffalo Point and Lost Valley and at various points along the river. The park's newest visitor center is at Tyler Bend near U.S. 65 in the middle river area. Tyler Bend has hiking trails and a canoe launch. Interpretive programs are offered here.

One of the most popular activities in the park is canoeing or floating the river. Visitors may enjoy anywhere from a half-day to a ten-day, 120-mile trip. Environments vary along the river, with wildernesslike areas between Carver and Woolum and a developed park-type setting around Buffalo Point. Thirty concessioners along the river rent canoes and related items. Most provide a shuttle service to various points along the river. A list of concessioners may be obtained by writing the park superintendent.

There are three congressionally designated wilderness areas within the park. Although there are no signed or maintained paths in these areas, the many miles of abandoned mining/farming/logging

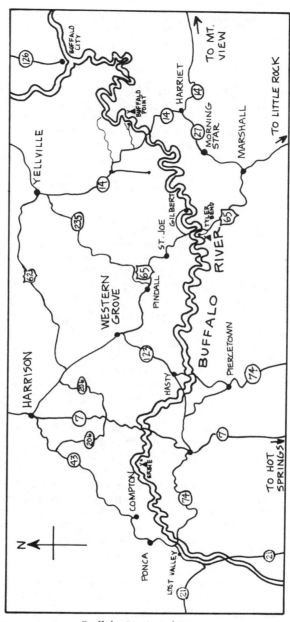

Buffalo National River

roads provide excellent hiking and backpacking opportunities. No motorized vehicles are allowed in these areas.

Facilities: Pit toilets and water are available at Lost Valley. No food service or lodging is provided in this part of the park, but both can be found in nearby communities. At Buffalo Point, a concessioner provides seven modern cottages and five rustic cottages. Meals and general merchandise also are available. For information, write Buffalo Point Concession, HCR #66, Box 388, Yellville, AR 72687 (501–449–6206).

Camping: A total of twelve campgrounds are scattered along the river. All have vault toilets. Steel Creek, Ozark, Kyles Landing, Erbie, Carver, Tyler Bend, Buffalo Point, and Rush have drinking water. The most developed campgrounds are at Tyler Bend (thirty-eight spaces, five group sites) and Buffalo Point (107 spaces, five group camps), which offer tables, grills, hookups, a dump station, flush toilets, and showers.

Fishing: Smallmouth and largemouth bass, catfish, and other varieties are available. An Arkansas license is required. Hunting is permitted with Arkansas Game and Fish Commission regulations and a few other restrictions imposed by the park.

FORT SMITH NATIONAL HISTORIC SITE
P.O. Box 1406
Fort Smith, AR 72902
(501) 783–3961

Fort Smith, which contains seventy-three acres, was incorporated into the National Park System in 1961 to preserve the site of two of the most famous United States military posts in the Louisiana Territory. Fort Smith later became a center of territorial law and order as the frontier moved westward. The park is located on Rogers Avenue in downtown Fort Smith, Arkansas. It is reached from U.S. 64 (Garrison Avenue) by turning one block south on Second Street.

On orders of the U.S. Army, construction on the first Fort Smith commenced in 1817. The purpose was to house troops that could help put an end to the Indian tribal wars taking place on the frontier. The fort was abandoned in 1824, and a second Fort Smith was built in 1838 100 yards east of the first site. As the frontier continued to move westward, Fort Smith lost much of its original importance, until it was abandoned by the U.S. Army in 1871.

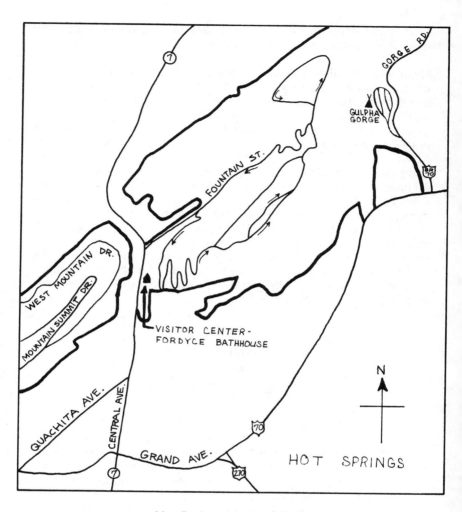

Hot Springs National Park

The end of Indian troubles was replaced by an era of general lawlessness as bands of outlaws and desperadoes rode the territory. The Federal Court for the Western District of Arkansas at Fort Smith was delegated to bring order to the region. Judge Isaac C. Parker arrived in 1875 as the youngest member of the federal judicial bench. During his twenty-one years on the bench, more than 9,000 defendants were convicted or pleaded guilty and 160 were sentenced to hang (yet only 79 were actually hanged). During this same period, more than one hundred deputy marshals were murdered. Parker gradually brought law to the Indian Territory; but as more settlers moved into the region, additional federal courts took much of his jurisdiction. Fort Smith's most famous citizen died in 1896 and is buried in Fort Smith National Cemetery.

A visitor center containing exhibits of the area's history is located in the old barracks building, which also contains Judge Parker's courtroom. The center is open daily except Christmas.

Facilities: Food and lodging are available a few blocks from the site. Restrooms and drinking water are in the visitor center.
Camping: No camping is permitted at the site. Two U.S. Army Corps of Engineers' campgrounds with tables, grills, water, and flush toilets are located nearby. One is 2 miles north of Barling, and the other is 1 mile west of Van Buren.
Fishing: Fishing in the Arkansas River is permitted with an Arkansas license.

HOT SPRINGS NATIONAL PARK
P.O. Box 1860
Hot Springs National Park, AR 71901
(501) 624–3383

Hot Springs National Park, which was designated a reservation in 1832 and added to the park system in 1921, contains 4,791 acres. It is famous for the forty-seven hot springs that provide millions of gallons of water for thermal bathing. The park is located in central Arkansas, approximately 50 miles southwest of Little Rock via Interstate 30 and U.S. 70. It may also be reached on Arkansas Highway 7 and U.S. 270.

The hot springs of Arkansas were used by local Indians long before white people came into the region. Permanent settlement began after the United States purchased the Louisiana Territory from France in 1803. In 1832, the springs were made into a federal reservation.

The rainwater that soaks through fractured rocks northwest of the springs is heated as it comes into contact with hot rock deep beneath the earth's crust. Each day, approximately 850,000 gallons of water heated to 143 degrees Fahrenheit flow from the park's forty-seven springs. The water—which is naturally sterile and entirely free of bad odors and taste—is collected, cooled, and piped to central reservoirs for bathhouse use. Two springs, accessible from Bathhouse Row or the Grand Promenade, are open for display to visitors, in addition to a larger display at the Tufa Terrace, where the flow of the upper springs built up a thick mineral deposit. The remainder have been capped to prevent contamination.

The park's visitor center, in the rehabilitated Fordyce Bathhouse, provides exhibits of the history and geology of the area. A fifteen-minute movie program is presented in the auditorium. Nearby—on Reserve Avenue, Bathhouse Row, and the Grand Promenade—drinking fountains provide free thermal water. Water from natural cold water springs is available on Fountain Street and on Whittington Avenue.

Visitors may take baths, sit in a whirlpool, or have a massage at a number of bathhouses operated by concessioners and permittees in accordance with Park Service regulations. A list of facilities and locations is available at the visitor center.

Numerous trails wander around the park's mountains and through its dense oak–hickory forests. Many of these begin from the scenic paved road that climbs Hot Springs Mountain and North Mountain. Conducted walks and campfire programs take place in the summer. The Fordyce Bathhouse Visitor Center is open year round, except for Christmas and New Year's Day.

Facilities: No food service or lodging is provided in the park, but nearly any type of facility can be found in the city of Hot Springs, which adjoins the park. Modern restrooms are provided in the visitor center, on Bathhouse Row and the Grand Promenade, and at the campground.

Camping: A single campground (forty-seven spaces) is located at Gulpha Gorge in the northeast corner of the park. Although the sites are fairly close together, the campground is quite nice. Tables, fireplaces, water, flush toilets, and a dump station are provided. The campground is open year round.

Fishing: No fishing is available in the park, but nearby Lakes Catherine, Hamilton, and Ouachita provide good possibilities. Boats and sporting supplies are available at the lakes.

PEA RIDGE NATIONAL MILITARY PARK
Pea Ridge, AR 72751
(501) 451–8122

Pea Ridge National Military Park, which contains 4,300 acres, was authorized in 1956 to memorialize the site of one of the major Civil War military engagements that took place west of the Mississippi River. The park is located in northwestern Arkansas, 10 miles northeast of Rogers and 30 miles northeast of Fayetteville via U.S. Highway 62.

The battle of Pea Ridge was fought during a two-day period in March 1862. Late in the previous year, the new commander of Federal forces in southwest Missouri initiated an aggressive policy of pushing pro-Confederate forces out of the state. Many of these men moved south near Fayetteville and joined a large force of Confederate soldiers. The combined group of 16,000 set out northward into Missouri with an eventual goal of St. Louis. Between their position and St. Louis, the new Federal commander stood with 10,500 soldiers at Pea Ridge.

The Confederate commander decided to circle the area and attack from the north. After two days of fighting, the Confederates ran short of ammunition while located near the Elkhorn Tavern and retreated eastward down the Old Huntsville Road. By noon, the battle was ended with an overall Federal victory. Reported casualties were 203 Union troops and 1,000 Confederates killed. The state of Missouri was saved for the Union.

A visitor center near the park entrance contains exhibits to help visitors interpret the park. Personnel are on duty from 8:00 A.M. until 5:00 P.M. to answer questions. A terrace at the back of the building permits visitors a sweeping view of the battlefield. Near the visitor center is a short (7-mile) self-guiding auto road to significant battlefield sites. Visitors with a little extra time should visit the unique town of Eureka Springs, 22 miles east on U.S. 62.

Facilities: No lodging or food service is available at the park, but both can be found in Rogers. Water and restrooms are located in the visitor center. A picnic area with tables, fireplaces, and water is nearby.
Camping: No camping is permitted in the park, but public campgrounds are available at Beaver Reservoir, 20 miles away.
Fishing: No fishing is available at Pea Ridge National Military Park.

California

CABRILLO NATIONAL MONUMENT
P.O. Box 6670
San Diego, CA 92166
(619) 293–5450

*Cabrillo is a 144-acre monument established in 1913 to com-
memorate Juan Rodriguez Cabrillo, the explorer who claimed the
West Coast of the United States for Spain in 1542. The monument
is located on Point Loma in the city of San Diego. It can be
reached by following Rosecrans Street (California 209) to Canon
Street, following Canon to Catalina Boulevard, and driving south
on Catalina to the end of Point Loma.*

The Cabrillo expedition sailed from Navidad, Mexico, on June 27, 1542,
to explore the unknown lands along the Pacific Coast. After frequent
stops for bad weather, supplies, and information from Indians, present-
day San Diego was reached on September 28. The expedition left on
October 3 to explore farther north, and on January 3, 1543, Cabrillo died
from injuries sustained in a fall several weeks earlier. The force eventually reached the southern boundary of Oregon before returning to
Navidad in the spring of 1543. The voyage helped open the way for later
expeditions that gained Spain a foothold in the New World.

The monument is open daily from 9:00 A.M. to 5:15 P.M., with
extended hours during summer months. A visitor center near the park
entrance contains exhibits and interpretative programs and offers an
exceptional view of San Diego and San Diego harbor. Make this your
initial stop. An old lighthouse, constructed in 1854 and abandoned in
1891, is open to the public. A recorded message center is located
nearby.

Overlooks and walkways at the monument present views of Mexico and the Pacific coastline. Tidepools on the coastal side of Point Loma
contain sealife such as starfish, sea anemones, crabs, and sea hares.

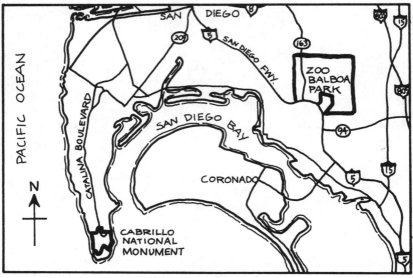
Cabrillo National Monument

Bayside Trail presents the hiker with views of wildlife, splendid vistas, and remnants of a coastal artillery system dating from World Wars I and II. From December through February, hundreds of gray whales migrate from the Arctic Ocean to the lagoons of Baja California. Ten- to fifteen-foot spouts may be seen from the whale-watching station where a tape-recorded message explains the migration.

Facilities: No food or lodging is available at the monument, but both are located nearby. Water and modern restrooms are at the visitor center.
Camping: No camping is permitted in the monument. Private camp-grounds can be found on Mission Bay north of the monument.
Fishing: Surf fishing is available on the west side of the monument off Gatchell Road. A California license is required and bait must be brought to the monument. Fishing is fair with catches of bass, halibut, opaleye, and shark. A bit of scrambling is required to reach the shoreline. Extreme care is necessary because of unstable sandstone cliffs.

CHANNEL ISLANDS NATIONAL PARK
1901 Spinnaker Drive
Ventura, CA 93001
(805) 644–8262

Channel Islands National Monument was established in 1938 but was expanded and had its status changed to "National Park" in 1980. It now contains more than 249,000 acres of land and water with large rookeries of sea lions, nesting sea birds, and unique plants and animals. The Channel Islands extend about 150 miles from the latitude of San Diego to that of Santa Barbara and from 10 to 70 miles offshore. Access to the islands is by private boat or public transportation.

Millions of years ago, mountains rose from the sea and large areas along the continent cracked. Land masses rose above the ocean and then slowly sank back beneath the water. A great land mass along the western edge of North America eventually submerged, leaving only the mountaintops now known as the Channel Islands.

For many thousands of years the islands were inhabited by the Chumash and other tribes of Indians. These people were skilled in making ornaments out of shells inlaid by means of asphalt. They also built large seagoing canoes of planks lashed together with thongs and caulked with native asphalt. The ancient Indian burial and village sites on some of the Channel Islands possess considerable archeological information covering the past 10,000 years.

Anacapa Island, at the eastern end of Santa Barbara Channel, is 11 miles from the mainland. It is actually a chain of three closely-linked islets combining to a length of approximately 5 miles. Anacapa's rocky shoreline is highlighted by sheer cliffs, and the only beach not submerged at high tide is at Frenchy's Cove. Here, a day-use area is near tide pools containing a variety of marine life. On East Anacapa Island are found the ranger station, the campground, nature trails, and a small museum, all within the setting of an old Coast Guard station. In neither location are there docking facilities, and a small craft is required to go ashore. There is no safe anchorage at East Island, and public transportation is advised for those wishing to visit this portion of Anacapa.

Santa Barbara Island (630 acres), 42 miles off the coast, is surrounded by kelp beds abounding in marine life. The island is composed of rolling, grass-covered hills that are edged by high cliffs from the sea. Anchorage is rough and landing in the rocky cove is hazardous. A Park Service ranger is stationed throughout the year on both Anacapa and Santa Barbara Islands.

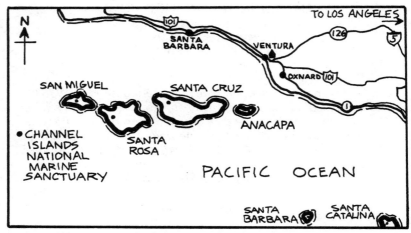

Channel Islands National Park

Santa Cruz is the largest island in the park and is especially important for its diversity of habitat. The National Park Service owns a portion of east Santa Cruz. The western part is owned by the Nature Conservancy. Landing on the island requires a permit from the landowners. The island's western portion may be reached by day-trips provided by the Nature Conservancy. Write Santa Cruz Island Project Office, 213 Sterns Wharf, Santa Barbara, CA 93101 (805–962–9111).

Santa Rosa is the park's second largest island and exhibits a variety of natural features including cliffs, high mountains, fossil beds, grasslands, rolling hills, beaches, and a marsh. Harbor seals breed on the island's beaches. Landing requires advance permission from the National Park Service.

San Miguel has outstanding natural and cultural features, including the best examples of caliche (a mineral sandcasting). The island hosts large numbers and varieties of seals and sea lions, and the island's largest mammal, the island fox, can be seen here. San Miguel contains more than 500 relatively undisturbed archeological sites, some dating back thousands of years. Visitors may land on the beach at Cuylor Harbor with a permit obtained by writing the park superintendent.

Facilities: No accommodations, concessioner facilities, fuel, or other services are available on the islands managed by the National Park Service. Pit toilets, but no drinking water, are located at the primitive campgrounds on Anacapa, Santa Barbara, and Santa Rosa Islands.
Camping: Four campgrounds, one each on Anacapa, Santa Barbara, San Miguel, and Santa Rosa islands, are very primitive. Maximum

capacity at each site is thirty persons, and reservations are required. Campers need to take water, camping gear, food, cooking equipment, and fuel for cooking. No campfires are permitted. Pit toilets and picnic tables are available on the islands.

Fishing: Fishing is permitted in accordance with California regulations, unless further restricted by federal law. Sea bass, barracuda, bonito, and yellowtail are among the varieties of fish living in the surrounding Pacific waters.

DEATH VALLEY NATIONAL MONUMENT
Death Valley, CA 92328
(714) 786–2331

Death Valley, which contains 2,067,875 acres, was established in 1933 to preserve a large desert containing the lowest point in the Western Hemisphere. The major part of the monument is located in southeastern California, with the remaining portion in southern Nevada. Four paved roads enter the park from the east and two enter from the west. The major road through the monument is California Highway 190. The visitor center is approximately 135 miles from Las Vegas.

Death Valley is a special place. The harsh environment with an average annual rainfall of as little as two inches requires hardy varieties of plants, animals, and humans. Most life revolves around permanent water sources such as springs. Higher elevations have cooler temperatures and more moisture, resulting in a greater variety of plants and animals. In spite of hordes of prospectors seeking precious metals over the years, even man has been unable to establish much of a life in this area.

The focal point at the monument is the Furnace Creek Visitor Center. Here visitors may view exhibits and obtain information on self-guided auto tours and trails. An illustrated slide program is available, and programs are presented by rangers during winter months. Guided walks are conducted on weekends and activity schedules are posted.

Seeing the park requires a considerable amount of driving. Some of the more interesting places (with numbers keyed to the map) are:

1. Scotty's Castle is a desert mansion built by Death Valley Scotty and a millionaire friend. A forty-five-minute tour of the castle leaves frequently during the day.

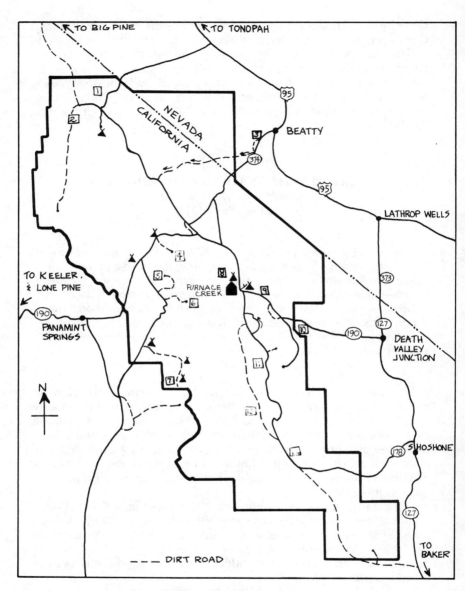

Death Valley National Monument

2. A volcanic crater ½-mile across and 500 feet deep.
3. Ruins of Rhyolite, an old mining town.
4. Mosaic Canyon is a small canyon containing interesting rock formations.
5. The ruins of Skidoo, an old mining town.
6. Aguereberry Point provides a grand view of the valley and the east mountains.
7. A 7.6-mile trail from the Mahogany Flat Campground leads to Telescope Peak, which at 11,049 feet is the park's highest point.
8. Harmony Borax Works is an old borax processing plant.
9. Zabriskie Point presents a view of colorful and dramatically eroded hills.
10. Ryan is an old mining town.
11. Badwater, at 280 feet below sea level, is the lowest point to which a motorist can drive in the Western Hemisphere.
12. Ashford Mill is the ruins of an old gold mill.
13. Westside Valley Road provides a scenic trip along the valley floor. This is the historic route of the twenty-mule- team borax wagons.

Facilities: Furnace Creek Inn and Ranch provides rooms, food service, a store, service station, swimming, and horses from early November through Easter. For information write Fred Harvey, Death Valley, CA 92328. Scotty's Castle offers food service, gasoline, and souvenirs, but no lodging. Stove Pipe Wells Village provides motel rooms, food, store, service station, swimming, and horses. Services are limited from May through October.

Camping: Eight campgrounds are located within the monument. Furnace Creek (200 spaces) and Texas Spring (ninety-three spaces, November–April) each offer tables, grills, water, flush toilets, and a dump station. Campsites at Furnace Creek and two group campsites in Texas Spring may be reserved through Ticketron, P.O. Box 617516, Chicago, IL 60661 (800–452–1111). Emigrant (ten sites, April–October) offers tables, grills, water, and flush toilets. Sunset (1,000 sites, November–April) and Stovepipe Wells (200 sites, November–April) offer water and flush toilets. Wildrose (thirty-six sites) offers tables, grills, and pit toilets. Thorndike (eight sites) and Mahogany Flat (ten sites) are open from March to November and offer tables, grills, and pit toilets. The roads to these last three are not passable for trailers, campers, or motor homes.

Fishing: No fishing is available in Death Valley National Monument.

DEVILS POSTPILE NATIONAL MONUMENT
c/o Sequoia and Kings Canyon National Parks
Three Rivers, CA 93271
(619) 934–2289

Devils Postpile is nearly 800 acres in size and was established in 1911 to preserve a great symmetrical formation of dark gray lava columns that fit together like the pipes of a large pipe organ. The monument is located southeast of Yosemite National Park (no connecting road) and is reached via a 16-mile paved road from U.S. 395. The intersection of the park's entrance road with U.S. 395 is 38 miles north of Bishop. A shuttle bus (fee) operates over the last 7 miles of the narrow mountain road that connects Minaret Summit with the monument. From early morning until late afternoon all visitors other than campers must ride the shuttle.

Less than 100,000 years ago, basalt lava, which was to become Devils Postpile, erupted in the already glaciated valley of the Middle Fork of the San Joaquin River. The lava cracked as it cooled, with each subsequent crack crossing others until the columns were formed. About 10,000 years ago, glaciers up to 1,000 feet thick flowed through the area and overrode the solidified lava. Much of the lava mass was quarried away, leaving only the more resistant parts such as Devils Postpile. One side of the Postpile was quarried away, and a sheer wall of columns forty to sixty feet high was left exposed. Many of the columns have broken away and lie on the slope below.

A ranger station by the parking area and shuttle stop has booklets about the monument. A short, steep hike along a well-used trail leads visitors to the top surface of the Postpile. Here the columns have been worn level and polished by the grinding of the glacier. Exposed cross-sections of the three- to seven-sided columns have the appearance of mosaic.

Devils Postpile National Monument has numerous short trails and is one of the key points on the John Muir Trail that stretches between Yosemite and Sequoia national parks. Two miles down the river trail from the Postpile, Rainbow Falls makes a drop of 101 feet into a deep green pool. During the middle of the day a rainbow forms to add to the beauty. A short, steep trail leads to the bottom of the falls where a garden of trees, flowers, and grasses is found. Cars may be driven to within 1.25 miles of the Falls via the road to Reds Meadow. A bubbling hot spring at Reds Meadow is evidence of the lava that still exists underground in this area.

The shuttle bus stops at a number of locations in addition to the Postpile, including Reds Meadow and Sotcher Lake. Visitors are free to ride the shuttle as much as they desire so long as they don't leave the valley. The narrow access road combined with the valley's traffic congestion make the shuttle an excellent way to see the monument and the surrounding scenery.

Facilities: Outside monument boundaries, about two miles from the campground, are the Reds Meadow Resort and Store, where gasoline, groceries, meals, cabins, a telephone, and saddle and pack horses are available. Water and flush toilets are at the monument's campground. Full services are available thirteen miles away in the town of Mammoth.

Camping: A campground (twenty-one sites) with tables and flush toilets is open from June 15 to October 1. Campers may ride the shuttle to Reds Meadow for supplies or meals. A number of U.S. Forest Service campgrounds are located outside the monument in Inyo National Forest. Additional Forest Service campgrounds are at Mammoth Lakes.

Fishing: The Middle Fork of the San Joaquin River contains rainbow, brook, and brown trout. Fishing is only a short walk from the campground and from several of the shuttle stops. A California license is required for persons over sixteen years of age.

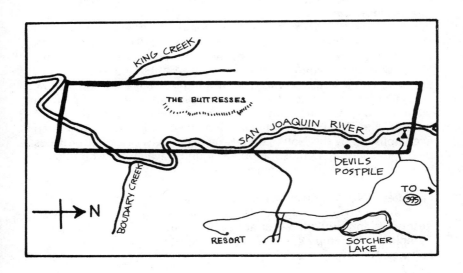

Devils Postpile National Monument

EUGENE O'NEILL NATIONAL HISTORIC SITE
c/o 4202 Alhambra Avenue
Martinez, CA 94553
(415) 228–8860

Eugene O'Neill National Historic Site was established in 1976 to commemorate the contribution of Eugene O'Neill to American literature and drama. The park is located in Danville, California, 30 miles east of San Francisco. Tours are by reservation only.

Nestled in the foothills of the San Ramon Valley is a concrete block structure sitting prominently amongst the natural landscape. The site at one time provided this country's only Nobel Prize-winning playwright a sanctuary in which to create masterpieces of American drama.

Built in 1937, the home today serves as a memorial to Eugene O'Neill's contribution to our country's vast cultural heritage. Named Tao House (symbolically referring to the Chinese philosophy) by O'Neill and his wife, Carlotta, it was to serve as their home for six years. While residing at Tao House Eugene O'Neill wrote the last five plays of his successful career. The most notable was *Long Day's Journey into Night.*

Free guided tours of the historic home and grounds are offered Wednesday through Sunday, at 10:00 A.M. and 12:30 P.M. Reservations are required, and the Park Service recommends making reservations about two weeks prior to the desired date (415–838–0249). Access to the site is by Park Service van. The two-and-one-half-hour tours allow visitors a glimpse into the personal and professional life of an internationally famous man and his surroundings. The tour route includes the Tao House, where much preservation work has been accomplished by the National Park Service. A visitor center provides displays and a self-guided grounds tour is available. Comfortable walking shoes are recommended.

Facilities: No overnight accommodations are available within the park, but food and lodging are available in nearby communities. Restrooms and drinking water are available in the visitor center.
Camping: No camping is permitted at the site.
Fishing: No fishing is available.

FORT POINT NATIONAL HISTORIC SITE
P.O. Box 29333
Presidio of San Francisco, CA 94129
(415) 556–1693

Fort Point contains twenty-nine acres and was established as a national historic site in 1970 to preserve a classic brick and granite mid-nineteenth-century coastal fortification. The fort sits just under the south end of the Golden Gate Bridge. From U.S. 101 going south, take the 25th Avenue exit at the tollgate. Northbound on 101, take the exit marked VIEW AREA, PRESIDIO, GOLDEN GATE NRA. From there, turn right to Lincoln, go left on Lincoln and left again at Long Avenue.

Fort Point was constructed during an eight-year period beginning in 1853 to bar the entrance of hostile ships into San Francisco Bay. The three-story brick structure was designed for 126 cannons and 600 soldiers. Guns with ranges of up to two miles fired cannon balls weighing from twenty-four to 128 pounds. The fort's walls average five to twelve feet in thickness. Fort Point was the only fort of its kind on the West Coast and one of the last built in the country.

In 1886 the fort was abandoned because more powerful guns made a brick structure such as this obsolete. From 1933 to 1937 it was used as a base of operations for building the Golden Gate Bridge, and during World War II the fort served as protection for a submarine net stretched across the entrance to San Francisco Bay.

The fort contains a visitor center and a small museum. Park personnel present historical demonstrations such as cannon loading and conduct half-hour guided tours of the fort throughout the day. Visitors may also take a self-guided tour. For guided tours and information, contact the information center in the fort.

Facilities: A drinking fountain and pit toilets are located just outside the fort. Other modern facilities are available 800 yards east of the fort near the Administrative Office.

Camping: No camping is permitted at Fort Point National Historic Site. A nice state park is 6 miles east of Point Reyes National Seashore (see camping section under Point Reyes).

Fishing: Fishing is permitted from the seawall surrounding Fort Point. Catches include perch, flounder, and an occasional bass. A California license is required to fish from the seawall but not from the nearby pier.

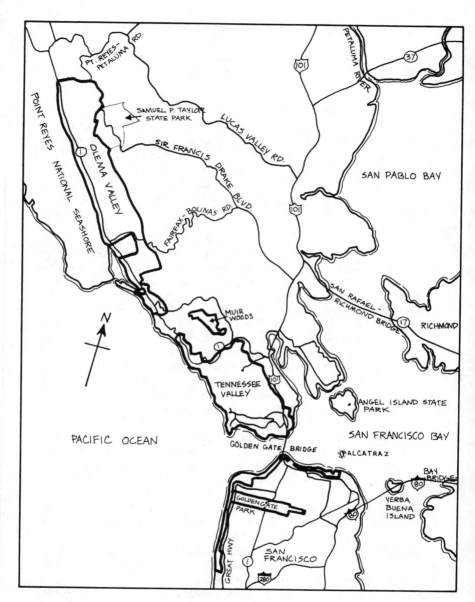

Golden Gate National Recreation Area

GOLDEN GATE NATIONAL RECREATION AREA
Fort Mason
San Francisco, CA 94123
(415) 556–0560

Golden Gate NRA was established in 1972 and contains 39,000 acres of ocean beaches, redwood forests, lagoons, marshes, and historical places of interest. The park is located along the western and northern perimeters of the city of San Francisco and north of the Golden Gate Bridge in the Marin Headlands.

Golden Gate National Recreation Area is a large, diverse, and spectacularly beautiful park that is made up of numerous individual areas. The park headquarters in Building 201 of Fort Mason in north San Francisco is a must stop for anyone intending to explore the park or sightsee in the city, and it is open from 8:00 A.M. to 5:00 P.M. on weekdays with personnel to answer questions. Picnic tables and fishing piers are available here for relaxation.

Transportation around the San Francisco section is available on the Municipal Railway (MUNI) system (683–MUNI), and access to areas across the Golden Gate is provided by Golden Gate Transportation (332–6600). Ferries from San Francisco Terminal provide access to Alcatraz (546–2805) and Angel Island (435–2131).

Because of the great diversity within Golden Gate National Recreation Area, it is not possible to cover each area and every activity available to visitors. Two of the more popular portions of the park follow.

San Francisco Area

Alcatraz: A one-and-a-half-mile guided tour of this former prison takes approximately two hours. A ferry leaves from Pier 43 at Fisherman's Wharf every forty-five minutes beginning at 9:00 A.M. Call 546–2805 for reservations.

National Maritime Museum: Models, photos, and historical items provide an account of San Francisco's nautical heritage. Ships at Hyde Street Pier may be boarded (556–8177).

Aquatic Park: Offers seating, lawns, a sandy shoreline, and beautiful scenery. Fishing and swimming are available in the lagoon (556–2904).

Fort Mason: Headquarters of this park offers a wide variety of cultural, educational, and recreational programs. A Liberty ship is docked at Pier 3 (441–5705).

Crissy Field: A quiet stretch of shoreline for hiking, fishing, or picnicking (556–1693).

Fort Point: See information under Fort Point National Historic Site on page 77.

Baker Beach: A sandy shoreline for hiking, swimming, or sunbathing with weekend tours (751–2519).

China Beach: A small beach nestled in a steep shoreline provides one of the best swimming areas in the city.

Land's End: A beautiful natural area with trees, birds, and vistas. Contains the route of an abandoned train to Cliff House and defense batteries of West Fort Miley (751–2519).

Cliff House: Excellent viewpoints of the coast with offshore Seal Rocks serving as home for sea lions and marine birds (751–1617).

Fort Funston: A loop trail with picnic areas provides vistas of coastal scenery. Hang gliders often use the cliffs and strong winds.

North of the Golden Gate

Marin Headlands: Wind-swept ridges, beaches, and protected valleys offer a major change from San Francisco's urban setting (561–7612).

Tennessee Valley: A narrow, secluded valley with a winding two-mile trail ending at a small beach (383–7717).

Muir Woods: See information under Muir Woods National Monument on page 97.

Mount Tamalpais: A number of hiking trails over mountainsides and through meadows and forests (388–2070).

Muir Beach and Stinson Beach: Vistas of the ocean and surrounding hills (868–0942).

Angel Island: A state park with picnicking, hiking, and beautiful scenery (435–1915).

Facilities: Lodging is available in San Francisco and surrounding communities. Food can be found at numerous locations within the park.

Camping: Camping is available at Point Reyes National Seashore (633–1092) and at Mt. Tamalpais State Park (388–2070). Private campgrounds are located along State Route 1. For additional information see the camping section under Point Reyes National Seashore.

Fishing: Surf fishing is possible at numerous locations along the beaches.

JOHN MUIR NATIONAL HISTORIC SITE
4202 Alhambra Avenue
Martinez, CA 94553
(415) 228–8860

John Muir National Historic Site was established in 1964 to preserve the home of John Muir and to commemorate his contributions to conservation and literature. The park is located near Martinez, California, approximately 25 miles northeast of Oakland.

John Muir emigrated to the United States from Scotland in 1849 when he was eleven years of age. After living in Wisconsin and acquiring an interest in both mechanics and biology, he started on his now-famous walks in 1867. Over the years his treks took him through much of wilderness America, and to Alaska, South America, Africa, India, the Orient, and Australia. His special place of interest was the Sierra Nevada.

Muir began writing in the 1870s and continued until his death in 1914. A great deal of the writing was undertaken at the house that is preserved at the site where Muir lived from 1890 until 1914 while he managed the fruit ranch of his father-in-law. Muir had resolved to do what he could to make the wilderness better-loved and preserved for future generations. He was an important influence in President Theodore Roosevelt's decisions to add 148 million acres of forests, twenty-three national monuments, and five national parks into our nation's forest and park system.

The National Park Service has restored the buildings and grounds to their appearance at the time John Muir lived here. The site is open Wednesday through Sunday from 10:00 A.M. to 4:30 P.M. except on Thanksgiving, Christmas, and New Year's Day. Park Service personnel are available to provide information, and a movie dealing with Muir's life is presented in the visitor center. Tours of the house are self-guided and a booklet is available in the visitor center.

Facilities: No facilities are available at the site but food and lodging can be found nearby. Drinking water and restrooms are in the visitor center. A picnic area is at Nancy Boyd Park, south of the historic site on Pleasant Hill Road.

Camping: No camping is permitted at the site and no campgrounds are in the immediate vicinity.

Fishing: No fishing is available at John Muir National Historic Site.

JOSHUA TREE NATIONAL MONUMENT
74485 National Monument Drive
Twentynine Palms, CA 92277
(619) 367–7511

Joshua Tree is a 560,000-acre national monument that was established in 1936 to preserve a section of California desert containing a notable variety of richness of vegetation. The monument is 140 miles east of Los Angeles. From the west it is approached via Interstate 10 to a point 15 miles east of Banning, where Highway 62 to Joshua Tree and Twentynine Palms fronts the north entrances. The south entrance is 25 miles east of Indio via U.S. 60 (Interstate 10).

At Joshua Tree National Monument, two desert ecosystems determined by different elevations converge. Desert plants in both systems have to be able to adapt to survive in a harsh environment. They must be able to go for prolonged periods without water and yet be able to absorb large amounts of moisture during brief rainstorms. Some plants spread roots close to the surface while others have roots growing deep into the earth.

One of the park's features is the Joshua tree. It grows to heights of forty feet and during March and April bears white blossoms in clusters eight to fourteen inches long. The tree is usually found at elevations above 3,000 feet in the central part of the monument.

The visitor will find five oases of California fan palms within the monument. The largest, in Lost Palms Canyon, contains more than one hundred palms. It is four miles by trail from the visitor center at Cottonwood Spring. The oasis at Fortynine Palms Canyon, just inside the northern boundary, is reached by a one-and-a-half-mile trail.

The main visitor center is just outside the north entrance near Twentynine Palms. Exhibits and a self-guided nature trail are located here. A small visitor center is also located at Cottonwood Spring. Other points of interest (keyed with numbers corresponding to those found on the map) are:

1. A one-and-a-half-mile moderately strenuous trail to Fortynine Palms Oasis, where water-loving plants thrive.
2. A half-mile nature trail is accessible from Indian Cove Campground.
3. A trail system winds between massive boulders and leads through a legendary cattle rustler's hideout.
4. Barker Dam forms a small reservoir. At one time the dam provided water for cattle and for mining use.
5. Lost Horse Mine is accessible via a 1½-mile trail.

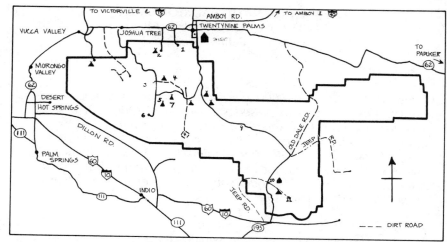

Joshua Tree National Monument

6. Key View, at 5,185 feet, provides a panoramic view.
7. A 1½-mile moderately strenuous trail to the Ryan Mountain summit provides several outstanding viewpoints.
8. An 18-mile self-guided motor nature tour winds through fascinating desert landscape. Four-wheel drive is required.
9. A self-guided nature trail contains some of the plants of the Colorado desert.
10. Cottonwood Spring is a manmade palm oasis noted for its birdlife.
11. A four-mile trail leads to the monument's largest group of palms.

Facilities: Overnight accommodations and food service are available in nearby towns but not in the monument. Water and flush toilets are available at the visitor center and at the campgrounds at Black Rock Canyon and Cottonwood Spring.

Camping: Nine campgrounds are available in the monument. The only locations with water and flush toilets are Black Rock Canyon (one hundred spaces) and Cottonwood Spring (sixty-two spaces) near the monument's south entrance. Reservations are available for Black Rock Canyon campground (open in season only). Write Ticketron, P.O. Box 617516, Chicago, IL 60661 (800–452–1111). Those with vault toilets and no water include Belle (twenty spaces), Hidden Valley (sixty-two spaces), Indian Cove (111 spaces and thirteen group sites), Jumbo Rocks (130 spaces), Ryan (twenty-seven spaces), Sheep Pass (six group sites, reservations only), and White Tank (twenty spaces).

Fishing: No fishing is available in Joshua Tree National Monument.

KINGS CANYON NATIONAL PARK;
SEQUOIA NATIONAL PARK
Three Rivers, CA 93271
(209) 565–3341

General Grant and Sequoia national parks were established in 1890. Kings Canyon National Park was established separately in 1940 and incorporated General Grant National Park. Today, the parks' combined 1,300 square miles are administered as a single unit. The parks are especially noted for groves of giant sequoias growing in canyons surrounded by the High Sierra. Sequoia and Kings Canyon are located in central California, between Yosemite and Death Valley. Access is from the west, with State Highway 180 from Fresno leading into Kings Canyon and Route 198 from Visalia entering Sequoia. No road crosses the Sierra Nevada range in either park.

The Sierra Nevada is the result of an uplifting of the earth's crust millions of years ago. Later, during the great ice age, glaciers quarried canyons and scooped basins, giving the mountains their present shape. Once the glaciers began melting, the basins turned into lakes and plant life returned to the region. The sequoias dominating the park were once widespread but now grow only on the western slope of the Sierra. Although not as tall as the related coastal redwoods, the sequoias are immense, with a trunk size that is simply amazing.

The parks' three major developed areas are Giant Forest, Grant Grove, and Cedar Grove. General's Highway connects Ash Mountain, Giant Forest, and Grant Grove. Entering at Ash Mountain, the road passes through Giant Forest, which contains some of the finest groups of giant sequoias including the General Sherman tree—the world's largest living thing. The area is covered with trails and short walks to Moro Rock, Beetle Rock, and Sunset Rock provide excellent viewpoints. A visitor center is at Lodgepole.

After leaving the park at Lost Grove the road wanders in a northwesterly direction to Grant Grove, an isolated section of Kings Canyon. Here, the visitor can see the General Grant—the nation's Christmas tree. Nearby are other large sequoias, and a visitor center with exhibits and a slide presentation is about a mile away. Be sure to visit this area of giant trees. Big Stump Basin, where large trees were cut during the logging era before the basin became part of Kings Canyon National Park, is reached via a self-guided trail near the south entrance. The Grant Grove area is convenient to both Cedar Grove and Giant Forest (about 30 miles to each), which makes it a good place to stay if you have only limited time. The road from Grant Grove to

Cedar Grove (30 miles) is open from about May 1 to November 1 and the view of the canyon is something not to be missed. Cedar Grove is one of the centers of activity in Kings Canyon. Visitors will find it considerably warmer than Grant Grove. Here peaks rise to a mile or more above the south fork of the Kings River. The river is fair for fishing, but because of the swift current and very cold water, it is not suitable for swimming or rafting. The end of the road is the site of major trailheads to the high country (long-term parking is available). A self-guided nature trail is nearby. The trailhead to Mount Whitney, the highest mountain in the continental United States, is reached along a paved road from Lone Pine on the park's east side.

Living history demonstrations and ranger-guided walks to areas of interest in both parks are provided throughout the year. Schedules are posted in lodges, campgrounds, and visitor centers. Campfire programs are presented nightly at Lodgepole, Giant Forest, Grant Grove, Dorst, and Cedar Grove and less often at Mineral King. Saddle horses and pack animals may be rented at corrals near Wolverton, Mineral King, Grant Grove, Cedar Grove, and at various locations on the park's east side. More than 700 miles of trails are open to horses. Limited tours (fee required) of Crystal Cave are scheduled Friday through Monday during May and September and on a daily basis during summer months. A steep half-mile trail leads to the cave entrance.

Winter season at Sequoia and Kings Canyon is from December through March. Downhill skiing is available at Wolverton, where there are two rope tows, a platter lift, and a ski rental shop with instruction. A three-mile marked trail from Wolverton to Giant Forest is provided for cross-country skiing. Sleds, tubes, and platters are permitted at Wolverton and Grant Grove.

Facilities: Lodging is available all year at Giant Forest and Grant Grove lodges, and from late May to October at Stony Creek Lodge. Camp Kaweah at Giant Forest has cabins and motel-type rooms, while Wilsonia provides cabins on private land inside the park. Housekeeping cabins are available at Camp Kaweah in Giant Forest, Meadow Camp in Grant Grove, and Silver City in Mineral King. Bearpaw Meadow Camp, eleven and a half miles from Giant Forest on the High Sierra Trail, provides wood-platform tents and meals from late June to early September. For reservations write Guest Services, Inc., Sequoia National Park, CA 93262 (209–565–3373). At Wilsonia write Kings Canyon National Park, CA 93633 (209–335–2310). For Silver City reservations write P.O. Box 56, Three Rivers, CA 93271 (209–561–3223).

Restaurants are open year round at Giant Forest, Grant Grove, and Wilsonia. From late May to October food service is also available at Cedar Grove, Giant Forest Lodge, and Stony Creek. General supplies are available at Cedar Creek, Giant Forest, Grant Grove, Stony Creek, and Wilsonia.

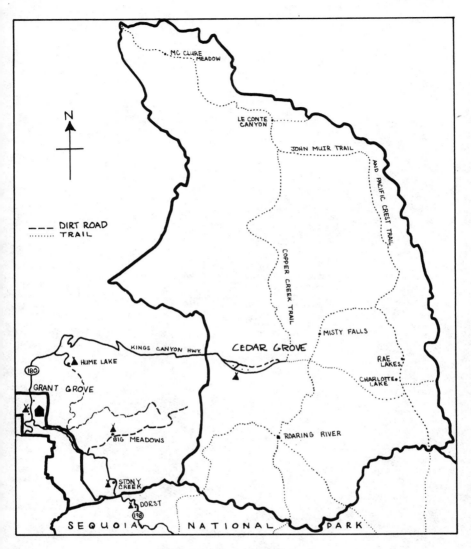

Kings Canyon National Park

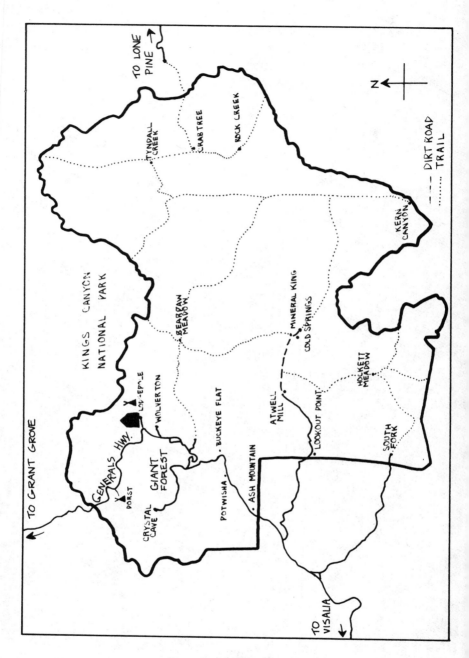

Sequoia National Park

Camping: A variety of campgrounds are located within the two parks. Most offer tables, grills, water, and flush toilets. In Sequoia, the Giant Forest area has Lodgepole (260 spaces, dump station, pay showers, store) and Dorst (238 spaces, seven group sites, dump station). Lodgepole fills first and reservations are available by writing Ticketron, P.O. Box 617516, Chicago, IL 60661 (800–842–1111). In the Mineral King area, Atwell Mill (twenty-three spaces) and Cold Springs (thirty-seven spaces) have pit toilets. No trailers are permitted in either campground. At lower elevations in Sequoia are Buckeye Flat (twenty-eight spaces, no trailers or recreation vehicles), Potwisha (forty-four spaces, dump station, swimming), and South Fork (thirteen spaces, pit toilet, trailers not recommended).

In Kings Canyon, the Grant Grove area has Azalea (113 spaces, dump station), Crystal Springs (sixty-three spaces), and Sunset (192 spaces, limited trailer space). A market and pay showers are within walking distance of these campgrounds. In the Cedar Grove area are Canyon View (thirty-seven spaces, four group sites), Moraine (120 spaces), Sentinel (eighty-three spaces), and Sheep Creek (111 spaces, dump station). Of these, Sentinel generally fills first and is the most crowded, while Moraine has somewhat less shade and is the least crowded. The amphitheater and ranger station are at Sentinel Campground.

Fishing: Many wilderness lakes and streams contain golden, rainbow, brook, and brown trout. The most popular fishing spots are along the Kings River and the forks of the Kaweah River. A California license is required and may be purchased at the stores.

LASSEN VOLCANIC NATIONAL PARK
Mineral, CA 96063
(916) 595–4444

Lassen Volcanic National Park contains 106,000 acres and was established as a national monument in 1907 (changed to a national park in 1916) to protect hot springs, fumaroles, mud pots, and sulfurous vents surrounding a volcano last active around 1921. The park is located in north-central California, about 42 miles east of Redding on State Highway 44.

Lassen is a beautiful and relatively uncrowded mountainous area of forests, lakes, and extinct and inactive volcanoes. Centered toward the west side of the park is Lassen Peak, a 10,457-foot plug-dome volcano that last erupted during a seven-year period beginning in 1914. In addition to Lassen Peak, an inactive cinder cone and active hot springs are in evidence.

A single main paved road, California 89 (summer only) winds in a north-south direction through the west side of the park. The southwest entrance has an entrance station, chalet, nature trail, and a seasonal winter-sports center. The northern entrance at Manzanita Lake includes a nature trail and small visitor center. Between these two centers visitors will find a variety of things to do and see.

Many of the park's 150 miles of trails begin from the roadside. A 1½-mile self-guided trail to Bumpass Hell begins seven miles inside of the southwest boundary. This leads to the park's best area in which to observe thermal activity. In addition to the trail to the Lassen Peak summit, there is also the five-mile (round trip) Cinder Cone Trail, which climbs to the top of a 700-foot cinder cone. This latter trail begins at the Butte Lake Ranger Station at the northeast corner of the park. Daily guided hikes of both half-day and full-day length take place throughout the summer. Most of these begin from various points along the main road. Two-hour naturalist-conducted walks leave the campgrounds during most days. The walk around Manzanita Lake is delightful and relatively easy.

The winter sports area is near the Sulphur Works Entrance Station. Facilities (open on weekends) include the 1,100-foot Poma lift, a 400-foot rope tow, and a 200-foot rope tow for beginners. A ski shop with rentals and instruction is also located here. Snowmobiling on unplowed roadways is allowed by permit only and tobogganing is on an unsupervised basis.

Facilities: Only minimal accommodations are present in Lassen. A general store operating near the Manzanita Lake campground during

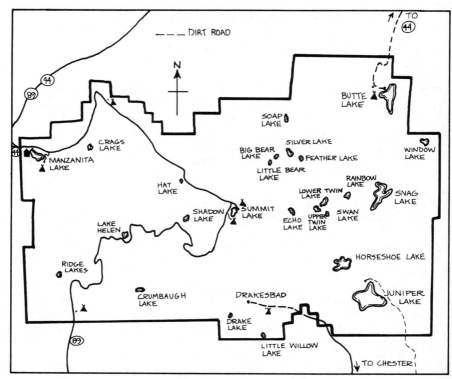

Lassen Volcanic National Park

summer months provides fast food, groceries, and gasoline. Limited food service is available at Lassen Chalet near the southwest entrance station during the summer months. Overnight accommodations are available at Drakesbad Guest Ranch during July and August. Write California Guest Services, Mineral, CA 96063 (916–595–3306). Ranger stations are located at Manzanita Lake, Summit Lake, Butte Lake, Horseshoe Lake, Juniper Lake, Warner Valley, and Sulphur Works.

Camping: Improved campgrounds are located at Manzanita Lake (179 spaces, pay showers), Summit Lake (ninety-four spaces), Butte Lake (ninety-eight spaces), and Sulphur Works (twenty-five spaces). The latter has campsites located approximately one hundred yards from parking facilities, but the first three can accommodate trailers and motorhomes. All of these camps have fire grates, picnic tables, water, and flush toilets. Summit Lake usually fills earlier than the other three. Less improved campsites (pit toilets, tables, fireplaces) are at Crags (forty-five overflow spaces), Warner Valley (fifteen spaces), and Juniper Lake (eighteen spaces). Juniper Lake is not recommended for trailers.

Fishing: Fishing is permitted anywhere except Emerald Lake, Manzanita Creek, and within 150 feet of the inlet to Manzanita Lake. A California license is required and possibilities include brown, brook, and rainbow trout. Grassy Creek connecting Horseshoe and Snag lakes is closed from October 1 to June 15.

LAVA BEDS NATIONAL MONUMENT
P.O. Box 867
Tulelake, CA 96134
(916) 667–2282

Lava Beds contains 46,500 acres, and it was established as a national monument in 1925 to preserve a rugged landscape formed by volcanic activity. The monument is located in extreme north-central California, 58 miles south of Klamath Falls, Oregon. It is reached by paved roads from California Highway 139.

Centuries ago, a group of vents spewed great masses of molten basaltic lava over this region of the country. As the rivers of liquid rock cooled and hardened, the landscape of Lava Beds National Monument was born. Cinder cones are scattered throughout the area and both smooth and rough (such as Devil's Homestead and Schonchin Flow) lava flows cover the monument. A number of these lava flows created lava-tube caves that are found throughout the area. Twenty-one caves are developed for visitors.

The only major Indian war to be fought in California took place in the lava beds. In 1872, a small band of Modoc Indians took refuge at what is now called Captain Jacks Stronghold after disagreements with settlers. The group of Indians was able to hold off federal and volunteer troops for nearly six months. A self-guided trail (half hour with booklets) is at the stronghold. Canbys Cross marks the spot where peace negotiations were held, and Gillems Camp was U.S. Army headquarters during the later phases of the war.

A visitor center is located three to four miles inside of the southeast entrance where a small museum explains the history and geology of the area. During summer months, park rangers give guided walks and campfire programs. A loop road south of headquarters provides access to many of the developed lava-tube caves. Numerous trails are located throughout the monument. Schonchin Butte, one of the largest cinder cones, can be climbed and a trail leads to Black Crater.

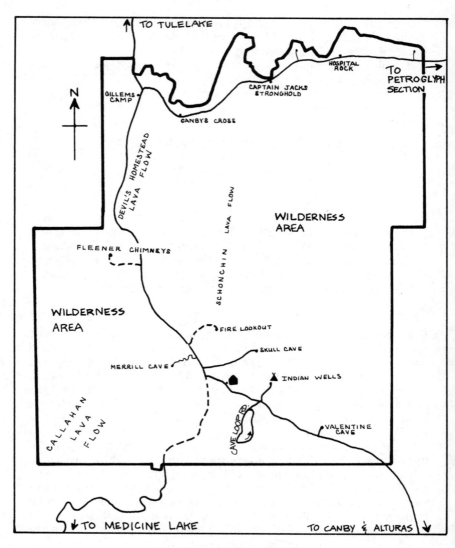

Lava Beds National Monument

Near the visitor center, Mushpot Cave is lighted for an easy self-guided tour that takes about twenty minutes. The tour is worth-while and should be a visitor's first order of business after viewing the visitor center exhibits. The remainder of the caves are without lighting so flashlights must be used. These may be borrowed at the visitor center. For those with even a mild interest in caves, a trip through one or more of these is a must. It is a unique experience that by itself makes a trip to the monument memorable.

Facilities: Food and lodging are not available within the monument, but both can be found in either Tulelake or Klamath Falls. Water and modern restrooms are located at headquarters and at the campground (during summer months). The picnic areas at Fleener Chimneys and Captain Jack's Stronghold have no water.

Camping: Indian Well Campground (forty-five spaces) is open all year and grills, tables, water, and flush toilets (summer only) are provided. The campground is located a short distance from the visitor center with sites interspersed among juniper trees that provide some shade for campers but not much for their vehicles.

Fishing: No fishing is available at Lava Beds National Monument. Thirty miles south of the park on U.S. Forest Service land, Medicine Lake provides excellent trout fishing. A California license is required and an area map showing the location of the lake is available in the Lava Beds visitor center.

MUIR WOODS NATIONAL MONUMENT
Mill Valley, CA 94941
(415) 388–2595

Muir Woods was established in 1908 and contains more than 550 acres of forest with a beautiful virgin stand of coastal redwoods. The park is located 17 miles north of San Francisco via U.S. 101 and California 1. See the area map of Muir Woods under Golden Gate National Recreation Area in this section.

Millions of years ago a giant tree related to today's redwood and sequoia grew throughout the northern hemisphere. Today, the red-wood grows only in a 540-mile-long, 30-mile-wide belt along the Pacific coast from just south of Monterey to the southwestern corner of Oregon. This is where the Pacific produces fog and damp climate in selected areas such as Muir Woods. In this park some specimens have

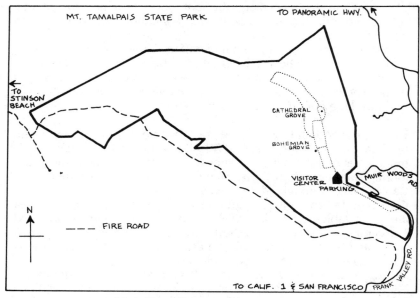

Muir Woods National Monument

reached over 250 feet in height, while farther north in the state, trees exceed 360 feet.

The redwood's ability to grow large and live a long life results from its resistance to fire, insects, and fungi. The wood is high in moisture content, contains almost no flammable pitch, and has a thick, asbestos-like bark. The last large fire in Muir Woods occurred in the middle 1800s. The wood also contains chemicals that make it resistant to insects and fungi. The tree's root system is surprisingly shallow but may radiate for up to one hundred feet.

The park is open from 8:00 A.M. to sunset. The visitor center is located in the park's southeast corner. The monument is designed primarily to be seen by hiking. The main walking trails are paved and therefore accessible to wheelchairs. Six miles of trails connect with those of Mt. Tamalpais State Park to provide the visitor with many hours of exercise, enjoyment, and quiet. Bridges along Redwood Creek make short loops possible, and trailside exhibits, signs, and markers are placed throughout the monument. A self-guided portion of the trail (with booklet) lies between the second and third bridge.

Be prewarned that the monument is quite crowded during summer months and on winter weekends with nice weather. During summer weekends the park is packed. The result is that parking is often difficult and solitude on the loop trails is elusive. It is best to visit early in the morning or later in the afternoon and get off the main walking path onto some of the trails.

Facilities: The park's only facility is a concession shop near the visitor center that sells snacks and souvenirs. Drinking water and restrooms are located at the visitor center.

Camping: No camping or picnicking facilities are in the monument. Mt. Tamalpais State Park surrounding Muir Woods provides walk-in tent-style camping with tables, grills, water, and restrooms. Automobile parking is about one hundred yards from the camping sites. To reach this area at Pantoll, take the Panoramic Highway north after leaving Muir Woods. Another state park is twenty-six miles northwest via Highway 1. See the camping section under Point Reyes National Seashore.

Fishing: No fishing is permitted in Muir Woods.

PINNACLES NATIONAL MONUMENT
Paicines, CA 95043
(408) 389–4578

Pinnacles National Monument was established in 1908 and contains the remains of an ancient volcano that has been eroded by wind, water, and freezing into spectacular pinnacles and spires. The park is located in west-central California, approximately 83 miles southeast of San Jose. The major part of the monument must be approached from the east via California Highways 25 and 146. The entrance to the west side of the monument, from U.S. 101 at Soledad, is not a through road and will not accommodate trailers or campers.

More than 23 million years ago, pressures within the earth caused cracks to appear along the western edge of the North American continent. A volcano in the Pinnacles region blew tons of rock and lava through the fissures and covered the countryside.

The rugged slopes of Pinnacles are covered by a brushy plant cover known as chaparral. The plants thrive in the hot, dry summers and sparse rainfall (fifteen inches) found in this area of California. This pygmy forest provides shelter for a variety of wildlife including black-tailed deer, rabbits, raccoons, bobcats, and gray fox. Frequently seen birds include the acorn woodpecker, brown towhee, California quail, and turkey vulture.

The visitor center, about 2 miles from the east entrance, contains a small museum where a park naturalist is on duty to help visitors.

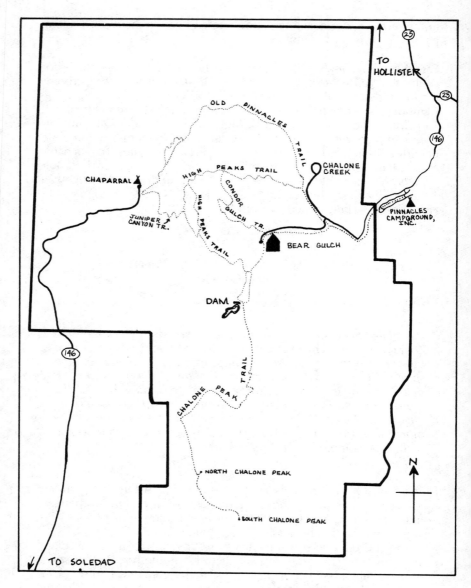

Pinnacles National Monument

Although the monument is open all year, its main seasons are spring and fall. Winter months bring the wet season and summer months are quite hot with daytime temperatures often exceeding 100 degrees Fahrenheit.

One of the park's main activities is hiking, and a number of trails are located throughout Pinnacles including:

1. High Peaks Trail (5.4 miles, five to six hours) begins at the Chalone Creek picnic area or at the parking area at the end of Bear Gulch picnic area. The 1,650-foot climb presents viewpoints of the entire park.
2. Condor Gulch Trail (1.7 miles, one and a half hours) connects the visitor center with the High Peaks Trail.
3. Bear Gulch Trail (1.7 miles, one hour) is a self-guided trail connecting the visitor center with the Chalone Creek picnic area.
4. Chalone Peak Trail (round trip: 10½ miles, seven hours) wanders through stands of chaparral on an uphill trip from Bear Gulch to a fire lookout at the top of Chalone Peak.
5. Moses Spring Nature Trail (1¾ miles, one and a half hours) begins at the parking lot next to the picnic area and leads to the foot of the reservoir dam. The trail is self-guided and leaflets are available at the trailhead. Return via the Caves Trail, which takes you between and under boulders (take a flashlight).
6. Balconies Trail (one way: 1.2 miles, two hours) connects Chalone Creek picnic area with Chaparral Campground on the park's west side. The trail is level and relatively easy to walk.

Facilities: No food services or accommodations are available in the monument. A camper store is located just outside the east entrance (short hours during summer weekdays). Drinking water and modern restrooms are available at the visitor center and in the picnic areas. On the west side, the nearest services are in Soledad.

Camping: On the park's west side, Chaparral Campground (twenty-three spaces) provides walk-in campsites with tables, grills, water, and vault toilets. No Park Service campgrounds are on the east side although a nice (125 sites) private campground is just outside the park. The sites offer some shade and are fairly widely spaced. The campground provides tables, grills, hot water, flush toilets, a swimming pool, showers (in poolhouse), and electric hookups. For information or reservations write Pinnacles Campground, Inc., 2400 Highway 146, Paicines, CA 95043 (408–389–4462).

Fishing: No fishing is available in Pinnacles National Monument.

POINT REYES NATIONAL SEASHORE
Point Reyes, CA 94956
(415) 663–1092

Point Reyes was added to the National Park System in 1962 and contains more than 70,000 acres of beaches, lagoons, and forested ridges backed by tall cliffs. The seashore's southern end is located approximately 22 miles northeast of San Francisco via California Highway 1. Park headquarters at Bear Valley is located near the town of Olema, 8 miles from the southern boundary.

Point Reyes National Seashore is a peninsula providing a habitat for more than 400 species of birds, seventy-two species of mammals, many types of other land and marine animals, and a great variety of plant life. The park is an "island" that has been separated from the mainland by the San Andreas Fault. Periodic movement along the fault has resulted in completely different types and ages of rocks on the peninsula as compared to those found on the mainland in the same area. During the 1906 earthquake, land on the west side of the fault moved as much as 21 feet northward. A short self-guided trail (thirty-five minutes) along the fault begins across the parking lot from the Bear Valley Visitor Center.

The island has seen a wide variety of people crossing its beaches. In 1579, Sir Francis Drake stopped over to make repairs to his ship and claimed the land for Queen Elizabeth. Don Sebastian Vizcaino, another explorer, landed here in 1603 and named it La Punta de los Reyes ("Point of the Kings"). By 1776, Point Reyes was under the control of Spain.

Park headquarters is located one fourth of a mile west of Olema on Bear Valley Road. Here the Bear Valley Visitor Center contains 250 natural history exhibits, an auditorium, 150 plant and animal specimens, and exhibits about the San Andreas Fault. Demonstrations, talks, and nature walks are conducted in the Bear Valley area during summer months. From Bear Valley a paved road heads northwest through Inverness and then splits, with one road going north past Tomales Bay State Park and on to McClures Beach, where tidepools can be seen. The other branch leads to Drakes Beach (a good swimming beach) and Point Reyes. The historic Point Reyes Lighthouse is no longer operating but is open to the public. A visit here is worth the drive but the long stairway down to the lighthouse requires some effort. The road to Limantour Beach begins a short distance north of Bear Valley.

Bear Valley Trailhead, near headquarters, is a gateway to more than 140 miles of trails. The most popular route is the 4.4-mile Bear

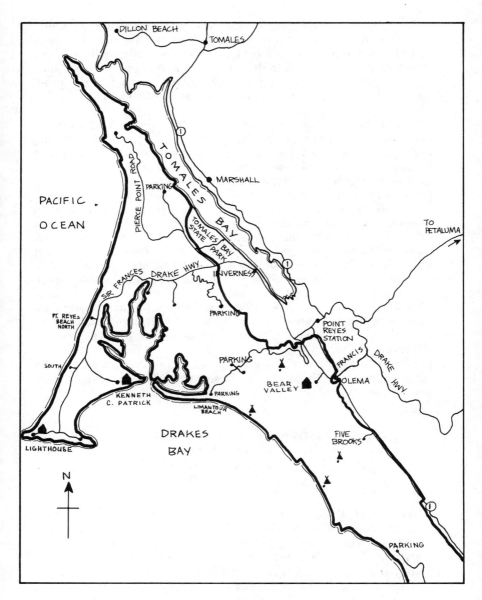

Point Reyes National Seashore

Valley Trail that winds through meadows and forests to the sea. Other trails branch from this main route and ascend into the high country of Inverness Ridge and the southern portion of the seashore. Bicycle use is restricted to designated trails so riders should check at Bear Valley Visitor Center for specific information. Horses are permitted on all trails except Bear Valley Trail on weekends and holidays.

Facilities: No overnight accommodations or complete food service is available within the park, but both can be found nearby. Drinking water and modern restrooms are located at park headquarters and at Drakes Beach. Limited food service is available at Drakes Beach.

Camping: Four hike-in campgrounds are open year round. Coast, Sky, Glen Camp, and Wildcat Group Camp have water, restrooms, tables, and grills. Sites may be reserved and are nearly always full on weekends and holidays during summer weekends. Reservations can be made up to sixty days in advance by calling 415–663–1092, Monday through Friday, 9:00 A.M. to noon. Users must register at Bear Valley Visitor Center and obtain a camping permit. No camping is permitted at Tomales Bay State Park but a fairly large private campground is located on California Highway 1 in Olema. Six miles east of Olema on Sir Francis Drake Highway, Samuel P. Taylor State Park provides camping (sixty-eight spaces) with tables, grills, water, flush toilets, and hot showers. The park encompasses a large grove of redwoods.

Fishing: Surf fishing is permitted on all beaches and a California license is required. There is some freshwater fishing in several small ponds.

REDWOOD NATIONAL PARK
1111 Second Street
Crescent City, CA 95531
(707) 464–6101

Redwood National Park was established in 1968 and contains nearly 106,000 acres of coastal redwood forests with ancient groves of trees averaging 500 to 700 years of age and growing to more than 300 feet in height. The park includes 40 miles of rugged and beautiful Pacific shoreline. Redwood National Park lies along U.S. 101 on the extreme northern coast of California. From the east the park is approached on U.S. 199 from Grants Pass, Oregon.

The redwoods of the Pacific Coast are nearly overpowering to someone viewing them for the first time. The world's tallest trees, some individual redwoods live as long as 2,000 years. In addition to the featured redwoods, a visitor will find oak, cedar, and Douglas fir at the higher elevations, and cedar, alder, maple, and hemlock along the streams and rivers. Varied wildlife including Roosevelt elk, fox, bobcat, cougar, black-tailed deer, and black bear can be found in various locations within the park's boundaries. Birding is a popular activity as well, with both ocean-going and forest birds.

The park encompasses three California state parks (Jedediah Smith, Del Norte Coast, and Prairie Creek Redwoods) established prior to the national park. Approximately forty-five miles long, Redwood is only seven miles wide at its widest point on the south end. U.S. 101 extends the entire length of the park, and additional roads and trails provide access to some of the scenic backcountry areas. Bald Hills Road near•the south entrance at Orick leads to Lady Bird Johnson Grove and the Redwood Creek trailhead. One of the more scenic drives begins near Klamath on Coastal Drive. This eight-mile road along bluffs and headlands is part gravel. Near the park's north entrance, the unpaved Howland Hill Road winds its way through a lush redwood forest and leads to the Stout Grove along the wild and scenic Smith River.

Numerous hiking trails are scattered throughout the park including almost unlimited walking along the Coastal Trail System. The Coastal Trail is thirty-five miles long, between Crescent Beach in the north and Orick in the south. Viewpoints, exhibits, and beach access are provided as the trail winds along bluffs overlooking the Pacific Ocean. The Redwood Creek Trail, east of Orick, provides an eight-and-a-half-mile path to the Tall Trees Grove. This grove contains the tallest known tree in the world, a twin-trunk giant towering 367.8 feet in height. The grove is also reached via a seventeen-mile drive from the Redwood Information Center and a three-mile hike. One mile beyond Redwood Creek trailhead, visitors may park and take a slow half-mile walk to the park's dedication site at Lady Bird Johnson Grove. This includes a self-guided nature trail. Park rangers present evening programs and guided walks in summer throughout the park. Information centers are located at Hiouchi, Crescent City, Crescent Beach, and Orick.

Facilities: A number of motels and food outlets are available along U.S. Highway 101. A hostel is seventeen miles south of Crescent City (707–482–8265). Most modern accommodations are in towns located near park boundaries, Crescent City to the north and Orick to the south. Eureka, a relatively large town, is approximately forty-five miles south of the park's south entrance.

Camping: Four walk-in campgrounds are provided by Redwood National Park, and four drive-in camping areas are provided in the state parks. Depending on individual taste, a visitor might enjoy camping at Gold Bluff Beach on the Pacific Ocean. This site is located

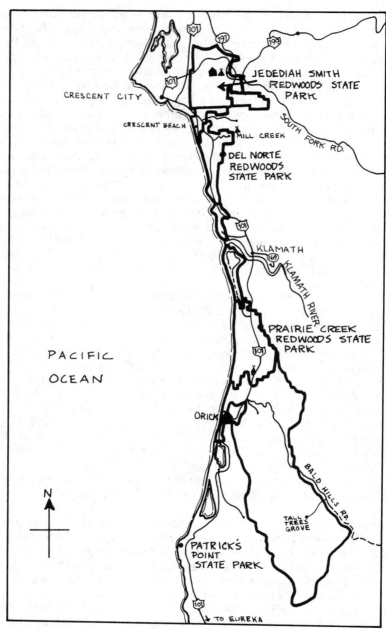

Redwood National Park

near the south entrance via a four-mile unpaved road. The location is breezy and cool in summer. Prairie Creek Campground is located a few miles north of Gold Bluff Beach on Highway 101. Two additional campgrounds at the north end of the park can be reserved by writing MISTIX, P.O. Box 85705, San Diego, CA 92138 (800–444–7275 and 619–452–1950).

Twenty miles south of Orick at the south entrance, Patricks Point State Park contains an improved campground. In addition, Six Rivers National Forest contains four campgrounds with a total of eighty-seven sites for tents, campers, and small trailers. These are located about thirty minutes east of Highway 101 on U.S. 199. Other more distant campgrounds are located in Klamath and Trinity National Forests. Camping is also available at private campgrounds and trailer parks along Highway 101.

Fishing: This is an excellent area for salmon and steelhead trout. Surfcasting for red-tail perch is also a popular activity. A California license is mandatory for both ocean and freshwater fishing. California regulations apply throughout the area.

SAN FRANCISCO MARITIME NATIONAL HISTORICAL PARK
Fort Mason
San Francisco, CA 94123
(415) 556–3002

This park of fifty acres was established in 1988 to preserve and celebrate the maritime history of the Pacific Coast. The historical park includes museum exhibits, historic ships, an aquatic park, research collections, and a maritime store. San Francisco Maritime National Historical Park is located just west of Fisherman's Wharf on San Francisco Bay in the city of San Francisco. The park is best reached via public transportation (municipal bus or the Powell and Hyde cable car), as parking is in short supply in this area of the city.

A visit to San Francisco Maritime National Historical Park is a trip to this historic city's past. The heart of the park is the Maritime Museum (556–2904) near the terminus of Beach Street across from Ghirardelli Square. Here visitors will find exhibits on the technology of steamships, models of historic ships, and exhibits from the days of the California Gold Rush.

Hyde Street Pier (556–3002) is the location of five historic merchant ships, including a vessel that carried lumber from the Pacific

Northwest (1895), a sidewheel ferry (1890), an ocean-going tug (1907), a paddle tug (1914), and the last San Francisco Bay scow schooner still afloat (1891). The Maritime Store (775–2665) at the entrance of Hyde Street Pier contains books, posters, cards, and gifts appropriate to maritime history.

Within walking distance of the Hyde Street Pier is a World War II submarine (Pier 45, east of Fisherman's Wharf) and the last unaltered survivor of 2,751 World War II Liberty Ships (Pier 3, west of the Municipal Pier). For those with more time, a 3½-mile walk along the shoreline from the museum to Fort Point provides both exercise and relaxation.

Fort Mason Center contains three research collections, which include an extensive maritime library, archives, manuscripts, logbooks, ship plans, and historic photographs. Park personnel schedule numerous activities including talks, guided walks, ship tours, and classes and workshops. Visitors should check at the museum for a current schedule.

Facilities: Food and lodging are abundant in the wharf area. Although natives normally stay away from this area, many visitors enjoy trying seafood offered by the many outdoor vendors. An American Youth Hostel at Fort Mason (771–7277) provides low-cost lodging for recreational travelers of all ages. Visitors may picnic in Aquatic Park at the terminus of the Powell and Hyde cable car.

Camping: See the camping section under Golden Gate National Recreation Area (California).

Fishing: Fishing is permitted along the waterfront.

SANTA MONICA MOUNTAINS NATIONAL RECREATION AREA
30401 Agoura Rd., Suite 100
Agoura Hills, CA 91301
(818) 597–1036

Santa Monica Mountains National Recreation Area was established in 1978 and contains 150,000 acres of rugged landscape and shoreline within easy reach of millions of nearby residents. The park is located between the cities of Los Angeles and Oxnard in an east-west corridor bordered on the north by U.S. 101 and on the south by the Pacific Ocean.

Santa Monica Mountains NRA is the culmination of years of effort toward the goal of establishing parklands and preserving open spaces in a heavily populated and rapidly growing area. The Santa Monica Mountains are a coastal range stretching fifty miles west of Los Angeles. The area contains mountains, grasslands, hardwood groves, freshwater and saltwater marshes, and plunging waterfalls. Wildlife includes mountain lions, deer, bobcats, red tail hawks, and golden eagles. One excellent way of seeing much of the recreation area is to drive fifty winding miles through the park on scenic Mulholland Drive.

With the widespread nature and diversity of activities available in the park, it is impossible to provide even a short sketch of each point of interest. Some of the more popular locations are:

Circle X Ranch: Offers camping with a full range of facilities for individuals and groups. Spectacular backcountry with trails to mountain peaks.

Point Mugu State Park (706–1310): Beaches, cliffs, picnic areas, and campgrounds along 5 miles of ocean shoreline. This park provides seventy miles of hiking and riding trails through canyons and across rugged uplands.

Franklin Canyon Ranch: A few miles north of Sunset Boulevard, offers trails, picnicking, and an opportunity to observe wildlife in a natural oasis surrounded by the city.

Leo Carrillo State Beach (706–1310): Over a mile of ocean beach fronted by cave-riddled bluffs. Three campgrounds for tenters and RV owners.

Rancho Sierra Vista: An 838-acre site with hiking trails, an Indian Cultural Center, and picnic areas.

Paramount Ranch (888–3770): A 336-acre area where movies were formerly filmed now provides a place for walking, riding horses, and picnicking. A western town movie set is still in use.

Malibu Creek State Park (991–1827): An area of rugged cliffs and gorges containing waterfalls, slopes of chaparral, grasslands, and live oak groves. Fifteen miles of hiking and riding trails wind through the park.

Will Rogers State Historic Park (454–8212): Will Rogers's home for the seven years prior to his death in 1935, the park has a visitor center, nature center, and hiking trails in addition to the historic grounds and ranch house.

Griffith Park (665–5188): A 44,000-acre city park contains fifty-three miles of hiking and equestrian trails, a planetarium, science center, and the Los Angeles Zoo.

Facilities: A variety of facilities including food and lodging are available along roads through and bordering the park.

Camping: Camping is available in both Point Mugu State Park (150 spaces) and Leo Carrillo State Beach (138 spaces). Both parks can accept trailers and campers of up to thirty-one feet. From March through September reservations are requested. Write Ticketron, P.O. Box 617516, Chicago, IL 60661 (800–452–1111).

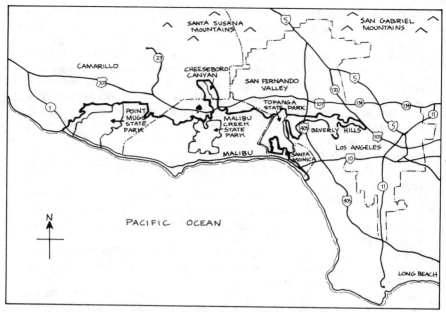

Santa Monica Mountains National Recreation Area

Fishing: Fishing is available throughout the park with a California license. Public fishing piers are located along the beaches of Malibu and Santa Monica. Fishing is also permitted in both state parks listed in the camping section.

WHISKEYTOWN–SHASTA–TRINITY
NATIONAL RECREATION AREA
P.O. Box 188
Whiskeytown, CA 96095
(916) 241–6584

Whiskeytown-Shasta-Trinity was established in 1965 and contains 403,000 acres of some of the most beautiful scenery in northern California. Whiskeytown Lake, the most developed and only one of the three areas operated by the National Park Service, is an excellent source of water-related activities. The lake is located in north-central California, approximately 230 miles from San Fran-

cisco. The three unit area is bisected by Interstate 5 running from Sacramento, California to Portland, Oregon.

Clair A. Hill Whiskeytown Dam and Whiskeytown Lake are on Clear Creek, a tributary of the Sacramento River, and are designed to store and regulate imported water of the Bureau of Reclamation's Central Valley Project. Water enters the area through pipes to the Judge Francis J. Carr Powerplant at the northwest tip of the lake. Surplus water is either released through another tunnel to the Keswick Powerplant or else diverted back into Clear Creek through bilevel outlets in the earthfill dam. The outlets allow the Bureau of Reclamation to regulate temperature for the maximum benefit of the salmon and steelhead trout that use Clear Creek as a spawning ground. Below the dam, on the south side of the lake, Clear Creek winds through steep gorges and rocky hills. Gold was discovered near here in the 1800s. A historical museum is open daily at Shasta, 2 miles east of Whiskeytown Lake.

The Clair Engle and Shasta lake areas extend into Shasta and Trinity National Forests, and are administered by the U.S. Forest Service. Write Shasta-Trinity National Forest, 2400 Washington Ave., Redding, CA 96001 for information on these areas. Trinity and Shasta dams are north of Redding, approximately 40 miles and 10 miles, respectively.

The five square miles of open water, extensive shoreline, and numerous coves make Whiskeytown Lake an inviting place for nearly any type of water activity. Boat launching ramps are provided at Whiskey Creek, Brandy Creek, and Oak Bottom, but swimming beaches are available only at the latter two locations. The lake's shallow areas begin to warm by late May or early June, but deeper waters remain cold all year.

There are about 50 miles of back-country roads open for use. These are graded dirt and gravel and, although some require four-wheel-drive vehicles, most are passable with passenger cars. The summit of Shasta Bally (6,209 feet) is 5,000 feet above lake level and may be reached on foot or by four-wheel-drive auto. More detailed information on back-country road conditions can be obtained at the visitor information station just off Highway 299 on the east side of the lake.

Facilities: A small store and post office are at Whiskeytown. Snack bars, camper stores, and boat rentals are available at Oak Bottom and Brandy Creek in summer. Restaurants and overnight accommodations are available eight miles east in Redding. Modern restrooms are at both marinas, the information station, and Oak Bottom Campground.
Camping: Brandy Creek (thirty-seven spaces) has no restrooms and is for self-contained vehicles only. Oak Bottom (155 spaces) has flush

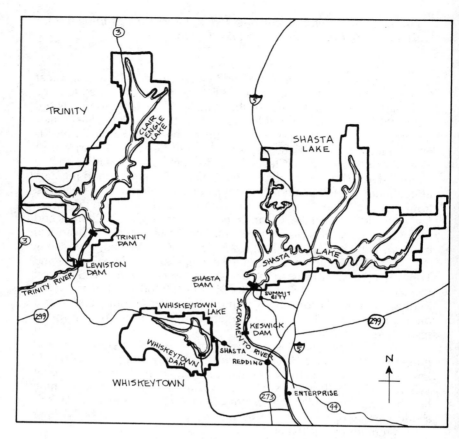

Whiskeytown–Shasta–Trinity National Recreation Area

toilets, water, and a dump station, and tables and grills are provided at tent sites. Cold showers are at the beach. The best camping at Oak Bottom is for tenters, because all other camping units are required to stay in a paved parking facility that has no shade, tables, or grills. The dump stations at Brandy Creek and Oak Bottom are closed in winter. For groups, Dry Creek has camping with pit toilets. Reservations are required. The U.S. Forest Service offers better camping facilities in the Trinity–Shasta areas. A map to these areas may be picked up in a Forest Service visitor center or at the National Park Service visitor center at the east end of Whiskeytown Lake.

Fishing: Fishing is good either from a boat or from shore. The lake is stocked with rainbow and brown trout, largemouth, smallmouth, and spotted bass, and kokanee. A California license is required.

YOSEMITE NATIONAL PARK
P.O. Box 577
Yosemite National Park, CA 95389
(209) 372–4461

Yosemite National Park was established in 1890 and contains what may be the most beautiful 761,000 acres in the United States. Granite peaks and domes rise above green or snow-covered meadows in the heart of the Sierra Nevada. The park is located in east-central California, approximately 190 miles due east of San Francisco via Interstate 5 and California Highway 120 east and west, Highway 140 from Merced, and Highway 41 from Fresno. While in the Yosemite area, consider exploring California Highway 49 on the park's west side. Here you will wander through many areas made famous by gold-seekers in 1849. On the park's east side, the ghost town of Bodie, near Mono Lake, is super. Bodie is a state park managed by the California State Department of Parks and Recreation.

Yosemite represents all that is good and most that is bad with the National Park System. The scenery is quite possibly the best of any national park. Yosemite contains beautiful valleys, high-country meadows, sparkling lakes, and spectacular waterfalls. The park's elevations range from 2,000 feet to more than 13,000 feet above sea level, which produces an outstanding variety of both animal and plant life. The bad part is that because of the area's beauty, visitors and campers have nearly loved parts of the park to death. Yosemite Valley is especially heavily used.

There are four major entrances into Yosemite National Park—two from the west and one each from the south and east. A single road—California 120—bisects the park in an east-west direction. To experience the high elevations it is necessary to use the road because the high country is toward the east side and away from Yosemite Valley. The road is closed in winter.

Most organized activity at Yosemite is in Yosemite Valley. Yosemite Village contains a visitor center and most modern conveniences that can be found in any small town. The entrance road follows the Merced River (good for small rafts or inner tubes) to all the main buildings and valley campsites. Shuttle-bus service is available and greatly simplifies getting around the congested valley floor. This service was introduced to reduce auto emissions and congestion. Free parking is available at Curry Village for day-use visitors. The valley is open all year and contains often-photographed features such as El

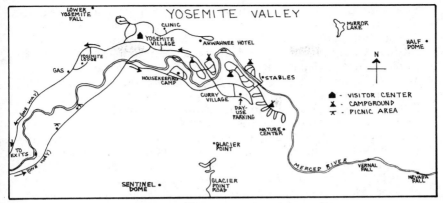

Yosemite National Park—Yosemite Valley

Capitan, Half Dome, Yosemite Falls, and Bridalveil Falls. The falls are most active in the early summer months.

Although most visitors spend the majority of time in the valley, Yosemite contains many other worthwhile features. A large grove of giant sequoias is located near the south entrance. Two smaller giant sequoia groves can be found near Crane Flat on the west side of the park. Near the south entrance at Wawona is the Pioneer Yosemite History Center—an exhibit of historic buildings, horse-drawn vehicles, and living history demonstrations.

Fifty-five miles from the valley across Tioga Road is Tuolumne Meadows. At an elevation of 8,600 feet, this is the largest subalpine meadow in the High Sierra. It is also a center for high-country pack trips and hikes.

Perhaps the best-known activity at Yosemite is rock climbing. A lesser-known but equally exciting activity is hang gliding. If these are too dangerous, visitors can try some of the 700 miles of hiking trails. Horses may be rented at Wawona, Yosemite Valley, White Wolf, and Tuolumne Meadows. Swimming is available in the park's rivers or at lodge swimming pools. Nightly interpretive programs are available at campgrounds and at concessioner facilities.

Winter activities at Yosemite include downhill skiing at Badger Pass with four T-bars, one chairlift, a rental shop, and ski school. Several trails are available for cross-country skiing and a guide map is available. Other winter activities include snowshoeing, ice skating, and snowcat tours in Badger Pass.

Facilities: Nearly anything can be found somewhere in Yosemite. Lodging, restaurants, and stores are located at Wawona, El Portal, Crane Flat, Tuolumne Meadows, White Wolf, and in Yosemite Valley.

Reservations are advised for all overnight accommodations. Write to the park to receive additional information regarding reservations. Dental and medical facilities are provided in Yosemite at Yosemite Medical Group. A self-service laundry is open during the summer at Curry Village and pay showers are at Tuolumne Meadows and in Yosemite Valley. Filling stations can be found throughout the park with those at Wawona and Yosemite Lodge open all year. Other facilities in the valley include barber and beauty shops, kennels, photographic studios, saddle and pack horses, and tours.

Camping: Developed campgrounds are located throughout the park with the eight in the valley usually filling very early. There are nearly 750 spaces in Yosemite Valley with the largest campgrounds at Upper Pines (226 spaces) and Lower Pines (165 spaces). Lower Pines is open all year. All of these have picnic tables, fire grates, and flush toilets and each is near a shuttlebus line. Dump stations are located at the Lower River and Upper Pines campgrounds. The valley campgrounds are very crowded, sometimes resembling giant parking lots. The park's other improved campgrounds are at Bridalveil Creek (110 spaces), Crane Flat (165 spaces), Hodgdon Meadow (110 spaces), Tenaya Lake (fifty walk-in spaces), Tuolumne Backpacker (twenty-five walk-in spaces), Tuolumne Meadows (350 spaces), Wawona (ninety-nine spaces, store and dump station nearby), and White Wolf (eighty-six spaces). Unimproved campgrounds are located at Porcupine Flat (seventy-five spaces), Tamarack Flat (eighty spaces), and Yosemite Creek (one hundred spaces). A large number of back-country firesites are available for camping. Reservations for Valley campsites are required from May to October. Write Ticketron, P.O. Box 617516, Chicago, IL 60661 (800–452–1111). A limited number of campsites made available by cancellations are offered on a first-come, first-served basis at a small station in the day-use parking area near Curry Village.

Fishing: Five species of trout including brook, brown, cutthroat, golden, and rainbow are found in Yosemite waters. Rainbow and brook are most abundant. A state license is required and the season is year round.

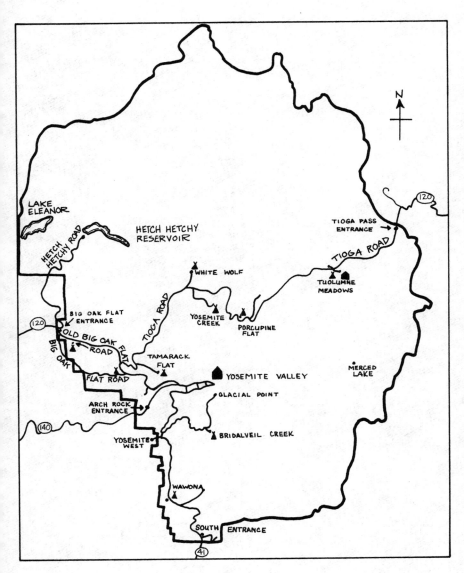

Yosemite National Park

Colorado

BENT'S OLD FORT NATIONAL HISTORIC SITE
35110 Highway 194 East
La Junta, CO 81051
(303) 384–2596

Bent's Old Fort National Historic Site contains 800 acres and became part of the National Park Service in 1960 to commemorate a principal Anglo-American outpost on the Southwestern Plains in the early 1800s. The park is in southeastern Colorado, 8 miles east of La Junta and 15 miles west of Las Animas on Colorado Highway 194.

The early 1800s saw an influx of traders into the Santa Fe and Taos area of what is now New Mexico. Caravans from Independence, Missouri, the main staging point, traveled to Santa Fe by two routes. The main trail ran across the Kansas plains to the Cimarron Crossing of the Arkansas River. At this point the trail broke into two branches. The Cimarron Cutoff crossed the Comanche-infested Cimarron Desert and offered little water. The Mountain Branch continued along the Arkansas River and turned southwest near Timpas Creek. The second route was longer, but it offered greater safety and more trees and water.

It was on the Mountain Branch that the two Bent brothers and a friend decided in the late 1820s to build a trading establishment. Because of the location, the men knew that a strong fort would be required. The enclosed adobe structure took a hundred men three years to construct.

Over a period of years, the merchants became trusted friends of the Indians and built a booming business. Finished goods were brought to the fort from St. Louis, where they were exchanged for beaver pelts and other furs. The men opened additional stores in Santa Fe and Taos. The annexation of Texas in 1845 brought turmoil to the region because U.S. troops used the fort as a staging area for invasions

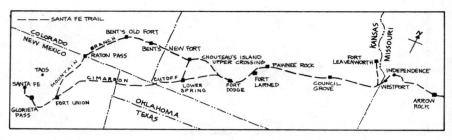

Bent's Old Fort National Historic Site and Fort Larned National Historic Site

of New Mexico. The influx of soldiers, settlers, and adventurers resulted in conflict with the once-peaceful Indians, and trade eventually came to a halt. It is thought that reduced trade and a cholera epidemic among the Indians caused William Bent to set fire to the fort and move 38 miles down the Arkansas River. There he built a structure that became known as Bent's New Fort (hence, the present name for the initial structure). Although the old fort was temporarily rehabilitated for use as a stage station, it was once again abandoned so that by 1915 only parts of the old walls were still standing.

During 1975 and 1976, Bent's Old Fort was reconstructed on the original foundation to its 1845–46 appearance. Interpretive Park Service and volunteer personnel are on duty daily inside the fort. Guided walks and a twenty-five-minute slide presentation are offered periodically throughout the day.

Facilities: Water and restrooms are located in the reconstructed fort. Food services and lodging are in La Junta and Las Animas.
Camping: No camping is permitted in the park. Private campgrounds are nearby in La Junta. For travelers on Highway 50, the Corps of Engineers' John Martin Reservoir provides pleasant camping (fifty-one mostly shaded sites, water, flush toilets, no showers, no hookups) 3 miles south of the town of Hasty. Hasty is approximately 32 miles east of Bent's Old Fort.
Fishing: No fishing is available in the park. Fishing is permitted at John Martin Reservoir (see camping section).

BLACK CANYON OF THE GUNNISON NATIONAL MONUMENT
Box 2233 East Main Street
Montrose, CO 81401
(303) 249–7036

*Black Canyon of the Gunnison was added to the park system in
1933 to preserve 13 miles of a spectacular and unspoiled canyon
that has been cut by the Gunnison River. The monument is
located in west-central Colorado, with both rims accessible by
automobile. The north rim is reached over a 14-mile gravel road
originating from Colorado Highway 92, east of Crawford. The
south rim is 5 miles north of U.S. 50 via a paved road beginning
6 miles east of Montrose.*

The Black Canyon has been formed over a period of 2 million years by
the continuous erosive forces of the Gunnison River. The river and its
seasonal floods have produced a canyon with depths ranging from
1,730 to 2,425 feet and widths of as little as 1,300 feet (at the
Narrows). The erosive Gunnison has cut faster than its tributaries,
resulting in canyons hanging high over the main gorge. The lack of
sunlight into the narrow canyon produces dark walls with heavy
shadows—hence, the name.

The river established its course by cutting through soft volcanic
rocks. It then continued to carve into the hard crystalline rocks of the
present canyon. Pinnacles in the eastern area of the park have been
created with the assistance of the river, as its flow followed the layers
of less resistant rock.

Visitors should first stop at the visitor center, where information
and exhibits on the life and geology of the park are available. The
paved road following the south rim is seldom more than ½-mile from
the canyon. Spectacular views are available from numerous short foot
trails, beginning from parking areas along the road's side. Interpretive
signs are generally at the end of each trail, and a self-guiding trail is
located at Cedar Point. A printed guidebook to Rim Rock Nature Trail
may be obtained near the North Rim Campground. During summer
months, conducted walks and evening campfire programs take place
in the park.

Facilities: No overnight accommodations are available at the monument, but they can be found in nearby communities. Rim House on the
south rim provides lunches, refreshments, souvenirs, and limited
camping supplies during summer months. No facilities are available
on the north rim.

Camping: The park contains two campgrounds. North Rim Campground (thirteen spaces) at Chasm View provides tables, grills, water

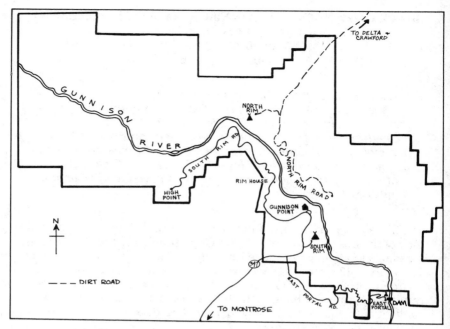

Black Canyon of the Gunnison National Monument

(trucked in), and pit toilets. South Rim Campground (102 spaces) has similar facilities. Both campgrounds are open from May through October. Commercial campgrounds are located in Montrose.

Fishing: Brown and rainbow trout, flannel-mouth sucker, and squawfish inhabit the Gunnison River, although access is difficult. A Colorado license is required.

COLORADO NATIONAL MONUMENT
Fruita, CO 81521
(303) 858–3617

Colorado National Monument was established as part of the National Park System in 1911. The park contains 20,454 acres of steep-walled canyons, monoliths, dinosaur fossils, and remains of prehistoric Indian cultures in a beautiful sandstone region. The park is located in west-central Colorado, just west of the town of Grand Junction via Interstate 70 or U.S. Highways 6 and 50.

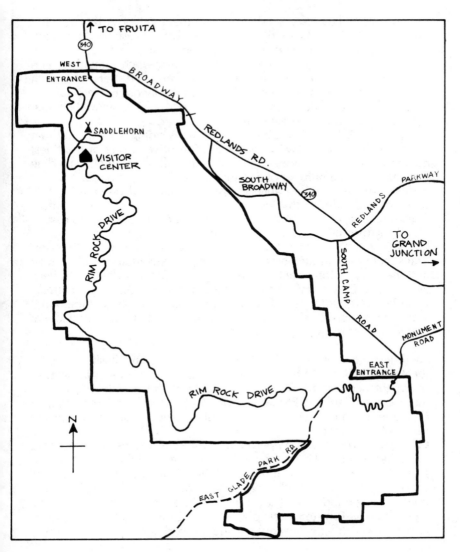

Colorado National Monument

Many western movie scenes shot in Monument Valley, Arizona, could just as easily have been filmed in Colorado National Monument. Water, wind, and freezing have produced some spectacular golden canyons. Even though the area's annual eleven-inch rainfall is relatively sparse, it generally occurs in concentrated bursts of such intensity as to have a pronounced effect on the landscape. Monument Canyon, in the park's northern end, is one of Colorado National Monument's most impressive areas.

Rim Rock Drive is a 22-mile, narrow, winding, paved road that connects the east and west entrances. The drive is one of the finest offered in any park in the country. Visitors will see many outstanding formations, and a number of parking overlooks are provided. A visitor center near the west entrance is open all year and provides a slide program and exhibits that explain the monument's history and geological formations. It is best to drive the park road from west to east so that the visitor center can be a first stop.

A number of hiking trails provide access to the park's interior. Trails include 2¼-mile Serpents Trail near Devils Kitchen Picnic Area and the longer Monument Canyon (6 miles), Black Ridge (5½ miles), and Liberty Cap (7 miles) trails. There are a number of short trails, including self-guiding trails at Window Rock (near the campground) and Coke Ovens. Daily programs and short guided hikes originate at the visitor center during summer months.

Facilities: Picnic areas with tables, grills, water, and flush toilets are located near both the east and west entrances. No food, gasoline, or overnight accommodations are available at the monument, but all three are available at Fruita (3 miles north of the west entrance) or Grand Junction (4 miles east of the east entrance). Ranger stations are near both entrances.

Camping: Saddlehorn Campground (eighty-one spaces), is adjacent to the visitor center, 4½ miles south of the west entrance. The campground is open all year and offers tables, charcoal grills, and flush toilets. Scrub juniper and pinyon trees provide some shade. Saddlehorn Campground provides campers with a spectacular view of the Grand Valley. Private campgrounds are in Grand Junction and Fruita.

Fishing: No fishing is available inside the park.

CURECANTI NATIONAL RECREATION AREA
102 Elk Creek
Gunnison, CO 81230
(303) 641–2337

*Curecanti National Recreation Area, administered under a coop-
erative agreement with the Bureau of Reclamation since 1965,
contains over 42,000 acres. The recreation area consists of three
reservoirs, known as the Wayne Aspinall Storage Unit, set in the
deep canyons of the Gunnison River. The park is paralleled by
U.S. 50 in west-central Colorado. The eastern border is approximately 8 miles west of the town of Gunnison.*

Curecanti National Recreation Area, part of the Colorado River Storage
Project, results from three dams constructed on the Gunnison River.
These dams provide visitors with a wide variety of water sports and
other outdoor activities amid the spectacular scenery of Colorado
mesa country. The land in this region has been shaped by volcanic
activity and the erosive forces of nature. Evidence of both is easily seen
along the shores of the lakes and on the walls of the surrounding cliffs.

Because of the cold winters, the normal visitor season is from
mid-May through mid-October. Evening naturalist programs are regularly scheduled during summer months, and activity schedules are
posted in visitor-use areas. The park's main visitor center is at Elk
Creek, where visitors can view a short slide presentation, a fish
observation pond, and exhibits. Naturalist activities are available here.
In Cimarron, there is an information station with a narrow-gauge
railroad exhibit. One mile away, visitors may take self-guiding tours of
an underground power plant. An 1881 trestle, a steam locomotive
(Engine 278 is one of three of this type left in the United States), and
several cars, including a caboose from the Denver and Rio Grande
Western Railroad, can be seen on the way to the plant.

A one-and-one-half-hour concessioner-operated, naturalist-staffed
boat tour of a dramatic, fjordlike canyon begins just below Blue Mesa
Dam on Morrow Point Lake. The early history of the region, including
accounts of the Ute Indians and the Denver and Rio Grande Railroad's
narrow gauge line, is discussed. The boat tours require reservations,
which may be made at Elk Creek Marina (303–641–0402). Reaching the
point of departure requires going down 232 steps and walking for half
an hour, but the views from the bottom of the 1,000-foot canyon are
outstanding.

Facilities: No overnight lodging is available in the park, but accommodations and most services are in Montrose, Gunnison, and other
nearby towns. A nice restaurant is located adjacent to the marina at Elk

COLORADO 125

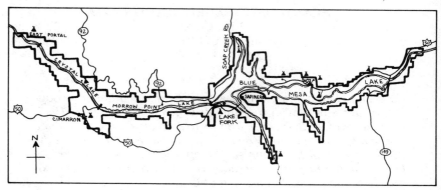

Curecanti National Recreation Area

Creek. Ranger stations and first aid help are at Cimarron, Lake Fork, and Elk Creek. Marinas at both Elk Creek and Lake Fork offer boat repairs and rentals, gasoline, guided fishing tours on Blue Mesa and Morrow Point, fishing tackle, and groceries.

Camping: The most developed campgrounds with tables, grills, water, flush toilets, and dump stations are at Cimarron (twenty-two spaces), Elk Creek (179 spaces, pay showers), and Lake Fork (eighty-seven spaces, pay showers). Campgrounds at Dry Gulch (ten spaces), East Portal (fifteen spaces), Gateview (seven spaces), Ponderosa (twenty-three spaces), Red Creek (seven spaces), and Stevens Creek (fifty-four spaces) have pit toilets. Only Cimarron and Elk Creek are open all year.

Fishing: Federal and state fish hatcheries annually stock nearly three million fish in the lakes. Anglers can enjoy year-round, high-country trout fishing at Curecanti. Ice fishing for rainbow and German brown trout is popular from December through March, and trolling and bank fishing become popular as soon as open water appears in the spring. Trolling fishermen find the rainbow, brown, and lake (mackinaw) trout fishing good throughout the season, with the best kokanee salmon fishing in late June, July, and August. A Colorado fishing license is required and may be purchased at the Elk Creek Marina.

DINOSAUR NATIONAL MONUMENT
Box 210
Dinosaur, CO 81610
(303) 374–2216

Dinosaur National Monument, established in 1915, contains fossil remains of dinosaurs and other ancient animals. The 211,000-acre park also includes spectacular canyons cut by the Green and Yampa rivers. The park straddles the border of northeast Utah and northwest Colorado. Access from U.S. 40 is via State Highway 149 at Jensen, which goes north to the Dinosaur Quarry and the main fossil area of the park. Access to the canyons is via Harpers Corner Road at monument headquarters, a few miles east of Dinosaur.

Dinosaur National Monument contains a deposit of the petrified bones of crocodiles, turtles, and dinosaurs. Excavation of the fossils is available to public view in the Dinosaur Quarry located 7 miles north of Jensen, Utah, in the southwestern portion of the monument. Here a wall of the quarry is enclosed, and visitors watch monument personnel cut away rock to expose ancient fossil bones. The center is open daily from 8:00 A.M. to 4:30 P.M. during winter, with somewhat longer hours during the busier summer season. It closes on Thanksgiving, Christmas, and New Year's Day.

In addition to the quarry area, Dinosaur offers some spectacularly wild and scenic country. A part of the park is reached by automobile, but most of it is available only to those willing to walk or raft. The 31-mile Harpers Corner Road winds north from monument headquarters, which is located 2 miles east of Dinosaur, Colorado. This road is paved and is generally open from April through October. The road ends with a 1-mile trail to view numerous canyons cut by the Green and Yampa rivers. No services are available on the road. Visitors should plan to spend from two to four hours for the round trip.

Backcountry roads are available for the more adventurous motorists, but they are impassable when wet. These are generally rough and dusty and lead to more remote areas. One of the most spectacular, Echo Park Road, begins just south of the park boundary on the Harpers Corner Road. This is a 13-mile dirt road that passes by Indian petroglyphs and Whispering Cave. No trailers, heavy vehicles, or low-clearance vehicles should be driven here because of steep grades and sharp turns. Generally accessible roads are available to the northern and eastern parts of the monument. Self-guiding nature trails are at Split Mountain Campground, Gates of Lodore, and Harpers Corner Road, and raft trips are available through private concession-

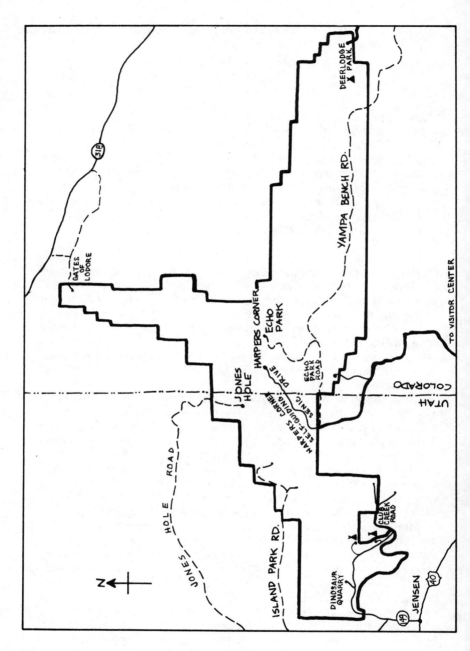

Dinosaur National Monument

ers. Information on river running is available at the visitor center. Private river runners are required to have a free river permit to navigate Dinosaur's rivers.

Facilities: Motels and cafes are available at Dinosaur, Rangely, Craig, and Vernal. Food, gas, and ice are available at these towns and at Jensen. Medical facilities are in Craig, Rangely, River Campground, and monument headquarters. Ranger stations are located at some public-use areas. Those at Deerlodge Park, Echo Park, and Jones Hole may be open in summer months.

Camping: The only two improved campgrounds are Split Mountain Gorge (thirty-five spaces) and Green River (ninety-nine spaces), both located on a paved road east of the Quarry Visitor Center. The campgrounds have picnic tables, fire grates, water, flush toilets, and programs some nights in summer. Green River Campground is more shady. Camping is available all year. Primitive campgrounds are located at Deerlodge Park (eight spaces, no water), Echo Park (twelve spaces), Gates of Lodore (seventeen spaces), and Rainbow Park (four spaces, no water). These have pit toilets and picnic tables.

Fishing: The Green and Yampa rivers are generally muddy, and fishing for catfish, at best, is fair. Trout fishing is occasionally good in Jones Creek. Either a Utah or Colorado license must be obtained, depending on where you fish.

FLORISSANT FOSSIL BEDS NATIONAL MONUMENT
P.O. Box 185
Florissant, CO 80816
(303) 748–3253

Florissant Fossil Beds, which contains nearly 6,000 acres, was added to the National Park System in 1969 to preserve the fossil insects, seeds, and leaves that are found here in abundance. Standing petrified sequoia stumps are also on display. The park is located in central Colorado, approximately 36 miles west of Colorado Springs on U.S. 24. From the small town of Florissant, turn south on Teller County Road No. 1.

Fossils in this area have been preserved in sedimentary rock at the bottom of an ancient lake that existed here approximately 30 million years ago. The lake was formed when mudflows from a nearby volcanic field dammed streams flowing through the valley. Later, as the volcanic activity showered materials through the air, a large variety

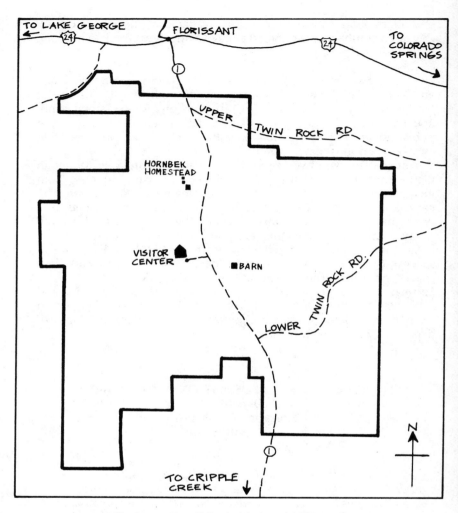

Florissant Fossil Beds National Monument

of plants and animals were caught and carried to the lake's bottom. Here they were buried in fine ash that eventually compacted to form shale, and the plants and animals became fossilized. Mudflows from this volcanic activity also buried trees surrounding the lake, so that they were petrified. Over time Lake Florissant filled with volcanic materials so that the shales were preserved, until erosion broke through the cover and exposed the lake bed.

The park is open from 8:00 A.M. to 7:00 P.M. (4:30 P.M. in winter) daily except Thanksgiving, Christmas, and New Year's Day. The visitor center provides a display of many of the impressions that have been found here. Included are dragonflies, beetles, ants, butterflies, spiders, fish, mammals, and birds. Also housed here are fossil leaves from earlier relatives of birches, maples, willows, beeches, and hickories. Giant petrified sequoia tree stumps have been excavated and can be seen along a 0.4-mile self-guiding trail behind the visitor center and along a 2.7-mile trail just north of the center. Park rangers present hourly interpretive talks and lead guided walks several times each day. The Hornbek Homestead, a short distance north of the visitor center, offers an excellent look at a restored homestead complex common in this region in the late 1800s and early 1900s. During winter months, cross-country skiing is available, but snowmobiling is prohibited.

Facilities: Neither food services nor overnight accommodations are available in the park. Nearby towns of Woodland Park, Divide, Florissant, Lake George, and Cripple Creek have motels, food, and fuel. The visitor center provides water and modern restrooms, and a picnic area is nearby.

Camping: No camping is permitted at the monument. Private camp-grounds are located in Cripple Creek and along U.S. 24 toward Colorado Springs. The U.S. Forest Service provides campgrounds near Lake George in Pike National Forest.

Fishing: Fishing is authorized at the monument with a Colorado license, but visitors probably will have more luck elsewhere in the surrounding area.

GREAT SAND DUNES NATIONAL MONUMENT
11500 Highway 150
Mosca, CO 81146
(719) 378–2312

Great Sand Dunes, which contains nearly 39,000 acres, was established in 1932 to preserve North America's tallest sand dunes. The park is located in south-central Colorado, 17 miles north of U.S. 160 via Colorado Highway 150. The monument is approximately 38 miles from Alamosa.

The desert floor of the San Luis Valley is surrounded to the east and northeast by the Sangre de Cristo Mountains, to the west by the San Juan Mountains, and to the south by the San Luis Hills. This trap, combined with the prevailing southwesterly winds and the sand and silt that for centuries have been carried into the basin, has produced sand dunes piled to heights of up to 700 feet. The winds produce some changes in the details of the dunes, but the main mass has changed relatively little over the years. The eastern boundary of the dunes is formed by Medano Creek. The small dunes found east of the creek have been formed from sand blowing across the stream bed when it is dry.

The visitor center contains exhibits on the history and geology of the area. Park personnel are on duty from 8:00 A.M. to 8:00 P.M. Memorial Day to Labor Day and from 8:00 A.M. to 5:00 P.M. the remainder of the year. The visitor center is closed all federal holidays in winter. Pets must be on a leash. Rangers conduct walks to the dunes and give evening campfire programs from Memorial Day to Labor Day. The Montville Nature Trail (¼ mile) is located north of the visitor center, and leaflets are provided for a nominal fee.

Medano Pass Primitive Road begins near the campground and provides access to four-wheel-drive vehicles. In addition, a concessioner operates four-wheel-drive tours over the road during summer months. For information, write Great Sand Dunes Oasis, Sand Dunes Road, Mosca, Colorado 81146 (719–378–2222).

The most popular activity in the monument is hiking on the dunes. Routes are optional because no trails are possible, however most hikes begin from the dunes parking area. Campers may start at the campground. During summer months, hiking in the morning or late afternoon is most pleasant. The sand can be quite hot; wear shoes when hiking. Watch for lightning.

Facilities: No lodging or food service is provided in the monument, but food, snacks, and gasoline are available just outside the south

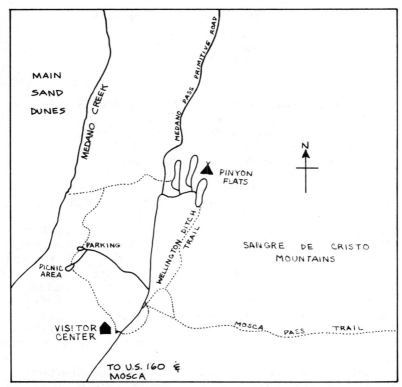

Great Sand Dunes National Monument

entrance. Overnight accommodations can be found nearby and in Alamosa. Water, tables, and fire grates are provided at the picnic area. Restrooms with flush toilets are at the picnic area and the visitor center.

Camping: Pinyon Flats Campground (eighty-eight spaces, three group sites) is open from April to October. It provides tables, grills, water, flush toilets, and a dump station. Facilities are limited in the off-season. A private campground near the park has full hookups. Back-country camping requires a free permit, which is available at the visitor center.

Fishing: Fishing is generally poor in the monument.

HOVENWEEP NATIONAL MONUMENT
McElmo Route
Cortez, CO 81321
(303) 529–4465

Hovenweep National Monument, which contains 785 acres, was established in 1923 to preserve six clusters of ruins of pre-Columbian Pueblo Indians. The monument straddles the Utah-Colorado border and is 45 miles from Cortez, Colorado. Approaches range from graded dirt to gravel roads.

The inhabitants of Hovenweep were prehistoric Pueblo Indians who occupied the Four Corners region until A.D. 1300. Their culture was similar to that of the inhabitants of Mesa Verde to the east. The Pueblos raised crops, gathered wild foods, and hunted. They also were excellent artists and craftsmen. For centuries they lived in small, scattered villages. During the early 1100s, however, they began moving into larger pueblos. By 1200, they had moved to the heads of the Hovenweep canyons and had built pueblos and towers, perhaps to protect the permanent springs. The long draws into the canyons could be terraced to hold back the soil and provide sheet-water irrigation for crops. By the late 1200s, the Hovenweep area was deserted after a long period of drought.

Today's piles of masonry indicate the sizable population that once lived at Hovenweep. The monument consists of six groups of ruins: the Square Tower Ruins and Cajon Ruins in Utah, and the Holly, Hackberry, Cutthroat Castle, and Goodman Point ruins in Colorado. These ruins are all noted for their square, oval, circular, and D-shaped towers, many of which are built on boulders or rim edges.

Square Tower is the best-preserved ruin and has a self-guided trail with a ranger on duty. A 4-mile hiking trail leads from here to Holly Ruin. The Cajon Ruins consist of two large pueblos that have been ravaged by both time and relic hunters. Holly, Hackberry, and Cutthroat Castle ruins contain towers and pueblos. Goodman Point includes a massive unexcavated pueblo and several small sites. All the ruins except Square Tower are isolated and difficult to reach.

Temperatures at the monument tend to be moderate, although summer daytime temperatures can exceed 100 degrees Fahrenheit. June is generally a good month to avoid because of the presence of small biting gnats. Fall is probably the best time to visit.

Facilities: No lodging or food service is available at the monument. Supplies can be purchased at Hatch Trading Post, 16 miles west, or at Ismay Trading Post, 14 miles southeast. The nearest overnight accom-

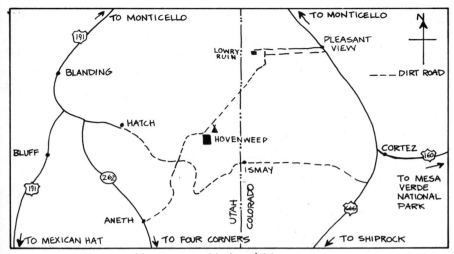

Hovenweep National Monument

modations are at Blanding and Bluff in Utah and Cortez in Colorado. Water and bathrooms are at the ranger station and the campground. Unleaded gas is available in Aneth (20 miles to the south), Blanding, and Cortez.

Camping: A campground (thirty-one spaces) near the ranger station is open all year and has tables, grills, and flush toilets. Restrooms are closed during winter months, and pit toilets are available. The campground is rarely filled.

Fishing: No fishing is available at Hovenweep National Monument.

MESA VERDE NATIONAL PARK
Mesa Verde National Park, CO 81330
(303) 529–4461

Mesa Verde National Park, which contains more than 52,000 acres, was established in 1906 to protect the most notable and best-preserved pre-Columbian cliff dwellings in the United States. The park is located in the southwestern corner of Colorado, 10 miles east of Cortez and 35 miles west of Durango on U.S. 160.

The Anasazi Indians of Mesa Verde went through three distinct stages. The earliest people, known as the Basket Makers, lived in clustered

COLORADO 135

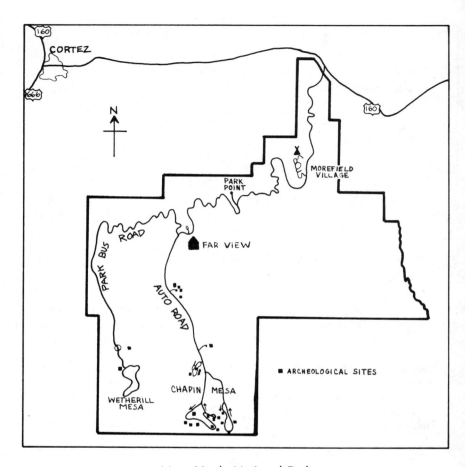

Mesa Verde National Park

dwellings dug into the ground ("pithouses") on mesa tops. Here they grew beans, squash, and corn in the rich soil. By the mid-700s, descendants of the Basket Makers (Pueblos) started building homes above ground by weaving sticks around wooden poles stuck in the ground. The walls and roof were weatherproofed with a thick coating of mud. By A.D. 1000, stone masonry construction began replacing mud mixture between poles. Sometime in the late 1100s, the Anasazi of Mesa Verde abandoned their homes on mesa tops and constructed cliff dwellings, for which this park is best noted. Exactly what prompted this construction is uncertain, although possible reasons include protection from the elements or enemies. The dwellings may also have been constructed for religious or psychological reasons. Less than one hundred years later, for reasons that are still uncertain, the Indians left Mesa Verde.

Far View Visitor Center, seventeen miles from the park entrance, contains displays of contemporary Indian arts and crafts. Approximately one-half way from the entrance to Far View is Park Point, which offers a viewpoint of the Four Corners region. The 12-mile drive from Far View to Wetherill Mesa (summer only) offers some excellent views of the park. An archeological museum at Chapin Mesa contains artifacts and exhibits of Indian life at Mesa Verde. Park personnel are located in each area to answer visitors' questions. During summer months, park rangers conduct trips through some of the ruins and present nightly programs at the campground. Schedules are at the visitor center or museum. During winter months, walks are guided only to Spruce Tree House.

Hiking in Mesa Verde is restricted. In the Morefield Area, Prater Ridge Trail (7.8 miles), Knife Edge Trail (1.5 miles), and Point Lookout Trail (2.3 miles) require no permit. In the headquarters area, hikers must register for Petroglyph Point Trail (2.8 miles) or Spruce Canyon Trail (2.1 miles).

Facilities: The only overnight lodging inside the park is at Far View Lodge. Meals also are served here. Reservations and information may be obtained by writing ARA Mesa Verde, P.O. Box 277, Mancos, CO 81328 (303–529–4421 summer; 303–533–7731 winter). Food service is available at Morefield, Spruce Tree Terrace, and Wetherill Mesa, as well as at Far View. Restrooms are provided at all four locations. Groceries may be purchased at Morefield, and gasoline is available at Morefield and Far View.

Camping: Morefield Campground (477 spaces and seventeen group camps) is 4 miles inside the park entrance. It provides tables, grills, water, a dump station, and flush toilets. Pay showers, a laundry, and a grocery are located within easy walking distance. The campground is open from early May until late October.

Fishing: No fishing is available at Mesa Verde National Park.

ROCKY MOUNTAIN NATIONAL PARK
Estes Park, CO 80517
(303) 586–2317

Rocky Mountain National Park, established in 1915, contains 265,197 acres of some of the most beautiful and easily accessible high-mountain country in North America. The park is located in north-central Colorado, with the main entrance near Estes Park, approximately 65 miles from Denver and 91 miles from Cheyenne. Rocky Mountain also may be approached from the town of Grand Lake through Arapaho National Recreation Area.

The area of the present-day Rocky Mountains was once covered by a great sea. More than 100 million years ago, the sea began to recede, and the ancestral Rockies gradually rose above the old sea bed. Over a period of millions of years, the mountains were eroded by the wind and water until only a high rolling plain was left. Approximately 60 million years ago, another gradual uplifting produced today's Rocky Mountains. The range began to erode almost immediately, and then about 1 million years ago, the ice age created giant glaciers that left U-shaped valleys, lakes, and moraines. Five small glaciers are still in the park today.

The most accessible parts of the park lie along Trail Ridge Road, a 50-mile paved road (open in summer only) connecting Estes Park with Grand Lake, which reaches a height of more than 12,000 feet. Before driving the road, a stop at one of the visitor centers (Estes Park or Grand Lake) will prove worthwhile. Trail Ridge Road stays above timberline for 11 miles and provides numerous viewpoints, and the Alpine Visitor Center at Fall River Pass offers exhibits to help interpret this part of the park. Fall River Road is a section of the original road crossing the mountains and is open from Horseshoe Park Junction to Fall River Pass. West of Endovalley, the gravel road is one way uphill.

The paved road to Bear Lake offers easy but congested access to a high mountain basin. Here, a beautiful lake is combined with a number of the park's trail heads. The parking lots here and at Glacier Gorge Junction often fill early during summer months. Two of the more popular trails beginning here are Dream Lake (2 miles round trip) and Emerald Lake (3 miles round trip). The park has more than 355 miles of trails, and horses are allowed on many of them. Winter sports are concentrated at Hidden Valley.

Facilities: No lodging is available inside the park, but accommodations are available in both Estes Park and Grand Lake. For information,

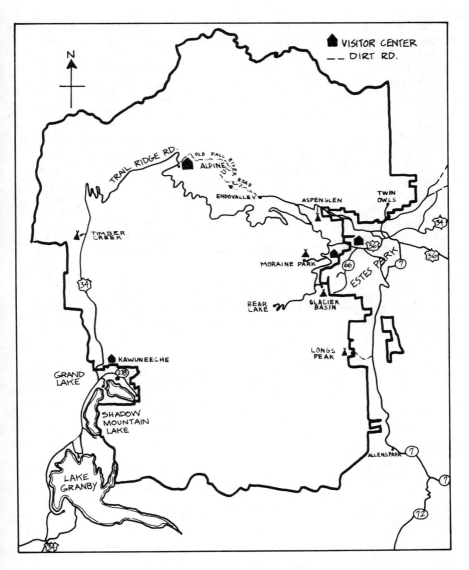

Rocky Mountain National Park

write the Chamber of Commerce in Estes Park, CO 80517 or Grand Lake, CO 80447. Food service is provided by a concessioner at both the Fall River Pass store (summer only) and Hidden Valley (winter only). Water and restrooms are available at various locations, including the visitor centers and campgrounds. During summer, horses with guides can be hired at two locations inside the park on the east side or from a number of liveries outside both the east and west park boundaries.

Camping: Aspenglen (twenty-three spaces), Glacier Basin (152 spaces, eighteen group camps, dump station), Longs Peak (thirty spaces, tents only), Moraine Park (250 spaces, dump station), and Timber Creek (one hundred spaces, dump station) all provide tables, grills, water, and flush toilets. Camping limit is seven days parkwide. At Long's Peak it is three days. Moraine Park, Longs Peak, and Timber Creek are open all year. Campsites at Glacier Basin and Moraine Park may be reserved. Write Ticketron, P.O. Box 617516, Chicago, IL 60661 (800–452–1111). Numerous trail camps are located throughout the park.

Fishing: German brown, brook, rainbow, and cutthroat trout are maintained by natural reproduction in the mountain streams and lakes. The fish are generally not large, and live bait is prohibited except under special circumstances. Fishing is not permitted in Bear Lake. A Colorado license is required.

Guam

WAR IN THE PACIFIC NATIONAL HISTORICAL PARK
P.O. Box 3441
Agana, GU 96910
(671) 477–8528

War in the Pacific National Historical Park contains nearly 2,000 acres. It was authorized in 1978 to interpret events in the Pacific theater of World War II. The park includes major historic sites associated with the 1944 battle for Guam and consists of seven separate units on the west side of the island.

Guam was captured by the Japanese only a few days after the December 1941 attack on Pearl Harbor. The island remained under Japanese control for two and a half years until the July 1944 invasion by American forces. Following 7,000 American and 17,500 Japanese casualties, Guam was recaptured by American troops in August of 1944.

The park's visitor center is located on Highway 1, in the Asan Island Unit near the town of Asan. Here visitors will find exhibits and audiovisual programs interpreting action in the Pacific theater. A patio behind the visitor center provides a view of the invasion beach used by American forces. Six other units around the park preserve beaches, cliffs, and ridges that were significant sites in the fighting.

Facilities: Food and lodging are found in nearby towns. Drinking water and restrooms are available in the visitor center.
Camping: No camping is available in the park.
Fishing: Fishing is permitted in units fronting on the Philippine Sea.

Hawaii

HALEAKALA NATIONAL PARK
P.O. Box 369
Makawao, Maui, HI 96768
(808) 572–9306

Haleakala National Park contains nearly 29,000 acres, and it was established in 1916 to preserve the outstanding features of Haleakala Crater—the remains of a 12,000-foot volcano in which the last activity occurred nearly 200 years ago. The park is located in the southeastern section of the island of Maui. The crater is a one-and-a-half-hour drive from Kalului via Highways 37, 377, and 378. The eastern section of the park may be reached by driving 62 miles (three hours) over Highway 36, a poor road that is only partially paved.

The island of Maui was formed by two volcanoes spewing lava and ash until they merged as one land mass. Haleakala, the largest of the two, once stood 12,000 feet above sea level and 30,000 feet above its base on the ocean floor. After the volcanoes became dormant, rain cut streams down the mountain's slopes and created large depressions near the summit. Later volcanic activity filled the stream beds with lava and formed vents in the crater. The last activity in Haleakala's crater occurred 500–1,000 years ago.

Park headquarters is located 1 mile inside the northwest entrance on Highway 378. Personnel are available to answer questions and provide permits and publications. Ten miles up the road, a visitor center has exhibits and provides an excellent view of the crater. Interpretive talks are given daily.

On the east side of the park, the abundant vegetation and tropical nature of the Kipahulu area stand in vivid contrast to the ash and cinder cones of the crater area. Sparkling pools connected by waterfalls are fed by a rain forest receiving up to 250 inches of rain annually.

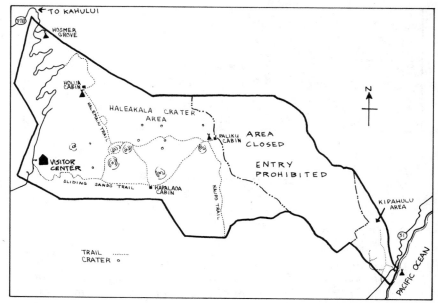

Haleakala National Park

A variety of trails and guided walks are available in the park. Short, self-guided walks are located in the crater area. Halemauu Trail views the Keanae Valley and Koolau Gap on the one-mile walk from the highway to the crater rim. At the northwest corner of the park, the ¼-mile Hosmer Grove Nature Trail displays the interplay between native and exotic plants and animals. A ¼-mile trail to the top of White Hill is located near the visitor center. Crater rim walks of one-half to two hours in length are conducted by rangers during the summer months. Self-guided day hikes through the crater are also available. In the Kipahulu area, self-guided walks include one from the parking area to the top pools and waterfall (½-mile) and the Waimoku Falls Trail (1½ miles) through a bamboo forest. Swimming in the pools at Oheo is quite popular.

Facilities: No overnight motel accommodations, food services, stores, or service stations are located within the park. From Kipahulu (Route 31 to Hana) these services are located approximately 10 miles north. From the Haleakala Crater entrance a service station is approximately eighteen miles away on Route 37, and restaurant and lodge facilities are located within 12 miles on Route 377. The visitor center has restroom facilities and drinking water.

Camping: Hosmer's Grove Campground (five spaces) in the northwest corner of the park has tables, fireplaces, drinking water, chemical toilets, and a cooking shelter with barbecue grills. Camping in the crater is permitted in two locations. Each of these is accessible by trail only. Two campgrounds—one near Holua cabin (twenty-five spaces) and one near Paliku cabin (twenty-five spaces)—offer primitive facilities including pit toilets and drinking water. Three crater cabins are available to winners of a lottery held ninety days prior to desired occupancy dates. Kipahulu Campground near Oheo Gulch offers a few tables, grills, and pit toilets, but no drinking water.

Fishing: The Kipahulu Campground and a picnic area are located near the Pacific Ocean and fishing is permitted here.

HAWAII VOLCANOES NATIONAL PARK
Hawaii Volcanoes National Park, HI 96718
(808) 967–7311

Hawaii Volcanoes contains 220,000 acres and was added to the National Park System in 1916. Active volcanism continues in the park. The most recent activity has been continuing since January 3, 1983 and has built the largest landform on the east rift zone, an 819-foot cinder and spatter cone. Hawaii Volcanoes National Park is located in the southeastern corner of the island of Hawaii. The visitor center is approximately 29 miles southwest of Hilo on Hawaii Highway 11, which bisects the park.

Millions of years ago a hotspot in the earth's mantle in the middle of the Pacific caused lava and gases to spurt from cracks 18,000 feet beneath the ocean's surface. As additional layers of lava were added, the island of Hawaii emerged from the sea. The island is ninety miles across at its base and measures nearly 32,000 feet from ocean floor to summit.

The most recent of the active volcanoes are 13,676-foot Mauna Loa and 4,690-foot Kilauea. Mauna Loa has been intermittently active during recent times, with large eruptions occurring in 1926, 1942, 1950, and most recently, in 1984. Kilauea, one of the most studied and best understood volcanoes in the world, has had its summit collapse to form a broad, shallow depression. Its eruptions have generally been characterized by mild and nonexplosive activity, except in 1790 and 1924.

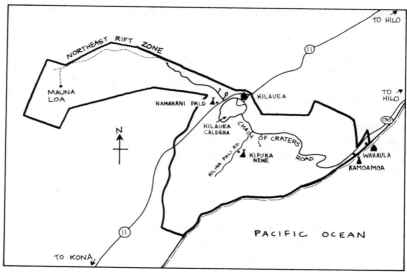

Hawaii Volcanoes National Park

Most of the park's activity centers around the Kilauea crater. Crater Rim Drive is an 11-mile paved road passing lush jungle, raw craters, and areas of devastation. Along the road are trails and overlooks such as Thurston Lava Tube, which has a trail through jungle and part of a tunnel through which once rushed glowing lava (0.3 mile, one quarter of an hour); the boardwalk Devastation Trail (0.6 mile, one half hour); and overlooks at Kilauea, Steaming Bluff, and the Hawaiian Volcano Observatory.

The ten-mile paved road from Kipuka Puaulu to an overlook part way up Mauna Loa is quite narrow but can be worthwhile on a clear day. A self-guided nature trail in Kipuka Puaulu (1.1 miles, one hour) leads into the open forest where many varieties of native trees grow. From a turnoff halfway down the Chain of Craters Road, visitors can drive to the top of Hilina Pali, a series of steep cliffs that provide a spectacular view of the southeast seacoast of the island.

A museum at park headquarters contains exhibits and paintings that help to tell the story of the island. Daily programs include talks by park personnel and a color film of recent volcanic activity. The Wahaula Visitor Center on the coast contains another museum explaining the human history of the area.

Facilities: Volcano House, on the rim of Kilauea crater, is operated year round by a concessioner. Information and reservations are available by writing Volcano House, Hawaii Volcanoes National Park, HI 96718 (808–967–7321). Food service is available at the hotel. Groceries, gasoline, and merchandise may be purchased in the town of Volcano, one mile outside the park on Highway 11. Groceries and meals are also available in Kalapana, four miles east of the park. Automobile repair facilities are twenty-one miles outside the park at Keaau.

Camping: Camping is limited to seven days annually at each of the park's three developed campgrounds. Namakani Paio (ten spaces, two group camps) offers camper cabins, eating shelters, fireplaces, and flush toilets. Kipuka Nene (six spaces) provides shelters, fireplaces, and pit toilets. Kamoamoa (ten spaces) has eating shelters, fireplaces, pit toilets and water.

Fishing: Fishing is restricted to native Hawaiians and their guests within the park, except for backcountry at Halape.

PU'UHONUA O HONAUNAU NATIONAL HISTORICAL PARK
P.O. Box 128
Honaunau, Kona, HI 96726
(808) 328–2326

Pu'uhonua o Honaunau (Place of Refuge of Honaunau) comprises 182 acres where, until 1819, vanquished Hawaiian warriors, noncombatants, and taboo breakers could escape death by reaching its sacred grounds ahead of their pursuers. The park is located in the southwestern section of the island of Hawaii, 111 miles from Hilo and 20 miles south of the resort center of Kailua-Kona. From Highway 11, turn west on Route 160, which goes by the park entrance.

The object of war in old Hawaii was to exterminate the enemy, including any members of the opposing side. Vanquished warriors and noncombatants on both sides could receive sanctuary in Hawaii's places of refuge. Although there were at least six refuges on the island of Hawaii at any one time and a number on other inhabited islands of the Hawaiian chain, the one contained in Pu'uhonua o Honaunau National Historical Park is historically the most important and the one still nearly intact. The refuge accepted all who sought sanctuary, including those who broke ancient laws. These individuals were absolved by priests before returning home in peace.

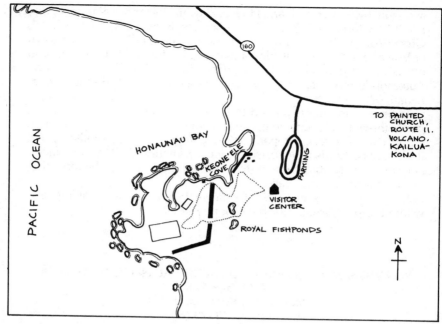

Pu'uhonua o Honaunau National Historical Park

The great wall surrounding the place of refuge was constructed around A.D. 1550 in order to provide physical protection to the refugees. Although the seaward end of the south wall has been battered by high surfs, it once probably extended almost to the sea. The wall was built without mortar. An ancient temple that at one time contained the bones of important chiefs and honored males (no females) has been restored by the National Park Service.

The park's visitor center is located beside the parking area. Cultural demonstrations on the grounds vary from day to day and may include canoe carving, thatching a grass hut, and fishing as the ancient Hawaiians did. Coves, cliffs, tidal pools, and associated marine life are easily visited along the shoreline.

Facilities: No lodging or food service is available at the site. Both may be found on nearby Highway 11. Water and restrooms are at the visitor center.
Camping: No camping is permitted at the site.
Fishing: Saltwater fishing from the shoreline is permitted.

PUUKOHOLA HEIAU NATIONAL HISTORIC SITE
P.O. Box 44340
Kawaihae, HI 96743
(808) 882–7218

Puukohola Heiau contains seventy-seven acres and was added to the National Park System in 1972 to preserve the ruins of the last major religious structure of the ancient Hawaiian culture built in the islands. The site is located in the northwestern section of the island of Hawaii. It is reached via State Route 270 and is about 12 miles from Waimea.

In 1782, Kamehameha became ruler of the northwest half of the island of Hawaii and unsuccessfully attempted to gain control of the remaining part. After he conquered the islands of Maui, Lanai, and Molokai, his aunt was told by a prophet that Kamehameha would control all the islands if he built a large temple to his family war god. The result was a temple atop Puukohola Hill started in 1790 and finished one year later. The prophecy was fulfilled in 1810 after years of war as Kamehameha became ruler of all the Hawaiian Islands. After Kamehameha's death in 1819, his son abandoned past religious traditions and ordered the temple destroyed.

The temple platform was constructed without the use of mortar by setting lava rocks and boulders together. Three long narrow steps cross the side that faces the sea so the interior could be viewed from canoes floating offshore. Recent earthquakes have begun to collapse the outer layers of rock and the temple site is currently closed to the public.

In addition to Puukohola Heiau, the park includes a number of other interesting features. On the hillside between Puukohola Heiau and the sea is the ruin of Mailekini Heiau, a temple used by Kamehameha's ancestors. Just offshore are the ruins of another temple, Hale-o-ka-puni Heiau, which was dedicated to the shark gods. The stone leaning post is a rock used by a high chief to lean against as he watched sharks circle about Hale-o-ka-puni Heiau before devouring the offerings he had placed there. Along the coast is Pelekane, the site of the king's residence at Kawaihae. In 1790, British sailor John Young was stranded on Hawaii and became a close friend of Kamehameha. The site of Young's home is north of Puukohola Heiau across State Road 270.

A small visitor center just off Highway 270 provides information and exhibits on Kamehameha and the park's history. A relatively rugged, steep trail leads from this point to major features of the park. The lower area may be reached by auto via Spencer Beach Park Road.

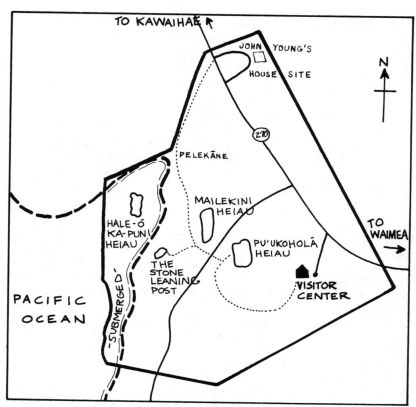

Puukohola Heiau National Historic Site

Facilities: No food service or lodging is available at the site. Gasoline and oil and a general store for supplies are one mile away. Water and restrooms are provided in the park's visitor center.

Camping: No camping is permitted at the site but camping and swimming are available nearby at Samuel Spencer County Park. Water and flush toilets are provided.

Fishing: The park's shoreline is a poor location for surf fishing. Better access is available at Samuel Spencer County Park.

USS *ARIZONA* MEMORIAL
1 Arizona Memorial Place
Honolulu, HI 96818
(808) 422–2771

The USS Arizona Memorial was established in 1962 as a memorial marking the spot where the Japanese sank the battleship USS Arizona during the December 7, 1941, attack on Pearl Harbor. The National Park Service took over the Memorial, visitor center, and tour operations in October 1980. The park is located on the island of Oahu, about twenty minutes west of downtown Honolulu on Kamehameha Highway.

On November 26, 1941, a Japanese task force of thirty-two ships plus twenty-seven submarines set out from Japan to the Hawaiian Islands. The purpose of the mission was to destroy America's Pacific Fleet. The first wave of Japanese aircraft arrived over their targets at 7:55 A.M. and, meeting virtually no opposition, strafed and bombed at will. In addition to the strike at Pearl Harbor, the Japanese attacked other installations such as Wheeler Air Field, Schofield Barracks, Kanehoe Naval Air Station, Hickam Airfield, Ewa Marine Corps Air Stations, and Bellows Airfield. The USS *Arizona* sank with a loss of more than 1,100 crew members only nine minutes after being hit by a 1,760-pound armor-piercing shell shortly after the attack commenced.

The park's visitor center is directly off Highway 99. Visitors should stop at the information desk and obtain tickets for the tour, which includes a film and boat trip to the Memorial. Tickets are issued on a first-come, first-served basis, and holders enter the theater and ride the boat in groups. The memorial is often crowded, so long waits can occur. Visitors may browse through exhibits at the visitor center and tour a nearby World War II submarine while waiting for their tour group to be called.

Facilities: A snack bar is available. A bookstore with military books and related material is operated by the non-profit Arizona Memorial Museum Association. Drinking water and restrooms are at the visitor center.
Camping: No camping is permitted in the park.
Fishing: No fishing is permitted in the park.

Idaho

CITY OF ROCKS NATIONAL RESERVE
P.O. Box 169
Almo, ID 83312
(208) 824–5519

City of Rocks National Reserve comprises slightly over 14,000 acres (half private, half public) and was established in 1988 to preserve significant cultural and natural resources including scenic granite spires, sculptured rock formations, and visible remnants of the California Trail. The reserve is located in south-central Idaho, 50 miles south of the town of Burley via Highway 27 from the west and Highway 77 from the east.

The monoliths, spires, and domes found in City of Rocks National Reserve are the result of millions of years of erosion from wind and water. As overlying rocks and granite cracked and fractured, underlying granite was eroded to form the shapes that can be seen today by visitors. Exposed formations range in age from relatively recent to over 2 billion years. The varied rock formations located in the reserve have made this one of the prime areas for climbers from around the world.

This area was once traversed by Shoshone and Bannock Indians. By 1843, emigrants traveled through City of Rocks via the California Trail that linked Sacramento, California, with St. Joseph, Missouri, and the Salt Lake Alternate Trail. It is estimated that fifty thousand people passed through in 1852 on their way to the California gold fields. Remnants of the California Trail are still visible.

City of Rocks is in the high desert, 5,000 to 6,000 feet above sea level, where the summer temperature can range from freezing to over one hundred degrees Fahrenheit. This environment supports aspen, Douglas fir, and lodgepole pine, and, at lower elevations, sagebrush, pinyon pine, and juniper. A variety of wildflowers can be seen in

◄ City of Rocks National Reserve   **IDAHO 153**

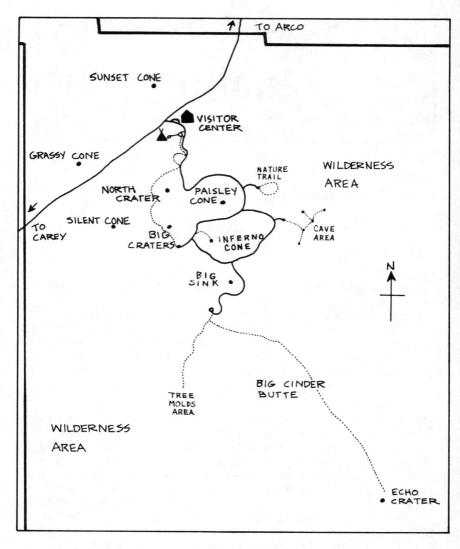

Craters of the Moon National Monument

spring and summer. Wildlife includes mule deer, mountain lions, bobcats, porcupines, and coyotes.

Facilities: Restrooms are at Bath Rock and Twin Sisters, and potable water is available only at a hand pump at the Emery Canyon Road summit, ¾ of a mile above Bath Rock. All other water should be boiled. Telephones and food supplies are at Alamo and Oakley, while the nearest full services are in Burley.

Camping: Only primitive camping is available in the reserve. Sites are at Parking Lot Rock, Elephant Rock, and Twin Sisters.

Fishing: No fishing is available in City of Rocks National Reserve.

CRATERS OF THE MOON NATIONAL MONUMENT
P.O. Box 29
Arco, ID 83213
(208) 527–3257

Craters of the Moon National Monument was incorporated into the National Park System in 1924 in order to protect 83,000 acres of volcanic cones, craters, lava flows, and caves. The park is located in south-central Idaho, approximately 18 miles southwest of Arco on U.S. 20/26/93.

Craters of the Moon is composed of vast lava fields containing large cinder cones that will remind visitors of a trip to the moon. Although vegetation was completely destroyed by the lava flows occurring as recently as 2,100 years ago, various types of plant and animal life have reestablished themselves.

Many interesting points in the park can be reached by means of a 7-mile paved loop drive that circles one of the park's major cinder cones. Seven trail heads lead from the road or one of its nearby side roads. Two of the longer trails lead into Craters of the Moon Wilderness Area, which contains the largest portion of the monument. The hike to the Tree Molds area will take about two hours and the trail to Echo Crater will consume considerably more time. The Devils Orchard Nature Trail begins at the end of a side road near the start of the loop. This ⅓-mile self-guided trail takes the hiker through a display of cinder fields and crater-wall fragments and requires approximately twenty minutes to complete. Another self-guided and easy-to-walk trail begins at a turnout just south of the campground. The turnout is also the beginning of a trail to North Crater and Big Craters. Although longer (one and three quarter miles) and quite rigorous, the views into the craters are spectacular.

One fascinating feature of the park is the cave area. This collection of caves are lava tubes and can be reached by hiking a short trail at the end of one of the side roads of the loop drive. The caves were formed when the surface area of lava flows cooled and hardened. This crust formed an insulating barrier so that the still molten material in the interior could continue to flow. Later, lava drained out of the tubes when the eruption stopped. The largest cave is the Indian Tunnel (800 feet). Beauty, Surprise, Dewdrop, and Boy Scout caves are smaller and more difficult to enter. The latter cave contains a floor of ice that can be quite slippery.

During summer months, ranger-guided hikes are conducted each day and campfire programs are presented each evening. Rangers are generally on duty in the visitor center to answer questions.

Facilities: Accommodations, food service, and gasoline are not available within the park, but can be found in the town of Arco. Modern restrooms and drinking water are at the visitor center and the campground.

Camping: A unique campground (fifty-one spaces) located near the visitor center just off the main highway is set in the volcanic field amid cinders and volcanic rocks. Fireplaces, tables, drinking water, and flush toilets are provided. Little shade is available. The campground is open from May to October.

Fishing: No fishing is available in Craters of the Moon National Monument.

NEZ PERCE NATIONAL HISTORICAL PARK
P.O. Box 93
Spalding, ID 83551
(208) 843–2261

Nez Perce National Historical Park was authorized in 1965. It comprises twenty-four historical sites scattered over a 12,000-square-mile area in northern Idaho. The individual sites, illustrating a chapter in the history and culture of the American Northwest, are generally close to U.S. Highways 12 and 95 southeast of Lewiston.

The natural resources of central Idaho attracted many groups of people during the settling of the American West. One of these groups—the

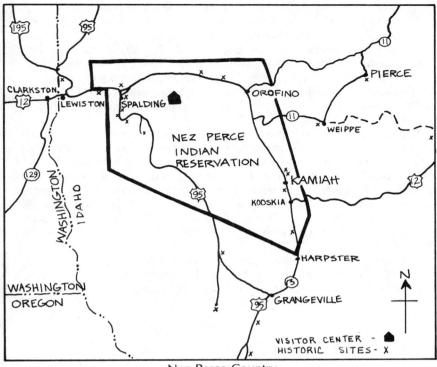

Nez Perce Country

Nez Perce Indians—encountered tragedy because of contacts with the white culture.

The Nez Perce inhabited north-central Idaho, northeastern Oregon, and southeastern Washington. For years they remained at peace while other tribes waged war with the growing number of explorers and settlers. After signing a treaty with the tribe in 1855, the federal government negotiated a new agreement in 1863 following the discovery of gold in 1860. Although the second treaty took almost ninety percent of the Nez Perce land from the 1855 agreement, many members of the tribe accepted the new treaty. In 1877, the federal government gave in to settlers' demands and decided to force the non-treaty Nez Perce bands onto the reservation. This resulted in a four-month-long war and an 1,800-mile fighting retreat that was stopped forty-two miles south of Canada. Many of these Indians were eventually placed on a reservation outside their ancestral lands.

The park commemorates and interprets not only the Nez Perce, but also the explorers, fur traders, missionaries, soldiers, settlers, gold miners, loggers, and farmers. Nez Perce National Historical Park is administered by the National Park Service, but the many detached historic sites are under a variety of ownerships and are managed under agreements with the U.S. Forest Service, the Bureau of Indian Affairs, the Idaho Department of Highways, the Idaho State Historical Society, the Nez Perce Tribe of Idaho, and several private organizations. A complete tour of all sites in the park is approximately a 400-mile trip. Park headquarters and a visitor center are in the town of Spalding.

Facilities: Various facilities including food and lodging are available in towns along the two major highways. Lewiston is a relatively large town eleven miles west of the park headquarters in Spalding.

Camping: Although no camping is provided by the Park Service, the area offers a diversity of camping opportunities. Clearwater, Nezperce, and Wallowa-Whitman national forests have campgrounds, as does the Corps of Engineers' Dworshak Reservoir. Winchester, Hellsgate, and Timothy state parks are all within thirty minutes' driving time of Spalding.

Fishing: A number of rivers, including the Potlatch, Clearwater, Snake, and the Salmon, are located near the various sites and provide excellent trout fishing. An Idaho license is required.

Iowa

EFFIGY MOUNDS NATIONAL MONUMENT
P.O. Box K
McGregor, IA 52157

Effigy Mounds comprises 1,475 acres. It was established in 1949 to preserve outstanding examples of prehistoric burial mounds in the shapes of birds and bears. The park is located in northeastern Iowa, 3 miles north of Marquette on Iowa Highway 76.

Effigy Mounds National Monument contains 191 known prehistoric mounds, of which twenty-nine are in the form of bear and bird effigies and the remainder are conical or linear shaped. The oldest mound excavated in the park, belonging to the Red Ocher Culture, has been dated to be about 2,500 years old. Burial offerings included large chipped blades, dart points, and spherical copper beads. Other mounds, from a culture dating from 100 B.C. to A.D. 600 have been excavated, revealing pottery and projectile points.

The Effigy Mounds people occupied this land from approximately A.D. 700 until historic times. They differed from the earlier mound builders not only in constructing mounds in effigy forms but also in using copper for tools instead of ornaments and in burying their dead with few lasting offerings. By about 1400, the Effigy Mounds people were replaced by Indians of the Oneota Culture.

The park's visitor center contains museum exhibits and an audio-visual presentation on the geology and history of Effigy Mounds. It is open daily (except Christmas) from 8:00 A.M. until 5:00 P.M. during winter and from 8:00 A.M. until 7:00 P.M. in summer. The one-hour, self-guiding Fire Point Trail provides access to some of the park's major points of interest, including some mounds and viewpoints on 300-foot bluffs along the Mississippi River. Trail markers and exhibits help interpret the walk. Ranger-guided walks are given frequently during

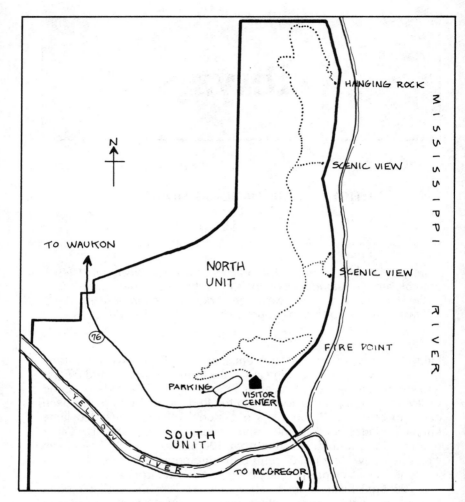

Effigy Mounds National Monument

summer months. A longer walk along the Hanging Rock Trail takes visitors to other points of interest.

Facilities: No lodging or food service is available in the park. Restrooms and drinking water are provided in the visitor center.

Camping: No camping is permitted at Effigy Mounds National Monument. Six miles south, on top of a bluff, Pikes Peak State Park offers sites with full hookups. Six miles northwest, Yellow River State Forest provides primitive camping and pit toilets.

Fishing: No fishing is available at the park. A trout stream is in Yellow River State Forest, 6 miles northwest of Effigy Mounds.

HERBERT HOOVER NATIONAL HISTORIC SITE
P.O. Box 607
West Branch, IA 52358
(319) 643–2541

Herbert Hoover National Historic Site comprises 187 acres and was established in 1965. The park includes the cottage where Hoover was born, his boyhood home, as well as his grave site. The historic site is located in West Branch, Iowa, 10 miles east of Iowa City on Interstate 80.

Herbert Hoover—mining engineer, humanitarian, statesman, and thirty-first president of the United States—was born August 10, 1874, in West Branch, Iowa. His father, a blacksmith, died when Herbert was only six years old. His mother died three years later. Herbert lived with relatives in West Branch until age eleven, when he moved to Oregon to live with an uncle and his family. At the age of seventeen, Hoover enrolled at Stanford University and in 1895 graduated with a degree in geology in the first class of the newly founded Stanford.

Hoover worked in the California gold mines and moved on to mining engineering projects in Australia, China, and England. He became very well known in international mining circles. During World War I, Hoover headed a variety of relief efforts that helped feed millions of people in thirty-three nations. He served as Secretary of Commerce for eight years and was then elected to the presidency in 1928. Following his unsuccessful effort at reelection, Hoover retired to California, where he devoted much of his time to the Hoover Institute on War, Revolution, and Peace at Stanford. He served on presidential commissions in 1946, 1947, and 1953 to study famine relief and recommend improvements in the executive branch of the federal government. Hoover died on October 20, 1964, and was buried on a hillside overlooking his birthplace.

In addition to the Hoover birthplace and grave site, the park contains a portion of the village of West Branch that is restored as a late nineteenth-century midwestern neighborhood. A blacksmith shop, schoolhouse, and meetinghouse are open to visitors. A visitor center is near the park's entrance on Parkside Drive and Main Street. The Presidential Library–Museum contains a collection of Hoover's presidential papers and many of the books and objects accumulated during his distinguished career. The park's buildings are open from 8:00 A.M. to 5:00 P.M. daily except Thanksgiving, Christmas, and New Year's Day. The library-museum and the site charge nominal fees for admission.

Facilities: No food or lodging is available in the park, but both are in nearby West Branch. Drinking water and restrooms are provided in the visitor center and the library-museum.

Camping: No camping is permitted in the park. Lake McBride State Park offers camping approximately 25 miles northwest of West Branch. Several private campgrounds also are located nearby.

Fishing: No fishing is available at the historic site.

Kansas

FORT LARNED NATIONAL HISTORIC SITE
Route 3
Larned, KS 67550
(316) 285–6911

Fort Larned, which comprises 718 acres, was incorporated into the National Park System in 1964 to protect the remains of a key military base along the Santa Fe Trail. The fort is located in southwestern Kansas, 6 miles west of the town of Larned on Kansas Highway 156. Also see the map under Bent's Old Fort National Historic Site (Colorado) in this book.

Named after Army Paymaster-General Benjamin Larned, Fort Larned was built in 1860 to protect travelers and the U.S. mail on the Santa Fe Trail from attacks by the Plains Indians. Seven adobe buildings were constructed at the fort during its first year, and in the winter of 1864–65 a stone blockhouse was added for protection. In 1866, additional appropriations allowed a renewed building program. Sandstone from quarries east of the fort was combined with pine timbers shipped from the East in the construction of nine new stone buildings around a quadrangular parade ground.

Following its use as a source of protection for those traveling the Santa Fe Trail, Fort Larned was used as a base of operations for the U.S. Army during the Indian War of 1867–68. By the end of 1868, organized Indian resistance had been broken. During the early 1870s, the fort housed soldiers who were to protect construction workers on the Santa Fe Railroad. The railroad was completed in 1872, and in July 1878 Fort Larned was abandoned.

Although the old adobe buildings are gone, the nine stone buildings are still standing. Several of the buildings are open to visitors, and guided tours and living history programs are presented during summer months. The visitor center—with a museum, audio-visual program, and exhibits—is housed in the barracks buildings next to the handicapped parking lot. A brochure for a self-guiding walk of the historic site is available in the visitor center. Four miles southeast a detached forty-acre unit of the historic site contains well-preserved wagon ruts of the Santa Fe Trail. A brochure is in the visitor center at the main unit. The park is open daily from 9:00 A.M. to 5:00 P.M. except Thanksgiving, Christmas, and New Year's Day.

Facilities: Drinking water and restrooms are in the visitor center. A shaded picnic area is located at the entrance to the site. Food and lodging are available in the town of Larned.

Camping: No camping is permitted at the site, but a private campground is in the town of Larned.

Fishing: No fishing is available.

FORT SCOTT NATIONAL HISTORIC SITE
Old Fort Boulevard
Fort Scott, KS 66701
(316) 223–0310

Fort Scott National Historic Site comprises seventeen acres. It was established as an area of the National Park Service in 1979, although federal planning and financial assistance was authorized in 1965 to help preserve and restore this important fort of the mid-1800s. Fort Scott is located in southeastern Kansas, 90 miles south of Kansas City and 60 miles north of Joplin, Missouri. In the town of Fort Scott, the site is located on Old Fort Boulevard.

Fort Scott was constructed in 1842 as part of a chain of posts designed to provide a frontier buffer zone between Indian Territory to the west and the developing states to the east. It was manned by cavalry that patrolled the border and policed the Indian Territory. After Congress opened more western territory to white settlement in the early 1850s, the frontier moved west and Fort Scott's importance diminished. In 1855, all of the army buildings were sold at a public auction, and they became part of the new town of Fort Scott. During the Civil War, the town was occupied by the Union Army, and the fort was reactivated. It was a major Federal supply base, communications center, and staging area for campaigns into Confederate territory.

The park's visitor center and bookstore are located in the restored post hospital, near the parking lot. The fort contains a number of other restored and reconstructed buildings open to visitors. Three areas of the park have been restored to natural tall grass prairie. Fort Scott is open daily from 8:00 A.M. to 5:00 P.M. (extended during summer) except Thanksgiving, Christmas, and New Year's Day.

Facilities: No lodging or food service is available in the park, but both can be found nearby. Restrooms and drinking water are located in the visitor center.

Camping: No camping is permitted in the park, but a state park with camping facilities is southwest on Highway 7 and a private campground is nearby.

Fishing: No fishing is available.

Louisiana

JEAN LAFITTE NATIONAL HISTORICAL PARK AND PRESERVE
Room 210, U.S. Customs House
423 Canal Street
New Orleans, LA 70130
(504) 589–3882

Jean Lafitte National Historical Park and Preserve was so designated in 1978 and includes the former Chalmette National Historical Park. The park contains four separate units in southern Louisiana that preserve significant examples of historical and natural resources of the Mississippi Delta Region. The Acadian Unit is in Lafayette, Louisiana, about 150 miles west of New Orleans. The other three units are located in and around the city of New Orleans.

The Mississippi Delta Region is rich in cultural and natural history. The river brought a stream of people and products from all parts of the globe to its point of drainage into the Gulf of Mexico. Jean Lafitte National Historical Park and Preserve, named for a well-known resident of New Orleans during the early 1800s, preserves four areas, showing the diversity of this history. The park is closed Christmas and New Year's Day. Some units may be closed for Mardi Gras.

Acadian Unit: This unit was added to the park in 1988 and preserves and interprets resources in several areas of the Acadian region of southern Louisiana. In addition to headquarters at Lafayette, the unit includes the Chitimacha Indian Tribe at Charenton, the Liberty Theatre at Eunice, and the Tunica-Biloxi Indian Tribe at Marksville. The assimilation and adaptation of the Cajuns resulted in distinctive lifestyles. There is a visitor center in Lafayette and at the Chitimacha Indian Reservation. In cooperation with the city of Eunice, the National Park Service sponsors a weekly live program devoted to

◀ **Chalmette Unit of Jean Lafitte**
National Historical Park and Preserve

Cajun culture. The program is conducted in Cajun French every Saturday evening from 6:00 P.M. to 8:00 P.M. at the Liberty Theatre.

Barataria Preserve Unit: Located on State Highway 45, about 12 miles south of New Orleans, this area of rich coastal wetlands includes bayous, live oak, alligators, and a number of important archaeological sites. There are about 8 miles of self-guiding trails that provide access to the sites and wetlands. Twelve miles of waterways are available for non-motorized craft such as canoes. Ranger-guided canoe tours are available on weekends and moonlit evenings. The visitor center offers audio-visual programs and exhibits on the area. The visitor center is open from 9:00 A.M. to 5:00 P.M. daily.

Chalmette Unit: Located six miles east of New Orleans off State Highway 46, this unit preserves the battlefield where Andrew Jackson's militia halted a British force of approximately 10,000 soldiers sent to attack New Orleans in 1814. The visitor center, open daily from 8:30 A.M. to 5:00 P.M., houses a small museum with uniforms and information about the military units that participated in the battle. There is a movie detailing the Battle of New Orleans. Programs about the battle are presented four times daily, and costumed demonstrations take place on Saturdays. An additional site administered by this unit is the Islenos Center, located 12 miles southeast of the Chalmette Unit.

French Quarter Unit: The unit's visitor center at 916 North Peters Street in downtown New Orleans provides exhibits, audio-visual programs, and demonstrations on the cultural diversity of the Mississippi Delta Region. From the visitor center, rangers lead a variety of walking tours of the French Quarter. The center is open daily from 9:00 A.M. to 5:00 P.M.

Facilities: No food or lodging is provided by the National Park Service, but both are available near the units.

Camping: No camping is permitted in the park. Public and private campgrounds are available in the two areas.

Fishing: Fishing is available in the Barataria Preserve Unit and the Chalmette Unit with a valid Louisiana fishing license.

Minnesota

GRAND PORTAGE NATIONAL MONUMENT
Box 668
Grand Marais, MN 55604
(218) 387–2788

Grand Portage was designated a national historic site in 1951 and was changed to a national monument in 1958. It contains 710 acres that were used as part of a principal route into the Northwest by Indians, explorers, missionaries, and fur traders. An old fur-trading depot is reconstructed here. The park is located in the northeastern tip of Minnesota, 151 miles northeast of Duluth on U.S. 61, a beautiful drive.

From 1779 to 1802, the wilderness outpost at Grand Portage served as an important meeting place for French trappers and traders along a route from Montreal to the Northwest. Blocked to the north by British dominance through Hudson's Bay Company, the French were forced to use this longer route. In 1763, the route was inherited by the British, who later used Grand Portage as the scene of an annual rendezvous. Here, traders with canoes full of goods from Montreal stopped on their way to Canada's interior. From the opposite direction came traders with furs for the East. In 1803, the post was abandoned after the United States gave notice that beginning the following year it would levy duties on all merchandise and furs passing over the portage.

The park is open all year to hiking and skiing; the reconstructed stockade, Great Hall, kitchen, and warehouse are open from mid-May to mid-October with park service personnel on duty. Guided tours, exhibits, and craft demonstrations are provided during summer months in the stockade area. From the dock, a boat leaves daily (summer only) for Isle Royale National Park, 22 miles offshore. Two hiking trails are available to visitors. Mount Rose Trail (one-half mile) climbs to the top of a knoll behind the stockade. A self-guiding trail leaflet is available

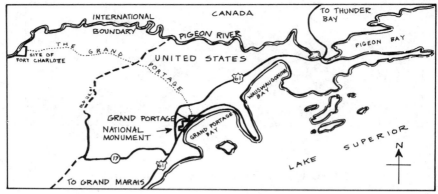
Grand Portage National Monument

at the trail head across the road from the parking lot. The longer Grand Portage (eight and one half miles) winds through the woods to the site of a former way station, Fort Charlotte, for furs en route to Grand Portage.

Facilities: Grand Portage Lodge and Conference Center provides full food service and overnight accommodations. Other limited services are nearby. Grand Marais (thirty-six miles) provides a greater variety of alternatives. Drinking water and modern restrooms are available at the monument.

Camping: No camping is permitted at the main Grand Portage site. Camping is permitted at Fort Charlotte with a free permit obtainable from the National Park Service. A Minnesota state park with camping facilities is approximately twenty miles southwest on Highway 61. Several private campgrounds can be found in the Grand Portage area. For those driving north, Middle Fall Provincial Park, just north of the Canadian border, is an attractive place to camp.

Fishing: Fishing is permitted in Lake Superior. A license is required from the State of Minnesota as well as the Grand Portage Band of Ojibwa Indians.

PIPESTONE NATIONAL MONUMENT
Box 727
Pipestone, MN 56164
(507) 825–5464

Pipestone, which contains 283 acres, was established in 1937 to preserve quarries where Indians obtained materials used in making peace pipes. The park is located in southwestern Minnesota, adjacent to the north side of the town of Pipestone. It may be reached via State Highways 30 and 23 or U.S. 75.

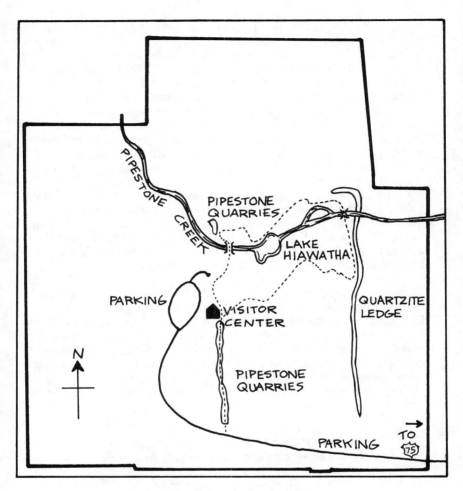

Pipestone National Monument

Millions of years ago, a thin clay layer was sandwiched between layers of sand deposited at the bottom of a sea. Later, additional sediment layers buried these deposits deep beneath the earth's surface, and pressure, heat, and chemical action changed the sand into quartzite and the red clay into stone. As the area was uplifted and eroded, a dense red mineral that today is called pipestone was exposed.

Centuries ago, many Indian tribes traveled thousands of miles to mine the pipestone. Although difficult to quarry, once extracted the red stone was easily carved with primitive tools. The rare material was traded over a wide area and was particularly used for ceremonial objects such as peace pipes. Today, only Indians are allowed to excavate the material.

The park's visitor center is open from 8:00 A.M. to 6:00 P.M. (until 8:00 P.M. on weekends and 5:00 P.M. in winter) and contains exhibits, an audio-visual program, and the Upper Midwest Indian Cultural Center. A ¾-mile self-guiding trail takes visitors past the quarries and through a small section of virgin prairie. Markers are placed along the trail, and guide booklets are available in the visitor center.

Facilities: Food and lodging are available in the town of Pipestone. Drinking water and restrooms are provided in the visitor center.
Camping: No camping is permitted in the park, but Split Rock Creek State Park (seventeen sites, pit toilets) is 8 miles south on Highway 23, and Blue Mounds State Park (seventy-six sites, flush toilets, showers, electricity, swimming beach) is 18 miles south on U.S. 75. A private campground is located just outside the park entrance.
Fishing: No fishing is available at Pipestone National Monument.

ST. CROIX NATIONAL SCENIC RIVERWAY;
Lower St. Croix National Scenic Riverway
P.O. Box 708
St. Croix Falls, WI 54024
(715) 483–3284

The St. Croix and Lower St. Croix National Scenic Riverways were separately established in 1968 and 1972 to preserve approximately 250 miles of riverways that show little evidence of disturbance by man. The parks begin near the sources of the St. Croix and Namekagon rivers in northern Wisconsin and follow the border between Wisconsin and Minnesota.

Thousands of years ago, this region of the United States was leveled by glacial ice flowing down from the north. As the climate warmed and

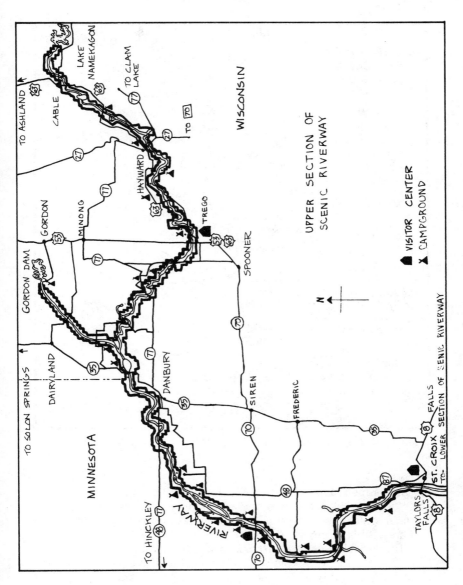

St. Croix National Scenic Riverway—Upper Section

St. Croix National Scenic Riverway—Lower Section

the glacier melted, much of the resulting water used the St. Croix basin as an escape. The scraping of the advancing ice sheet combined with the later water runoff exposed ancient rocks and volcanic formations that are visible along the rivers.

The French were the first Europeans to venture into this region. Here they found the Dakota and Chippewa tribes living in an area rich in both plant and wildlife. The St. Croix valley became an abundant source of beaver pelts for Europe until the early 1800s. After that, logging was to be the main industry until the 1920s. Today, much of the riverway cuts through second-growth hardwood forests.

Although the St. Croix and Lower St. Croix were established as two park areas, they actually constitute a single riverway and are administered jointly. The St. Croix section consists of 102 miles of the

St. Croix River and 98 miles of its Namekagon tributary (see map). The lower St. Croix carries the park an additional 52 miles from Taylors Falls to the Mississippi. The main visitor center and headquarters is at St. Croix Falls, and information stations are open in the summer near the towns of Grantsburg and Trego, Wisconsin, and in Stillwater, Minnesota.

Canoeing the rivers is one of the park's most popular activities. During late summer and fall, the water level is generally low and the lower sections of the river provide the best trips. A listing of the numerous canoe outfitters located along the riverway may be obtained by writing the park superintendent. Most visitors find that 10–20 miles of paddling downstream is a full day. The Lower St. Croix is popular for power-boating, water-skiing, and house-boating. State parks along this part of the riverway provide camping, picnicking, nature hikes, and interpretive exhibits.

Facilities: No food service or lodging is provided by the Park Service. Overnight accommodations and supplies are in nearby communities.
Camping: A number of primitive campgrounds are located along the riverway. Campgrounds with vault toilets and water are at Howell Landing and Earl Park.
Fishing: Bass, muskellunge, walleye pike, and sturgeon are in the rivers, and the Namekagon is noted for brown trout. A license is required. Where the river forms a boundary between the two states, a license from either is valid while fishing from a boat.

VOYAGEURS NATIONAL PARK
P.O. Box 50
International Falls, MN 56649
(218) 283–9821

Voyageurs National Park was authorized in 1971 and established in 1975 to preserve 217,000 acres of beautiful forested lake country that was once inhabited by French-Canadian fur traders. The park is located in northern Minnesota and stretches along the U.S.–Canadian border east of International Falls. Four roads along U.S. 53 provide access, although summer travel within the park is confined to boats.

Most of this land, which has been shaped by glaciers into a system of countless waterways, remains as undeveloped and wild as it was when French-Canadian voyageurs made their way through here from Montreal to the Northwest. The hardwood stands are broken only by lakes and occasional bogs, sand beaches, and cliffs. The south side of the

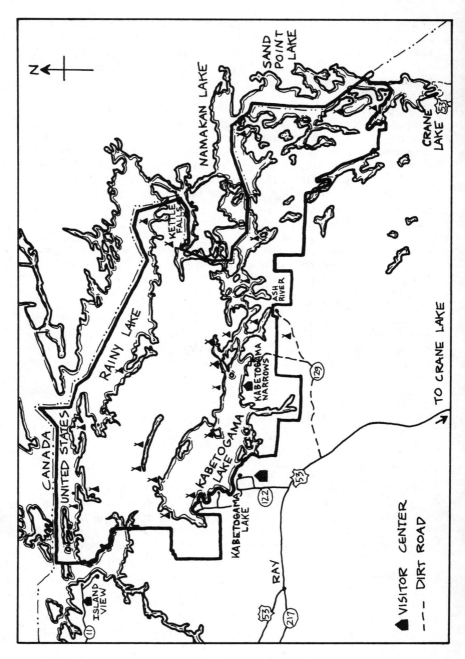

Voyageurs National Park

Kabetogama Peninsula is dotted with numerous islands, while the north shore is broken with many coves and small bays. The former fur company trading posts and forts were west of the park, near International Falls.

One of the park's visitor centers is at Kabetogama, approximately 3 miles north of U.S. 53 on Highways 122 and 123. Here visitors will find exhibits and information on the area. The Ash River Visitor Center is eleven miles east of Highway 53 on Highway 129. Both the Kabetogama and Ash River centers are open seasonally. The Rainy Lake Visitor Center is located 11 miles east on Minnesota Highway 11. A variety of interpretive programs are offered, including guided boat tours, canoe trips, and cross-country ski excursions. Boats, canoes, and guide services are available outside the park at Ash River, Crane Lake, Kabetogama, Kettle Falls, and Island View.

Facilities: Lodging, food, and full boating services are available only at Kettle Falls, inside the park. Kettle Falls is accessible only by boat. For information, write Kettle Falls Hotel, Ash River Trail, Orr, MN 55771 (218–374–3511) in summer; 622 Twelfth Avenue, International Falls, MN 56649 (218–283–2692) in winter. Groceries, restaurants, lodging, and gas are at Ash River, Crane Lake, Kabetogama, Island View, Orr, and International Falls.

Camping: One hundred primitive campsites, accessible only by boat, are located throughout the park. Public camping facilities are available nearby in Kabetogama State Forest, and private camping with hookups is available at Ash River, Crane Lake, Kabetogama, and Island View.

Fishing: Northern Minnesota is noted for sports fishing, especially walleye, northern pike, trout, bass, muskie, perch, and crappie. A Minnesota license is required.

Missouri

GEORGE WASHINGTON CARVER NATIONAL MONUMENT
P.O. Box 38
Diamond, MO 64840
(417) 325–4151

*George Washington Carver National Monument, which contains
210 acres, was established in 1943 to memorialize the birthplace
and childhood home of this famous educator and agronomist. The
monument is located in southwestern Missouri, approximately 10
miles southeast of Joplin. From either Neosho or Carthage, take
U.S. 71 Alternate to the town of Diamond. From here, drive 2
miles west on County Highway V and then south 1 mile.*

In the mid-1850s, Moses Carver and his wife purchased a black girl
named Mary to help with their 240-acre farm in southwestern Missouri.
Some time later, probably in the early 1860s, Mary gave birth to her
second boy, whom she named George. About this same time, the
outbreak of the Civil War brought a period of suffering to the people of
Missouri. Mary and her children were carried off by a group of raiders,
and, although George was eventually recovered by a small Union
Army contingent, his mother was never heard from again. Upon his
return to the farm, George worked and learned alongside the Carvers
before adopting their name and leaving for a black school in Neosho
just prior to reaching his teens.

The remainder of George Washington Carver's life was a testi-
mony to his initiative. After receiving honorable mention for a painting
entered in the 1893 Chicago World's Fair, he earned bachelor's and
master's degrees in botany from Iowa State University. In 1896, he
accepted a position at Tuskegee Normal and Industrial Institute in
Alabama, where he served for more than forty years. During this
period, Carver made significant contributions to southern agriculture
and received numerous awards.

A visitor center near the parking lot is the start of a self-guiding ¾-mile trail passing by a number of exhibits from Carver's boyhood. Among these are the cabin site where he was born, the relocated Moses Carver dwelling, and a statue of Carver as a boy. The visitor center contains a museum with exhibits that trace Carver's life and accomplishments. Two films concerning Carver are shown continuously in the visitor center.

Facilities: No food or lodging is available in the park, but both are in Diamond. Water and restrooms are located in the visitor center. A picnic area is available.
Camping: No camping is permitted. Roaring River State Park provides camping approximately 50 miles southeast, near Cassville.
Fishing: No fishing is available.

HARRY S TRUMAN NATIONAL HISTORIC SITE
223 North Main
Independence, MO 64050
(816) 254–2720

Harry S Truman National Historic Site was established in 1982 to preserve the home and memorialize the life of the thirty-third president of the United States. Truman's home is located in western Missouri in the town of Independence, near Kansas City. An information center with parking is at Main Street and Truman Road.

Harry Truman was born in Lamar, Missouri, in 1884 and moved to Independence as a six-year-old boy. It was in Independence that he met Bess Wallace, his future wife, and was graduated from high school. After working on the family farm, serving in the United States Army during World War I, and attempting a number of business ventures, Truman was elected Jackson County administrative judge in the early 1920s. By 1935, Harry Truman had been elected to the U.S. Senate and had moved to Washington. He was re-elected once before successfully running as Franklin Roosevelt's vice-president in 1944. Following Roosevelt's death in 1945, Truman assumed the presidency, to which he was elected in 1948. Deciding not to run again in 1952, Harry Truman returned to Independence in 1953, where he purchased the house at 219 North Delaware Street from his mother-in-law's estate. Truman had lived in the house from his marriage in 1919 and continued to live there until his death in 1972 at the age of eighty-eight. Truman's wife, Bess, continued to live at the residence until her death ten years later.

The Truman Home Ticket and Information Center, located at the intersection of Truman Road and Main Street, contains a twelve-minute audio-visual presentation about the home. The center operates daily from 8:30 A.M. to 5:00 P.M. except for Thanksgiving Day, Christmas, and New Year's Day. Guided tours of the Truman home do not take place on Mondays between Labor Day and Memorial Day. Guided-tour tickets are sold at the ticket center on a first-come, first-served basis, so arrive early in the day. Ticket sales are limited to four tickets per person. From the visitor center, the Truman home is five blocks west on Truman Road to Delaware Street. Parking in the Truman home neighborhood is extremely limited. Ask at the Ticket and Information Center for RV and trailer parking.

Other Truman-related sites in Independence include the Harry S Truman Library and Museum and the Jackson Country Courthouse, where Truman's political career began. The courthouse features a thirty-minute audio-visual program about the president's life. Between Memorial Day and Labor Day, park rangers conduct guided walks (no charge) at 10:00 A.M. and 2 P.M. through the Truman home neighborhood.

Facilities: Restrooms and drinking water are available at the ticket center, library, and railroad station. Food is available nearby on Independence Square, adjacent to the ticket center; lodging is available at the intersection of Interstate 70 and Noland Road. Neither is offered by the National Park Service.
Camping: No camping is available at the park.
Fishing: No fishing is available at the park.

JEFFERSON NATIONAL EXPANSION MEMORIAL
11 North Fourth Street
St. Louis, MO 63102
(314) 425–4465

Jefferson National Expansion Memorial contains ninety-one acres and was designated part of the National Park Service in 1935 to memorialize Thomas Jefferson and other American leaders who directed territorial expansion of the United States, as well as the pioneers who explored and settled the West. This park, highlighted by the famous 630-foot Gateway Arch, is located on the St. Louis riverfront, within easy walking distance of downtown. Parking is available along the riverfront, just to the east of the memorial.

As the people of the United States began moving westward following the Louisiana Purchase in 1803, St. Louis—with a strategic location on a cliff convenient to the Mississippi, Missouri, and other river approaches—became an important center of commerce, transportation, and culture. Along with being the headquarters of the western fur trade, the city was a congregating point for pioneers starting across the plains. Although most of this activity occurred along the riverfront, an 1849 fire destroyed most of the downtown area where the present park is located. Future growth moved uptown, and only two buildings, the Old Courthouse and the Old Cathedral, still stand within the park boundaries.

The central feature of the park is Eero Saarinen's 630-foot stainless steel arch, which was built to commemorate St. Louis's historic role as a gateway for the westward pioneers. A passenger tram (fee charged) with eight five-passenger cars built on the order of baskets on a ferris wheel, climbs each leg of the arch to an observation deck at the top. Beneath the arch, the Museum of Westward Expansion contains exhibits from the westward migration. Films about the westward expansion and the building of the arch are shown periodically throughout the day. Waits of an hour or more to take the tram are common, but visitors can make a tram reservation (do this immediately upon your arrival) and spend the waiting time viewing the exhibits and movies. The Old Courthouse, where Dred Scott sued for his freedom, has numerous exhibits on St. Louis history and is open daily.

Facilities: Fast food restaurants are in paddle-wheel boats along the riverfront, a short walk from the arch. Drinking water, soft-drink machines, and restrooms are in the visitation area beneath the arch. Food and lodging are a few blocks away in downtown St. Louis.
Camping: No camping is permitted at the memorial.
Fishing: Fishing is permitted in the Mississippi River across the road from the arch. Fishing access also is available ½ mile south and ½ mile north of the memorial.

OZARK NATIONAL SCENIC RIVERWAYS
P.O. Box 490
Van Buren, MO 63965
(314) 323–4236

Ozark National Scenic Riverways, established in 1964, includes nearly 80,000 acres that contain 134 miles of the beautiful Current and Jacks Fork rivers. The park is located in southeastern Missouri, 150 miles south of St. Louis.

The mountains of this region are remnants of a large range eroded by wind and water. In addition to surface erosion, underlying limestone has developed large pockets as a consequence of water dissolving the rock. The result is a large number of sinkholes, caverns, and springs for which this region is noted. One of the largest springs in the nation, Big Spring, is located south of Van Buren. Other large springs are Alley Springs on the Jacks Fork and Welch and Blue Springs on the Current River. Among the numerous caves along the riverways, Round Spring Cavern is one of the most popular. Many of the caves are large and beautifully decorated.

The major activity center on the Jacks Fork River is at Alley Spring, and major centers on the Current River are at Akers, Pulltite, Round Spring, and Big Spring. Evening programs on the area's geology and history are conducted during summer. Daytime craft demonstrations include john-boat-building, corn-milling, and quilt-making. Listings of programs and demonstrations are available at park headquarters and at the activity centers. Tours of Round Spring Cavern are available.

The most popular activity in the park is floating the rivers. Canoes and john boats (for fishing) may be rented (a rental agency takes the canoes to launch points and picks up floaters at a scheduled time and place). The upper stretches of the rivers generally are more fun to float during late winter and spring because of low water levels during summer. Special canoe demonstrations are conducted by park rangers, and maps and river guides to both rivers are sold in the park.

Facilities: Cabins, lodging, meals, and stores are located at Montauk State Park, Big Spring, Alley Spring, Round Spring, and nearby towns. Boat rentals are available at Akers Ferry, Pulltite, Round Spring, Two Rivers, Alley Spring, and nearby towns.

Camping: Campgrounds with tables, grills, water, and flush toilets are Cedar Grove (six spaces, vault toilets), Hawes (ten spaces, vault toilets), Akers (eighty-one spaces, eight group sites, vault toilets), Pulltite (fifty-five spaces, three group sites), Round Spring (sixty spaces, three group sites, dump station, showers, laundry), Two Rivers (twelve

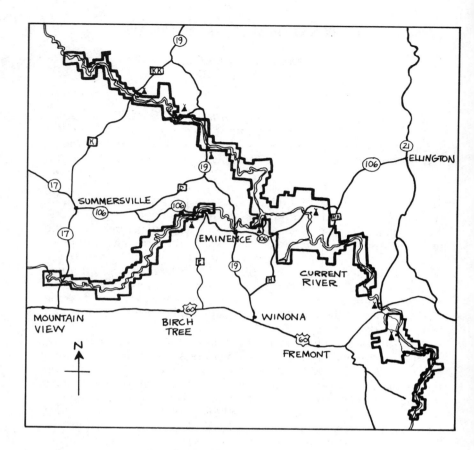

Ozark National Scenic Riverways

spaces, two group sites), Alley Spring (220 spaces, three group sites, dump station, showers), and Big Spring (205 spaces, four group sites, dump station, showers). Floaters may use gravel bars on both the Current and Jacks Fork rivers for camping.

Fishing: Rock bass and smallmouth bass are the most abundant fish caught. Largemouth bass, walleye (twenty-pounders have been caught), and chain pickerel are also fairly common. Trophy trout are in the Current River from the Montauk State Park boundary to Cedar Grove. A Missouri license is required. And if fishing for trout, a special stamp is required.

WILSON'S CREEK NATIONAL BATTLEFIELD
RR #2, Box 75
Republic, MO 65738
(417) 732–2662

Wilson's Creek, which contains 1,750 acres, was authorized in 1960 to commemorate the site of an 1861 Civil War battle for control of Missouri. The park is located in southwestern Missouri, 10 miles southwest of Springfield and 3 miles east of Republic. It is reached from Interstate 44 by going south at Exit 77 to U.S. 60, going west to Missouri M, south to Missouri ZZ, and south to the park.

Missouri's strategic location and resources made its allegiance an important concern following the outbreak of the Civil War. The state was divided in its loyalties, with the governor an active secessionist and Senator Blair a Unionist.

Hostilities came to a head on August 10, 1861, when 5,400 Union troops attacked a Confederate force of 12,000 camped near Wilson's Creek. The attackers surprised the Confederates and quickly occupied a ridge subsequently named "Bloody Hill." The battle raged for five hours before the Union forces retreated to Springfield. The Union commander, General Nathaniel Lyon, died during the battle, becoming the first Union general to die in battle in the Civil War.

Losses on both sides were heavy, with the North losing 1,317 men and the South losing 1,230. Though the Confederates held the field—and therefore won the battle—the Federals had helped their cause in Missouri. Due to the battle at Wilson's Creek and the battle at Pea Ridge seven months later, Missouri remained a Union state.

A visitor center built in 1982 features a thirteen-minute film, a spectacular battle map display, a museum, and a sales area. A 4.85-mile self-guiding driving tour features the restored 1852 Ray House, the 1863 Edwards' cabin, and a 1-mile-long walking trail at Bloody Hill. Weekend and holiday living-history programs are featured during the summer months.

Facilities: No facilities are located in the park, but food and lodging are available in the towns of Republic and Springfield. Drinking water and modern restrooms are in the visitor center.
Camping: No camping is permitted in the park. A variety of public campgrounds are available within the 30–60-mile range. Private camping is available approximately 5 miles from the park, near Interstate 44.
Fishing: Fishing is available but not recommended.

GEORGE A. CUSTER

LIEUT. COLONEL
BVT. MAJOR GENERAL
7 U. S. CAV.
FELL HERE
JUNE 25, 1876

Montana

BIG HOLE NATIONAL BATTLEFIELD
P.O. Box 237
Wisdom, MT 59761
(406) 689–3155

Big Hole National Battlefield contains 656 acres. It was authorized in 1910 to preserve the site of an 1877 battle between the U.S. Army and the Nez Perce Indians. The park is located in southwestern Montana, 89 miles southwest of Butte via Interstate 90, Interstate 15, and Montana 43. From Wisdom, drive 10 miles west on State Highway 43.

During the summer of 1877, a group of about 800 Nez Perce Indians began a journey from western Oregon and Idaho, over the Bitterroot Mountains, and into Montana Territory. The reason for the trip was the influx of settlers, miners, and stockmen into the area that had been reserved for the Nez Perce under two separate treaties. Because the Army was charged with returning the Indians to the reservation, the two groups faced each other in battle a number of times during the chase. One such conflict occurred in the Big Hole Valley. Although the Nez Perce were able to hold off the attacking Army troops and escape, their losses were large and their spirit was broken. Two months later, after failing to obtain help from the Shoshone and Crow, the Nez Perce surrendered in the Bear Paw Mountains in northern Montana.

A visitor center with exhibits and an audio-visual program is open from 8:00 A.M. to 8:00 P.M. from Memorial Day to Labor Day, and 8:00 A.M. to 5:00 P.M. the rest of the year. Ranger programs on the Nez Perce and on 1870s military life are presented at the visitor center. A short drive to the parking area provides access to two foot trails that lead to the battle area. Each trail takes about forty-five minutes to walk.

◀ **Headstone Marker in Custer Battlefield
National Monument**

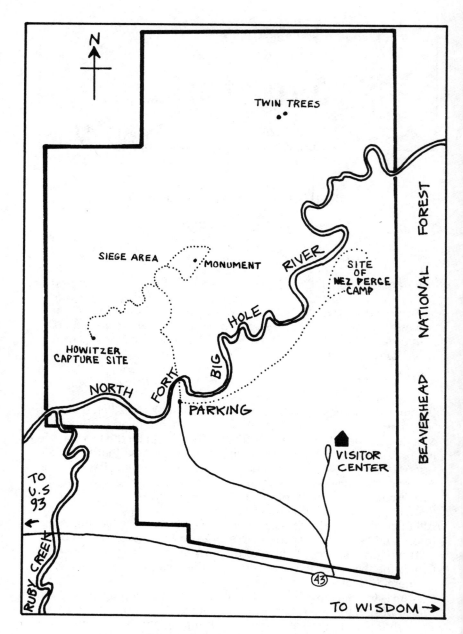

Big Hole National Battlefield

Another trail to the spot where a group of Indians captured an Army howitzer takes about thirty minutes.

Facilities: No food or lodging is available in the park. A gasoline station, grocery store, restaurant, and lodging are in Wisdom. Drinking water and restrooms are in the visitor center.

Camping: No camping is permitted in the park. A very nice May Creek National Forest Service campground is located seven and one quarter miles west on Highway 43. It has twenty-one mostly level sites with grills, fire pits, tables, water, and pit toilets.

Fishing: Trout fishing is permitted in the North Fork of the Big Hole River with a Montana license. Fishing is also available a short walk across the road from the above-mentioned campground.

BIGHORN CANYON NATIONAL RECREATION AREA
P.O. Box 458
Fort Smith, MT 59035
(406) 666–2412

Bighorn Canyon has been administered under a cooperative agreement with the Bureau of Reclamation since 1964. The park contains more than 120,000 acres, including the lower 47 miles of Bighorn Lake, which lies within a rugged, steep-walled canyon hundreds of feet deep. Bighorn Canyon is located in southeastern Montana and north-central Wyoming. The southern part of the park is reached via U.S. 14A from Sheridan, Wyoming, and by U.S. 310 from Billings, Montana. The northern portion and Yellowtail Dam are reached via Montana Highway 313 south 43 miles from Hardin, Montana.

Bighorn Canyon was cut over a period of thousands of years before the Yellowtail Dam was completed in 1965 to form seventy-one-mile-long Bighorn Lake. The result is the creation of all types of water-related activities on one of the country's most scenic manmade lakes. In addition to recreation, the reservoir is used for power generation, irrigation, water supply, and flood control.

The canyon cuts across the north end of the Bighorn Mountains in a region where the middle Rocky Mountains flow into the Great Plains. Upstream from the dam are half-mile high limestone cliffs containing fossils that began forming when this region was covered by a shallow sea. Nearby, in the Pryor Mountains, the Bureau of Land Management administers 32,000 acres that have been set aside as a wild horse

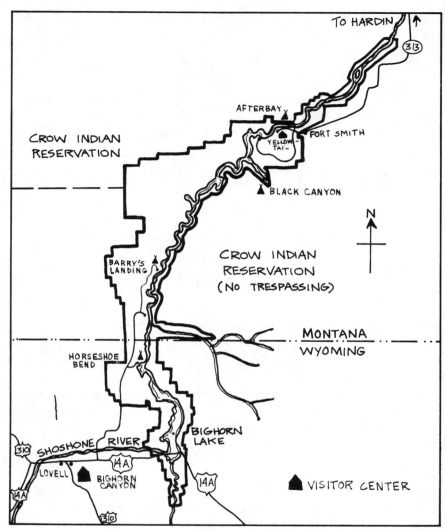

Bighorn Canyon National Recreation Area

range. Visitors may catch a glimpse of some of the 140 wild horses near Sykes or Britton Springs, or from the Sykes Ridge Road.

Fort Smith Visitor Center, located at Fort Smith in the north end of the park, concentrates on Crow Indian history. Tours of the Yellowtail Dam are available from Memorial Day to Labor Day. About three miles below the damsite, traces of the Bozeman Trail may be seen on the right bank of the river. This trail was used for transporting supplies between Fort Laramie, Wyoming, and Virginia City, Montana, after the discovery of gold in Montana.

At the park's south end, Bighorn Canyon Visitor Center provides an audio-visual presentation and exhibits. Here, visitors can find guided tours through a solar heating system and obtain information on tours of the Mason-Lovell Ranch Site. For those with boats, launching ramps are located at Afterbay, Barry's Landing, Horseshoe Bend, and Ok-A-Beh.

Facilities: Horseshoe Bend provides a swimming beach, picnic area, and food and marina provisions. Hotels, motels, restaurants, service stations, groceries, and sporting goods are available in Lovell, Wyoming, and Hardin, Montana. A motel, restaurant, grocery, and service station are in Fort Smith.

Camping: Afterbay (thirty spaces) and Horseshoe Bend (128 spaces) provide tables, grills, water, flush toilets, and dump stations. Barry's Landing (fourteen spaces) has more primitive facilities. Black Canyon (six spaces) has no water and is accessible only by boat.

Fishing: Bighorn Lake offers fishing for walleye (about 60 percent of all fish caught), rainbow and brown trout, perch, and black crappie. Bighorn River contains rainbow and brown trout. A Montana or Wyoming license is required depending upon the spot selected.

CUSTER BATTLEFIELD NATIONAL MONUMENT
P.O. Box 39
Crow Agency, MT 59022
(406) 638–2622

Custer Battlefield contains 765 acres and was established as a national cemetery in 1879 (changed to a national monument in 1946) to commemorate the site of the famous Battle of the Little Bighorn. The park is in southeastern Montana, approximately 1 mile from the intersection of Interstate 90 and U.S. 212.

Soon after the discovery of gold in the Black Hills in 1874, the areas reserved for the Cheyenne and Sioux were swarming with gold

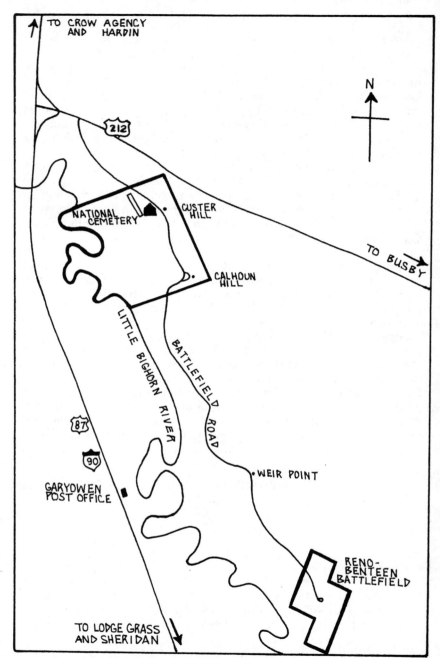

Custer Battlefield National Monument

seekers. When the Indians left the reservation, the Army was called upon to force their return. Lt. Col. George Custer was part of one of three separate expeditions sent to converge on the main body of Indians in southeastern Montana. He and the Seventh Cavalry were ordered to approach the Indian concentration on the Little Bighorn. Custer divided his regiment into three battalions and attacked. When the battle ended, Custer and the 225 men of his battalion were dead. An additional forty-seven men from the other two battalions were also killed. Indian losses are not known because the Indians removed most of their dead from the battlefield.

The park's visitor center contains historical exhibits and literature to help interpret the area. Veterans from Indian battles and more recent wars are buried in a national cemetery just west of the visitor center (Custer is buried at West Point). At Custer Hill, where a monument has been erected over the mass grave of soldiers killed in the battle, visitors have a view of most of the battlefield. Four miles beyond the main part of the park is a detached section where two other battalions fought the Indians. Guided walks, lectures, demonstrations, and an audio-visual presentation are presented daily during summer months.

Facilities: No lodging or food service is available in the park. Restrooms and drinking water are provided at the visitor center. A motel, restaurant, and gas station are located a short distance from the park entrance at the intersection of Interstate 90 and U.S. Highway 212.
Camping: No camping is permitted in the monument. A small private campground is located at the intersection of 90 and 212, about a mile from the park entrance. A larger private campground is in Hardin, fifteen miles north. Public camping facilities are available at Bighorn Canyon National Recreation Area, approximately forty miles away.
Fishing: Non-Indians are not permitted to fish in the Little Bighorn River, which is no longer stocked and only supports catfish. Nearby, the Bighorn River (also on the Crow Reservation) offers some of the finest trout fishing in the Northwest. Outfitters are available in the Fort Smith area of Bighorn Canyon National Recreation Area.

GLACIER NATIONAL PARK
West Glacier, MT 59936
(406) 888–5441

Glacier National Park was established in 1910 and contains more than 1 million acres of beautiful wilderness area including lakes, mountains, and nearly fifty glaciers. Some travelers who have seen much of the United States and many of the areas of the Park Service consider this to be the most outstanding park in the

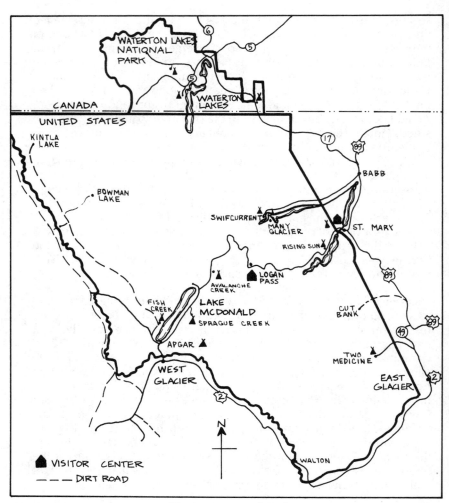

Glacier National Park

country. Glacier is located in northwestern Montana, with the west entrance 34 miles from Kalispell via U.S. 2 and the east entrance 62 miles west of Cut Bank via U.S. 2 and U.S 89.

The landscape of Glacier tells a story that began millions of years ago. Over a long period of time, compacted limestone was covered with sediments which, in turn, were covered with new layers of limestone. Approximately 70 million years ago, pressures within the earth caused the rock to warp and break until the western section was pushed over the eastern part. This overthrust lasted for millions of years until a 300-mile section of the earth's crust had been moved more than thirty-seven miles to the east. Much later, the park's surface was shaped by glaciers that formed numerous U-shaped valleys.

Glacier's three orientation centers at St. Mary (late May to mid-September), Apgar (late May to September), and Logan Pass (mid-June to early September) provide exhibits and information on the park. Glacier is crossed by the fifty-mile Going-to-the-Sun Road. This road, closed in winter, crosses through the heart of the Rockies at the treeline and provides one of America's most spectacular and scenic drives. Another worthwhile drive is along Many Glacier Road, which leaves U.S. 89 fourteen miles north of St. Mary at Babb.

Numerous outdoor activities are available in Glacier. Guided walks and campfire programs are offered on a daily basis from mid-June through August. Schedules are posted at ranger stations, visitor centers, and campgrounds. Horseback trips of from two hours to all day are operated out of Many Glacier, the Lake McDonald Lodge area, and Apgar. Information on guided backpacking trips and equipment rental may be obtained by writing Glacier Wilderness Guides, Box 535, West Glacier, MT 59936 (406–888–5333).

Boating on the many lakes found in the park is a popular activity. Motorboats are permitted only on Kintla, Bowman, Two Medicine Lakes, McDonald, Waterton, Sherburne, and St. Mary. Motors have a limit of ten h.p. on the first three. Boats may be rented at Many Glacier, Apgar, Two Medicine, and Lake McDonald Lodge. Excursion boat cruises are offered at Many Glacier, Rising Sun, Waterton Lake, Two Medicine, and Lake McDonald Lodge.

During winter months, cross-country skiing and snowshoeing have become increasingly popular. There is no downhill ski facility, and snowmobiling is not permitted. The park road from West Glacier to the Lake McDonald Lodge area (ten miles) is the only road open to automobile traffic in winter.

Facilities: Overnight accommodations are available at a number of locations inside the park, including Apgar, Lake McDonald, Many Glacier, and Swift Current. Information and reservations may be

obtained from Glacier Park Inc. From May 15 to September 15 write East Glacier Park, MT 59434 (406–226–9311). During the remainder of the year write Greyhound Towers Sta 5185, Tucson, AZ 85077 (602–795–0377). Sperry and Granite Park Chalets are open from July 1 through Labor Day and are accessible by trail only. The former is 6.5 miles from Lake McDonald Lodge, and Granite Park Chalet is 7.6 miles from Logan Pass. Rates and reservations may be obtained by writing Belton Chalets, Box 188, West Glacier, MT 59936 (406–888–5511).

Camping: Developed campgrounds with tables, grills, water, flush toilets, and dump stations are located at Apgar (196 spaces, ten group camps), Avalanche (eighty-seven spaces, hard-sided units only), Fish Creek (180 spaces), Many Glacier (117 spaces, hard-sided units only), Rising Sun (eighty-three spaces), Sprague Creek (twenty-five spaces, no dump station, tents and pickup campers only), St. Mary Lake (156 spaces, four group camps), and Two Medicine (ninety-nine spaces). Less-developed campgrounds with pit toilets are at Bowman Creek (six spaces, no water, no fee), Bowman Lake (forty-eight spaces, no large trailers), Cut Bank (nineteen spaces), Kintla Lake (nineteen spaces, no large trailers), Logging Creek (eight spaces, no large trailers), Quartz Creek (seven spaces), and River (seven spaces, no water, no large trailers). The camping limit at all these sites is seven days. Seventy back-country camps are accessible by trail only.

Fishing: Glacier has many good fishing lakes and many miles of streams. Rainbow, brook, and cutthroat trout are in Swiftcurrent, Josephine, and Grinnell lakes, as well as in the lakes of Upper Swiftcurrent Valley in the Many Glacier area and the Middle and North Forks of the Flathead River on the park's south and west boundaries. Grayling live in a few waters in the Belly River country. A Montana license is not needed to fish in Glacier National Park, but a free permit is required and may be obtained at visitor centers and ranger stations.

GRANT–KOHRS RANCH NATIONAL HISTORIC SITE
P.O. Box 790
Deer Lodge, MT 59722
(406) 846–2070

Grant–Kohrs Ranch contains 1,500 acres and was added to the National Park Service in 1972 to preserve the headquarters area of one of the largest and best-known nineteenth-century open range cattle-ranching businesses in the country. The site is located in western Montana, adjacent to the town of Deer Lodge. Exit off

◄ Grant–Kohrs Ranch—Lower Yard

Interstate 90 on U.S. 10 until reaching the fairgrounds. For travelers with an interest in the history of the Old West, this stop is a must.

The Grant–Kohrs Ranch saw its beginnings in the 1850s when Johnny Grant, a Canadian trapper and trader, settled in Deer Lodge Valley to become one of the area's early ranchers. Within a decade he and his family were running more than 2,000 cattle. In 1862, they constructed the largest home in Montana Territory. In 1866, the Grants sold the ranch to Conrad Kohrs, a butcher and Danish immigrant, for $19,200. From the open ranges of the 1860s and 1870s, Kohrs and his partner and half-brother, John Bielenberg, saw a gradual evolution of the cattle industry to an era of fencing, feed raising, and planted pastures. During this time the home ranch grew to 25,000 acres with between 8,000 and 10,000 cattle being shipped to Chicago annually.

Following the deaths of Kohrs and Bielenberg in the early 1920s, the ranch was operated by Kohrs's grandson, who preserved the house, its furnishings and outbuildings, and papers documenting its rich history.

The park is open daily except Thanksgiving, Christmas, and New Year's Day. A small visitor center with exhibits relating the ranch's history is located across U.S. 10 from the fairgrounds. From here, a self-guided trail takes visitors through the headquarters area. In addition, rangers conduct tours of the ranch house and outbuildings. A tour of the home with its outstanding and unique furnishings is worthwhile.

Facilities: No food or lodging is available in the park, but restaurants, motels, grocery stores, and gasoline stations are available within one mile in Deer Lodge. Water and restrooms are provided near the visitor center and at the ranch.

Camping: No camping is permitted at the site. Lost Creek State Park is approximately twenty-five miles away (northwest of Anaconda) and offers primitive camping facilities. Private campgrounds are in the town of Deer Lodge. For those traveling on Interstate 90, a nice campground (sixteen spaces, flush toilets, grills, water, and tables) in Montana's Beavertail Hill Recreation Area is fifty-three miles west of Deer Lodge.

Fishing: No fishing is available at the site, but there is good fishing at the nearby Clark Fork River.

Nebraska

AGATE FOSSIL BEDS NATIONAL MONUMENT
P.O. Box 27
Gering, NE 69341
(308) 436–4340

Agate Fossil Beds National Monument, which contains approximately 2,700 acres, was established in 1965 to preserve three renowned quarries that contain numerous well-preserved mammal fossils. The park is located in extreme western Nebraska on State Highway 29, approximately 23 miles south of the town of Harrison.

Agate Fossil Beds contains a concentration of fossils that were deposited as bones 13 to 25 million years ago during the Age of Mammals. The beds contain a variety of fossilized bones, the most common of which are those from a small two-horned rhinoceros that roamed the plain in huge numbers.

Initial excavation at Agate Fossil Beds occurred in 1904 when two scientists from the Carnegie Museum in Pittsburgh came here. One year later, a professor and four students from the University of Nebraska opened a quarry in University Hill. Subsequent excavations have occurred periodically since that time.

A visitor center with personnel, exhibits, and an audio-visual presentation is located about 3 miles east of Highway 29, between the park road and the Niobrara River. A self-guiding trail to an area of exposed fossils is nearby. A brochure is available.

Facilities: Although lodging and food are not available at the monument, they are in both Harrison and Mitchell. Drinking water is in the visitor center, and restrooms with flush toilets are available.
Camping: No camping facilities are available within the monument. A nice campground is at Fort Robinson State Park, 23 miles east of

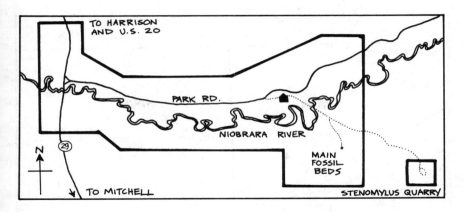

Agate Fossil Beds National Monument

Harrison on U.S. 20. For those heading south, city parks in Scotts Bluff and Gering provide campsites.

Fishing: The Niobrara River flows through the monument, and trout may be taken with a Nebraska license.

CHIMNEY ROCK NATIONAL HISTORIC SITE
P.O. Box 27
Gering, NE 69341
(308) 436–4340

Chimney Rock National Historic Site, which contains 83 acres, was designated an affiliated area of the National Park Service in 1956 to preserve the most famous landmark for pioneers traveling along the Oregon Trail. The site is located in western Nebraska, 3½ miles south of the town of Bayard. From near the intersection of U.S. 26 and State Highway 92, a 1½-mile gravel road leads to within ½ mile of the site.

Chimney Rock is one of the best-known natural landmarks in the United States. Located a little more than a mile south of the North Platte River, the 500-foot-high rock formation was used by settlers as a point of reference as far back as the early 1800s. It is most famous, however, as a landmark for westward emigrants along the Oregon Trail. The plains to the east of Chimney Rock made it visible to the

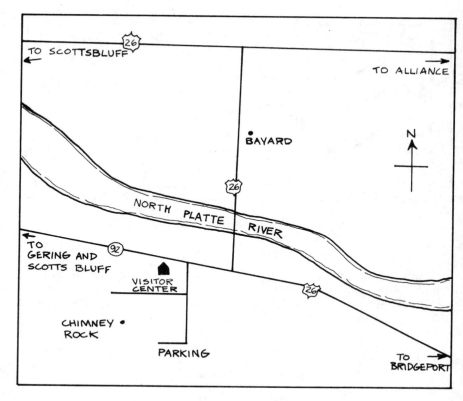

Chimney Rock National Historic Site

pioneers for many miles, and for them it warned of the mountains ahead.

A small visitor center operated by the Nebraska State Historical Society is located on State Road 92, near the site. The center is open from Memorial Day to Labor Day and contains exhibits on the history of Chimney Rock. Other exhibits on this park and on the passage along the Oregon Trail are in the visitor center at Scotts Bluff National Monument, 23 miles to the west. Visitors wishing to hike to the spire are advised to wear hiking boots and to watch for rattlesnakes. Information on possible routes may be obtained at the visitor center.

Facilities: There are no facilities at the site. Lodging and food are available along U.S. 26 and State Highway 92.
Camping: No camping is permitted at the site. Camping is available approximately 10 miles southeast in Bridgeport State Recreation Area.
Fishing: No fishing is available at the site.

HOMESTEAD NATIONAL MONUMENT OF AMERICA
Route 3
Beatrice, NE 68310
(402) 223–3514

Homestead National Monument was authorized in 1939 to commemorate the influence of the homestead movement on American history. It contains approximately 195 acres of prairie and woodland on the site of one of the first claims filed under the Homestead Act. The park is located in southeastern Nebraska, 40 miles southwest of Lincoln via U.S. 77 to Beatrice and 4½ miles west on Nebraska Highway 4.

After decades of pressure to donate public land to settlers, on May 20, 1862, President Abraham Lincoln signed into law the Homestead Act, which permitted any citizen to file a claim to 160 acres of unappropriated government land. To receive full title, a settler needed only to pay a small filing fee and to live on the land and cultivate it for five years. As settlement moved westward into more arid land, title to increased acreage was allowed. By 1935, the supply of public land suitable for homesteading was mostly exhausted, and remaining public lands were withdrawn from the program.

Although it is impossible to prove who was the nation's first homesteader, Daniel Freeman's homestead, on which the monument is located, was filed early during the first day (January 1, 1863) on which claims were permitted. Daniel Freeman and his wife are buried near the monument's eastern boundary. A trail to the grave site provides a panoramic view of the quarter-section homestead.

A visitor center near the monument entrance provides a short slide presentation along with displays of historic objects and pictures showing life during the homesteading years. Park Service personnel are present during daylight hours to answer visitors' questions. An old homestead cabin from a neighboring township was moved near the visitor center in 1950. A two-and-a-half-mile trail system leads from the visitor center to the original Freeman cabin, other Freeman buildings, the Freeman graves, and the squatters cabin site near Cub Creek. The trail meanders through prairie grasslands and is a worthwhile walk.

Freeman School, a furnished one-room schoolhouse, is part of the park and lies on Highway 4, a quarter mile west of the visitor center. Check at the visitor center for information on visiting the school that served the community for nearly one hundred years.

Facilities: Water and restrooms are provided in the visitor center. A small picnic area is available. Restaurants, motels, and supermarkets are located in Beatrice, four miles to the east.

Camping: No camping is permitted at the monument. The city of Beatrice (four miles east) has two city parks with camping facilities. Chatauqua Park—on the south side of town, three and a half blocks east off Highway 77 on Grable Street—has tables, water, electrical hookups, a dump station, and hot showers. Riverside Park—on the west side of Beatrice, four blocks north off Court on Sumner—has tables, water, electrical hookups, and a swimming pool.

Fishing: Although permitted in Cub Creek, which flows through the monument, fishing is pretty much a losing proposition. Your luck will be better in the Big Blue River.

SCOTTS BLUFF NATIONAL MONUMENT
P.O. Box 27
Gering, NE 69341
(308) 436–4340

Scotts Bluff National Monument, which comprises nearly 3,000 acres, was proclaimed a national monument in 1919 to preserve a series of massive sandstone and clay bluffs rising 800 feet above the North Platte River. These bluffs became an outstanding landmark for emigrants bound for Oregon and California. The park is located in western Nebraska, 3 miles west of Gering via Nebraska Highway 92. From Interstate 80, exit north on Nebraska 71 and drive 42 miles.

Scotts Bluff represents the remains of an ancient plain gradually eroded by wind and water. The dominant features of the bluffs made them memorable landmarks for thousands of explorers, trappers, traders, and settlers traveling along the valley cut by the North Platte River. The first white men passed this way in 1812, on the way to a fur post in Oregon.

The largest bluff was named for a fur trapper, Hiram Scott, who died in this vicinity in 1828. The landmark is most famous, however, as a signpost along the Oregon Trail. During the mid-1800s, a huge army of emigrants and gold seekers passed this way. Later, the Pony Express, Overland Stage, and Pacific Telegraph built stations near here. The completion of the transcontinental railroad in 1869 eliminated the need for most of the travel along this route.

A visitor center with exhibits and paintings is located on Highway 92. There are also exhibits pertaining to Chimney Rock, which lies twenty-five miles to the east. A one-and-six-tenths-mile paved road offers visitors access to the top of the bluff. A hiking trail to the top is also available. The depression or swale of the old Oregon Trail is still clearly visible from various points in the park and near the visitor center. Visitors may walk along part of the trail.

Facilities: Food and lodging are not available at the monument, but both are in Gering and Scotts Bluff. Drinking water and modern restrooms are located in the visitor center.

Camping: No camping is permitted at the monument. The town of Scotts Bluff maintains a campground in Riverside Park (southwest part of the city) that includes tables, grills, hookups, showers, and a dump station. A zoo is next to the campground. There is also camping available in the town of Gering.

Fishing: No fishing is available at the monument.

Nevada

GREAT BASIN NATIONAL PARK
Baker, NV 89311
(702) 234–7331

Great Basin National Park was established in 1986 to protect 77,109 acres of wild and rugged high desert country that includes spectacular mountains and an extensive cave system. The park is located near the Nevada-Utah border and park headquarters is 10 miles south of U.S. Highways 6 and 50, and 5 miles west of the small town of Baker, Nevada.

The West's Great Basin incorporates western Utah and nearly all of Nevada in a giant panorama of parallel north-south mountain ranges and sagebrush-covered valleys. Great Basin National Park, formed from what was previously Lehman Caves National Monument (established 1922) and Wheeler Peak Scenic Area, sits in the middle of this huge desert. The park's two main attractions are Wheeler Peak, which at 13,063 feet is one of the highest mountains in the Great Basin, and Lehman Caves, an extensive cavern system of gray and white marble decorated with stalactites and stalagmites.

The park's range of natural environments results from the great variations in elevation. Numerous types of plants and animals may be observed by visitors. Mule deer feed in the higher meadows, and coyotes and cougars are occasionally seen. Plant life depends on the season. Wildflowers begin blooming in the lower country during spring and gradually appear higher on the mountain as the summer progresses. In the fall, slopes are streaked with golden aspen leaves. During years of normal precipitation the higher peaks are covered with snow for more than six months.

The formation of Lehman Caves began millions of years ago when the mountains were higher and the climate was more humid than today. Water charged with carbon dioxide widened and enlarged cracks in the mountain's marble formation. The more soluble rock was

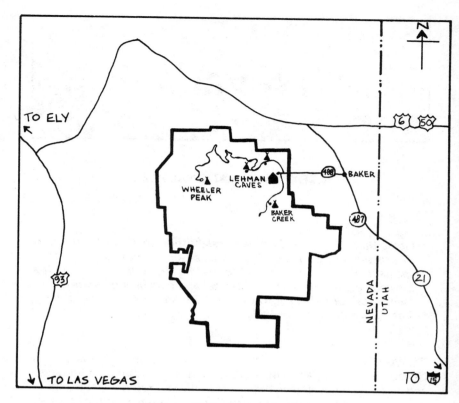

Great Basin National Park

dissolved, and as the water table gradually fell, the process of cave decoration began. Stalactites, stalagmites, columns, and shields (round discs of calcite) are all found in abundance throughout the caves. The caves take their name from rancher Absalom Lehman, who was probably the first white man to explore them. Lehman guided parties through the underground rooms from 1885 until his death in 1891.

The park is open daily except Thanksgiving, Christmas, and New Year's Day. Visitors with sufficient time should stop at the visitor center, take the cave tour, and drive the scenic paved road to the base of Wheeler Peak. Conducted tours of the cave (fee charged) require about one and one-half hours and cover approximately half a mile via a paved trail. Tours depart from the visitor center and warm clothing is suggested because of the cave's 50 degree Fahrenheit temperature. Photography is permitted in the cave.

The paved road to Wheeler Peak climbs approximately 3,000 feet from the visitor center. Large motorhomes and trailers are not recommended beyond Upper Lehman Creek. At the terminus of the road visitors will find a number of trails to lakes and to a bristlecone pine grove. The Wheeler Peak road is closed in winter.

Facilities: Refreshments, meals, and souvenirs are available at the visitor center from April through October. Modern restrooms and picnic tables are also located here. No overnight accommodations are within the park but restaurants, a small grocery, gasoline, and limited accommodations are in the town of Baker. Ely, Nevada, seventy miles west, is the nearest major town.

Camping: Three campgrounds are located along Wheeler Peak Scenic Drive. Lower Lehman Creek (eleven sites) and Upper Lehman Creek (twenty-four sites) are closest to the visitor center and generally fill first. Wheeler Peak (thirty-seven sites), at an elevation of 9,886 feet, is at the end of the scenic road. Baker Creek (twenty sites, pit toilets) is four miles south of the visitor center via a gravel road. All of the campgrounds offer tables, grills, and water, although water in some of the campgrounds must be boiled before drinking.

Fishing: No fishing is available at the park.

LAKE MEAD NATIONAL RECREATION AREA
601 Nevada Highway
Boulder City, NV 89005
(702) 293–8907

Lake Mead National Recreation Area was established in 1936 and contains almost 1.5 million acres of clear water and desert landscape, making it an attractive area for water-related activities. The park is located in southern Nevada and northwestern Arizona. Main access is via U.S. 93 from Las Vegas to Kingman, Arizona. When approaching on Interstate 15 from the west, take Highway 146 exit to Henderson, Nevada, and turn south on U.S. 93/95 to Boulder City. Buses from Las Vegas make regular trips to the recreation area and Hoover Dam.

Lake Mead and Lake Mohave combine to stretch for more than 180 miles. Both lakes have been formed from the construction of hydro-electric dams on the Colorado River. The most famous of these, Hoover Dam, was completed in 1935.

The park lies astride the Grand Wash Cliffs, which form a transition between two major geographical provinces in North America. To the east, the Colorado has carved a series of canyons (including the Grand Canyon) through high country known as the Colorado

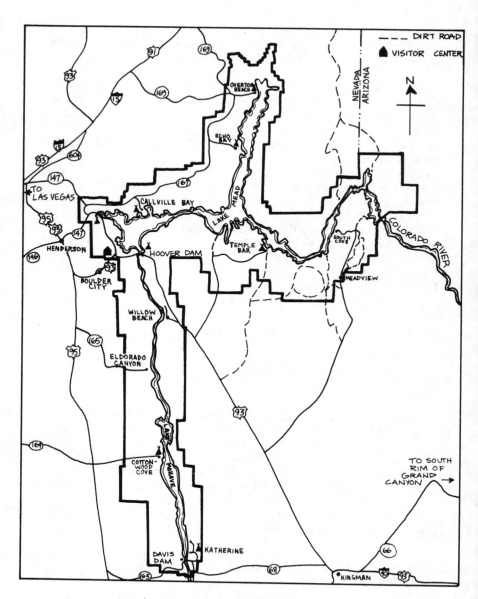

Lake Mead National Recreation Area

Plateau. After leaving the western portal of the Grand Canyon at Grand Wash Cliffs, north-south mountains of the Basin and Range province divert the river southward toward the Gulf of California. Broad enclosed valleys draining toward the river separate the mountain ranges of this region. In the Lake Mead section, the Colorado breached the mountains and provided the local basins with drainage to the south.

The park is open year round although daytime temperatures during summer months may rise above 110 degrees Fahrenheit. The main visitor center is a few miles northeast of Boulder City on U.S. 93. Daily tours of Hoover Dam are conducted by the Bureau of Reclamation, and self-guided tours can be taken at Davis Dam. Park personnel present ranger programs and hikes at various locations; schedules are posted at campgrounds and ranger stations. Much of the park's activity is water-related. Swimming beaches are open year round at Boulder Beach and Katherine. Concessioners offer boat trips to various locations, and docking facilities for private boats are located at a number of sites.

Facilities: Most modern facilities including lodging and food services are available in Boulder City, Henderson, Las Vegas, North Las Vegas, Searchlight, Overton, Bullhead City, and Kingman. Developed areas in the park are:

Boulder Beach: Ranger station, picnic shelter, launching ramp, boat dock, store, lodging, marine supplies, and restaurant. Write Lake Mead Resort, 322 Lakeshore Road, Boulder City, NV 89005 (702–293–3484). Motel only (702–293–2074); trailer village only (702–293–2540).

Callville Bay: Launching ramp, boat dock, store, trailer village, marine supplies, and restaurant. (702–565–8958)

Cottonwood Cove: Ranger station, picnic shelter, launching ramp, boat dock, store, lodging, marine supplies, trailer village, and restaurant. Write Cottonwood Cove Resort, P.O. Box 1000, Cottonwood Cove, NV 89046 (702–297–1464).

Echo Bay: Ranger station, launching ramp, boat dock, store, lodging, marine supplies, trailer village, and restaurant. Write Echo Bay Resort, Star Route No. 89010, Overton, NV 89040 (702–394–4066).

Katherine: Ranger station, lodging, trailer village, marina, restaurant, grocery, gasoline, laundry, houseboat rentals. Write Lake Mohave Resort, Bullhead City, AZ 86430 (602–754–3245).

Las Vegas Wash: Ranger station, marina, restaurant, grocery, gasoline, and laundry (702–565–9111).

Overton Beach: Ranger station, marina, trailer village, restaurant, grocery, marine fuel, and laundry (702–394–4040).

Temple Bar: Ranger station, lodging, trailer village, marina, restaurant, and marine fuel. Write Temple Bar Resort, Temple Bar, AZ 86443 (602–767–3211).

Willow Beach: Ranger station, lodging, trailer village, restaurant, grocery, gasoline, laundry. Write Willow Beach Resort, P.O. Box 187, Boulder City, NV 89005 (602–767–3311).

Camping: The park includes seven campgrounds. All have flush toilets and dump stations. All trailer villages listed below have hook-ups and are operated by private concessioners. Showers are also concessioner-operated. Stores are located at all campgrounds, except Echo Bay. Campgrounds in the park are Boulder Beach (154 spaces, five group camps, eighty trailer sites, showers, laundry), Callville Bay (eighty spaces, twenty trailer sites), Cottonwood Cove (149 spaces, seventy-five trailer sites, laundry), Echo Bay (166 spaces, fifty-eight trailer sites, laundry), Hemenway (184 spaces), Katherine (173 spaces, twenty-seven trailer sites, laundry), Las Vegas Wash (eighty-nine spaces), Overton Beach (five trailer sites, laundry), and Temple Bar (153 spaces, fourteen trailer sites, laundry).

Fishing: Lake Mead is especially noted for its largemouth bass, striped bass, and channel catfish. Lake Mohave contains rainbow trout in the upper end and largemouth bass farther down the lake. Sunfish and crappie are also taken in these lakes. A Nevada or Arizona fishing license is required and a stamp from the other state must be affixed to the license when fishing from a boat.

New Mexico

AZTEC RUINS NATIONAL MONUMENT
P.O. Box 640
Aztec, NM 87410
(505) 334–6174

Aztec Ruins, which comprises 319 acres, was established in 1923 to preserve the ruins of a large Pueblo Indian community. The park is located in northwestern New Mexico, north of the town of Aztec, near the junction of U.S. 550 and New Mexico Highway 44.

After the people of the Colorado Plateau region developed farming and a more sedentary lifestyle, the Anasazi cultural system now referred to as the Chaco Phenomenon began to grow. The West Ruin at Aztec, open to the public, is a Chaco-style greathouse of more than 400 rooms and kivas built in the early 1100s. Visitors may tour the West Ruin, which is actually only a portion of a larger community consisting of several other unexcavated greathouses, plazas, great kivas, tri-wall kivas, and smaller residential buildings. Prehistoric roadways, now barely visible, link the structures within this community. Short, well-defined road segments suggest a connection to hundreds of smaller residential sites along the Animas River valley and point toward other Chacoan communities in the Four Corners area. Aztec may have served as a major ceremonial, administrative, and trade center for the surrounding population. By the 1200s the Chaco system waned and a different cultural style emerged which had its roots in the Mesa Verde area to the north. Some remodeling of the pueblo occurred and the pueblo flourished in Mesa Verde style until it was abandoned by the early 1300s.

The visitor center contains exhibits such as pottery, baskets, and other items made by the Anasazi people who lived here. A self-guiding trail leads through the West Ruin and to the Hubbard tri-wall kiva. The great kiva in the West Ruin was reconstructed in 1933–34 by archaeologist Earl Morris. Visitors are cautioned to stay on the trails since the walls crumble easily. The park is open daily from 8:00 A.M. to 5:00 P.M. (longer during summer) except Christmas and New Year's Day.

NEW MEXICO 213

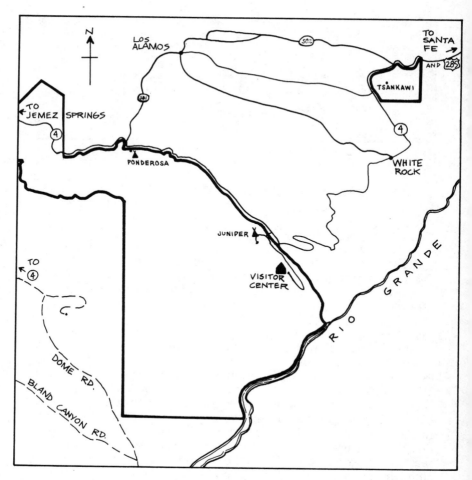

Bandelier National Monument

Facilities: Food and lodging are not available at the monument, but both may be found in Aztec. Drinking water and modern restrooms accessible to wheelchairs are located in the visitor center.
Camping: No camping is permitted at the monument. A city park with camping facilities is in Aztec.
Fishing: No fishing is available at the monument.

BANDELIER NATIONAL MONUMENT
HCR 1 Box 1 Suite 15
Los Alamos, NM 87544
(505) 672–3861

Bandelier, which contains 32,737 acres, was established in 1916 to preserve the ruins of many cliff houses of fifteenth-century Pueblo Indians. The monument is located in north-central New Mexico, 46 miles northwest of Santa Fe. From Sante Fe, drive north on U.S. 285 to Pojoaque and turn west on New Mexico Highway 502 to New Mexico Highway 4. Visitors to Bandelier should make an effort to spend time in the Scientific Museum at Los Alamos.

As the Southwest Indians attempted to escape the ravages of drought during the late thirteenth century, they sought locations with dependable water supplies. The ruins found today in Bandelier are the result of the Pueblo emigrants that settled here. The plateau that constitutes most of this area is composed of volcanic ash and lava spewed forth thousands of years ago by a giant volcano. As the volcano's interior was emptied by eruptions, the summit collapsed and formed a large saucer-shaped depression. Subsequently, the surrounding highland was carved by running water.

The features most accessible to visitors are in Frijoles Canyon. Here, along a stream at the bottom of a deep gorge, lie nearly 2 miles of cliff ruins. The masonry houses of from one to three stories contain many cave ruins carved from volcanic ash. Studies indicate that most of the ruins date from the late pre-Spanish period, although a few small ruins are from the twelfth century and earlier. For centuries the Indians honeycombed the cliffs with artificial caves and farmed the valley and the mesa top. During the 1500s, the dwellings were abandoned for reasons that are still not clear.

The monument's visitor center provides museum exhibits and an audio-visual presentation. Personnel are on duty during daylight hours to answer visitors' questions. Visitor center hours vary, depending on season and staffing. During summer months, rangers conduct guided walks and present evening campfire talks. A detached section of the park, Tsankawi, is located 11 miles north of Frijoles Canyon on Highway 4. Here a large unexcavated ruin is reached via a 2-mile self-guiding trail (1½ hours) beginning at the highway. The trail provides access to a number of interesting features, including petroglyphs (rock carvings) and cave structures.

Since most features of the park can be reached only by foot, the 70 miles of trails within Bandelier are well used. The main Frijoles Canyon ruins are accessible by loop trail (1 hour) from the visitor center, and most visitors take this walk first. A guide booklet describing the ruins is available. Other trails from the headquarters area, with round-trip distance and time required from each trail head, are Ceremonial Cave (2 miles, one hour), Lower Waterfall (3 miles, two and a half hours), and Rio Grande (5.5 miles, four hours). Trails are open during daylight hours.

Facilities: No lodging is available at the park, but motels are located in White Rock and Los Alamos. Drinking water and restrooms are provided at the visitor center and the campground. A curio store with a snack bar is located near the visitor center. An exceptionally lovely picnic area is a short distance away.

Camping: Juniper Campground (ninety-three spaces) provides tables, fireplaces, water, flush toilets, and a dump station. Juniper is closed from December through February. Ponderosa Campground (four spaces, four group camps) is located six miles west of the entrance and has tables, grills, water, and flush toilets. Ponderosa opens April 15, and closes November 1, although the dates are approximate, depending on weather. A number of wilderness campsites are located throughout the park, and a wilderness permit is required.

Fishing: Wild brook and rainbow trout inhabit Frijoles Creek near park headquarters, and there are brown trout in remote Capulin Creek. A New Mexico license is required.

CAPULIN MOUNTAIN NATIONAL MONUMENT
Capulin, NM 88414
(505) 278–2201

Capulin Mountain National Monument, which contains 790 acres, was established in 1916 to protect a symmetrical cinder cone rising high above the surrounding plain. The sighting of this prominent cinder cone by travelers some distance away makes it an important landmark today as it undoubtedly was for the early pioneers. The park is located in northeastern New Mexico, 3 miles north of the town of Capulin, just east off State Road 325.

Capulin Mountain (pronounced cah-poo-leen') is the cone of an extinct volcano that rises 1,000 feet above its relatively flat surroundings. The volcano was active about 10,000 years ago, and the mountain is composed primarily of cinders, ash, and rock debris from these explosions. From the highest part of the rim, where the crater drops approximately 415 feet, the visitor can see parts of New Mexico, Colorado, Oklahoma, and Texas.

A visitor center containing exhibits explaining volcanoes and the geographical area surrounding Capulin Mountain is located approximately ½ mile inside the park entrance. From here a two-mile mostly gravel road circles and climbs the mountain to a parking area near the rim. At this point, a one-mile self-guiding hiking trail follows the rim of the crater. The walk is fairly strenuous and takes approximately thirty-five minutes, but the time is well spent. It is probably less strenuous to walk the trail counterclockwise. There is also a one-fifth-mile trail from the parking area to the crater's bottom and a short (ten-minute) nature trail by the visitor center.

The monument contains a surprising variety of plants and wildlife. Porcupines, squirrels, and deer are relatively abundant, and golden eagles are seen on occasion. Extensive plant life is located both at the mountain's base and on Crater Rim Trail.

Facilities: Food and lodging are not available in the park. Both are in nearby Capulin, Des Moines, Clayton, and Raton. Both the visitor center and picnic area contain water and restrooms with flush toilets.
Camping: No camping is permitted at the monument. Camping is available in the towns of Capulin and Folsom and at Clayton Lake State Park, 10 miles northwest of Clayton on Highway 370. Camping is also available at Sugarite State Park, six miles north of Raton, and thirty-three miles west of Capulin.
Fishing: No fishing is available within the park.

CARLSBAD CAVERNS NATIONAL PARK
3225 National Parks Highway
Carlsbad, NM 88220
(505) 785–2232

Carlsbad Caverns National Park, which contains 46,775 acres, was established as a national monument in 1923 (changed to a national park in 1930). This series of caverns—one of the largest underground chambers yet discovered—contains many spectacular and strange formations. The park is located in southeastern New Mexico on U.S. 62/180, 20 miles southwest of the town of Carlsbad and 150 miles east of El Paso.

The caverns in this region have formed in limestone deposited near the edge of an ancient sea. The reef was built by lime-secreting marine organisms and precipitates from the water. When the reef stopped growing, it was buried by successive layers of sediments. Later, cracks in the rock allowed the entrance of rainwater charged with carbonic acid, which dissolved the limestone and formed large caverns. After the galleries were pushed above the water table during a period of general uplifting, the chambers filled with air. Then water and minerals began to filter in and decorate the rooms.

In addition to the seventy-six caves in the park, the rugged landscape in this region offers many interesting features. The range in elevation within the park (3,600 to 6,350 feet) results in a variety of plants and wildlife. A total of 740 species of plants, 59 species of mammals, 44 species of reptiles and amphibians, and 273 species of birds have been identified here.

A visitor center is located seven miles inside the park, near the cavern entrance. Roadside exhibits and panoramic views along the paved road add enjoyment to the drive. The center is open year round except Christmas Day. It offers exhibits and information services for visitors. Self-guiding trips through the caverns (8:00 A.M. to 3:30 P.M. in winter, later in summer; three-mile trips end at 2:00 P.M.) begin by walking in through the natural entrance (complete trip, 3 miles) or by taking an elevator and touring a single underground section of the caverns (complete trip, 1¼ miles). Both trips return to the surface by elevator. A jacket (56 degrees Fahrenheit inside temperature) and shoes with rubber heels and soles are strongly recommended. A fairly strenuous, primitive lantern trip (fee charged) into another cave called New Cave also is offered. Inquire at the visitor center.

Nature trails are located near the visitor center. Ranger-guided walks into the desert are scheduled during summer months. One of the park's most popular activities in the summer is watching the bats fly from the cavern entrance each evening just before sunset. These bats, which winter in Mexico, feed at night on flying insects.

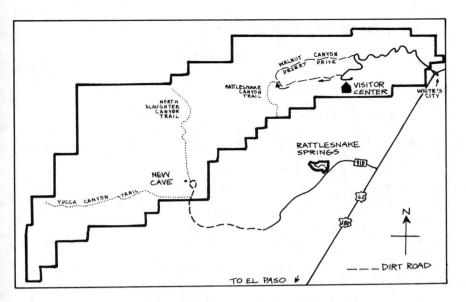

Carlsbad Caverns National Park

Facilities: A restaurant, gift shop, nursery, and kennel are located next to the visitor center. Food service is also provided in the caverns. No lodging is available in the park, but accommodations can be found in nearby communities. Water and restrooms are located in the visitor center. Picnic facilities are at the visitor center and at Rattlesnake Springs, 8 miles southwest of the park entrance on Slaughter Canyon Road.

Camping: No camping is permitted in the park, but private campgrounds are located in nearby communities. Brantley Lake State Park, fifteen miles north of Carlsbad via U.S. 285, has forty-nine sites with water, tables, grills, and electrical hookups.

Fishing: No fishing is available at the park.

CHACO CULTURE NATIONAL HISTORICAL PARK
Star Route 4, Box 6500
Bloomfield, NM 87413
(505) 786–5384

Chaco Culture National Historic Park, which contains nearly 34,000 acres, was established in 1907 to preserve numerous Indian ruins, including thirteen major ruins representing the highest point of Pueblo pre-Columbian culture. The park is located in northwestern New Mexico on State Highway 57. From the north, turn south at Blanco Trading Post and drive 29 miles on dirt Highway 57. From the south, turn north off Interstate 40 at Thoreau and drive 44 miles on paved Highway 57. Then take a marked turnoff that begins a 20-mile dirt road.

Chaco Canyon was inhabited 5,000 to 7,000 years ago by bands of hunters and gatherers. (It wasn't until the first century that farming became important.) Later, in the 600s, the Indians began to use irrigation and to build underground shelters called pithouses. During this period, they made pottery and constructed intricate baskets.

By the ninth century, a new pattern of life called the Pueblo culture emerged, and the Indians began constructing homes above ground from mud, rock, and poles. During the 1000s and 1100s, the population of Chaco Canyon reached its maximum of about 7,000 people. It was during this period that the main pueblos such as Chetro Ketl, Pueblo Bonito, and Pueblo del Arroyo were enlarged to their maximum size. Each of the pueblos contained at least one circular underground room, called a kiva, that was used for religious ceremonies. The most impressive kiva excavated in Chaco Canyon is in Casa Rinconada. During the middle 1100s, Indians began to leave this region, and by the late 1100s it was vacated. The Navajo Indians, who occupy much of the area today, began to move here in the 1700s.

The park's visitor center is located 1½ miles inside the south entrance. Museum displays and exhibits help explain the history and geology of Chaco Canyon and its inhabitants. The closest ruin, which is partially excavated, is Una Vida, a short walk from the visitor center. Self-guiding trails (one hour each) are also located at Pueblo Bonito, Chetro Ketl, Casa Rinconada, Kin Kletso, Hungo Pavi, and Pueblo del Arroyo. Guided walks are given regularly in the summer by rangers, and evening campfire programs are offered. Day hikes to Pueblo Alto, Wijiji, Penasco Blanco, and Tsin Kletsin are also available.

Facilities: No food, lodging, or telephone service is available at the park. On weekdays, limited supplies can be purchased at trading posts

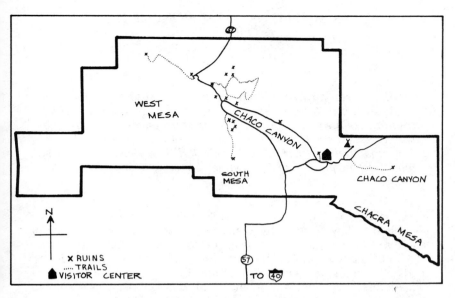

Chaco Culture National Historical Park

on Highway 44, but the nearest town is 60 miles away. Drinking water and restrooms are located in the visitor center.

Camping: Gallo Wash Campground (forty-six spaces, one group camp), 1 mile east of the visitor center, provides tables, fireplaces, flush toilets, and a dump station. The campground is open year round. Drinking water is available only in the visitor center. From mid-October to mid-April only pit toilets are usable. Spaces are unavailable for trailers longer than 30 feet.

Fishing: No fishing is available at the park.

EL MALPAIS NATIONAL MONUMENT
P.O. Box 939
Grants, NM 87020
(505) 285–4641

El Malpais National Monument contains 114,848 acres and was established in 1987 to preserve the geological and archaeological resources of a volcanic area that features ice caves and a 17-mile lava tube system. This area was also a home for Pueblo Indians. The monument is located in west-central New Mexico, approximately 10 miles south of the town of Grants via State Highways 53 or 117.

El Malpais (Spanish meaning "the badlands") National Monument is a lava-filled valley formed by centuries of volcanic activity. Major features of the monument can be accessed via State Highways 53 and 117 and County Road 42. High-clearance vehicles are advised for all roads other than State Highways 53 and 117.

Along State Highway 53, the Zuni-Acoma Trail was a Pueblo Indian trade route connecting two pueblos. The 7½-mile hike (one-way) crosses four major lava flows and a trail guide is available. Nearby, El Calderon is a forested area that includes a lava flow, a cave, a cinder cone, and a bat cave. Near the monument's west boundary is a large cinder cone and a lava tube that contains ice year round.

Along State Highway 117 visitors will drive along a ridge of sandstone that offers a view of the lava flows and surrounding countryside. Seven miles south of the bluffs, in El Malpais National Conservation Area, is the largest accessible arch in New Mexico. Just south of the arch, the highway passes through a narrow corridor formed by lava flow near the base of 500-foot sandstone cliffs.

Off County Road 42, which loops between the two state highways, visitors will find a trail that leads to several caves. Farther south are wilderness areas that present spectacular views of the monument.

Facilities: Picnic areas are at the south end of The Narrows on State Highway 117, Sandstone Bluff Overlook, and the Zuni-Acoma Trail parking area. Full services are available in Grants.
Camping: There are no campgrounds in the monument. Sixteen miles west of Bandera Crater, El Morro National Monument offers a small but nice campground. For more information, see the camping section under El Morro National Monument. For those traveling on Interstate 40, Bluewater Lake State Park offers water, electrical hookups, showers, fishing, boating, and swimming. The park is 19 miles northwest of Grants via Interstate 40 and State Highway 412.
Fishing: No fishing is available in the monument.

EL MORRO NATIONAL MONUMENT
Ramah, NM 87321
(505) 783–4226

El Morro National Monument, established in 1906, contains nearly 1,300 acres highlighted by "Inscription Rock," a soft sandstone monolith on which hundreds of inscriptions have been carved by explorers, emigrants, and settlers. The park is located in western New Mexico, 58 miles southeast of Gallup via State Highways 602 and 53, and 43 miles southwest of Grants via State Highway 53.

El Morro ("The Bluff") rises nearly 200 feet above the valley floor. It was named by the Spanish conquistadors who used this site and its natural water basin, filled by rain and melted snow, as a resting spot during the late sixteenth century through the seventeenth and eigh-teenth centuries. Before the Spanish came, Anasazi Indians had abandoned pueblos on the mesa. From the first Spanish inscription in 1605, the sandstone structure has served as a register for people and cultures in this area of the Southwest. The first Anglo-Americans to inscribe their names at El Morro were Lt. J. H. Simpson and artist R. H. Kern. Their inscriptions may still be seen. After their visit in 1849, numerous other individuals—including emigrants, traders, Indian agents, soldiers, surveyors, and settlers—added their names to the rock. On the top of El Morro are the ruins (mostly unexcavated) of Anasazi Indian pueblos.

A visitor center at the monument contains exhibits about the people and history of this area. Personnel are on duty to answer visitors' questions. A self-guiding trail, which begins back of the visitor center, leads along the base of the cliff where the inscriptions may be seen and then onto the top of the mesa where the pueblo ruins are located. A guide booklet covering both trails may be picked up in the visitor center. The first portion of the trail along the inscriptions involves a walk of about ½ mile and takes approximately forty-five minutes. If you climb to the top, you will have a total walk of 2 miles and spend about one and one-half hours. The walk to the top requires a 200-foot climb, and the trail on the mesa is more difficult.

Facilities: No food service or lodging is available in the park, but both can be obtained at Grants and Gallup. Camping supplies are available at Ramah, 13 miles west of the monument. Picnic tables are in front of the visitor center, where water and restrooms (with hot water) are provided.

Camping: An attractive small campground (nine spaces) is open year round, except for temporary closings forced by snowstorms, and offers tables, grills, water, and pit toilets. The campground is about 0.8 miles from the visitor center, and evening campfire programs are presented on weekends. It rarely fills except on weekends. There is no camping fee, and reservations are not taken.

Fishing: No fishing is available at the monument.

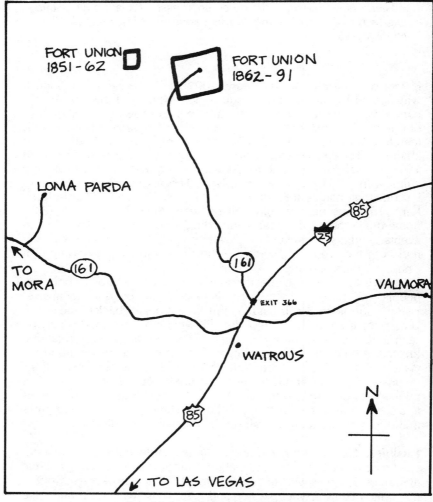

Fort Union National Monument

FORT UNION NATIONAL MONUMENT
Watrous, NM 87753
(505) 425–8025

Fort Union, which contains 720 acres, was added to the National Park System in 1956 to preserve the ruins of an important fort on the Santa Fe Trail during the period 1851 to 1891. The monument is located in northeastern New Mexico, 8 miles north of Interstate 25 (exit 366), at the end of State Highway 161. Fort Union is 28 miles northeast of Las Vegas, New Mexico.

Fort Union was established when the U.S. Army decided in 1851 to move its headquarters and depot out of Santa Fe. The log buildings of the first fort served as a station on the Santa Fe Trail and as the principal quartermaster depot of the Southwest. From 1854 until the beginning of the Civil War in 1861, soldiers from Fort Union battled Apaches, Utes, Kiowas, and Comanches. Concern of a Confederate invasion of New Mexico resulted in the construction of an earthwork fortification in 1861. Although the fort was never attacked, soldiers from the fort were involved in major clashes that secured New Mexico for the Union.

Following the war, Fort Union was again rebuilt, this time as a large supply installation designed to hold far more men. From this point until its abandonment in 1891, following completion of the Santa Fe Railroad in 1880, the fort was used as a staging area for army battles with Indians.

The park is open from 8:00 A.M. to 5:00 P.M. during the winter except Christmas and New Year's Day and from 8:00 A.M. to 6:00 P.M. during the summer. While walking among the ruins, keep in mind that the fort consisted of three parts. Military activities were conducted in the post, and the depot was concerned with transportation and supply of other southwestern forts. The third part of Fort Union, the arsenal, stored and distributed arms and ammunition. As was typical with forts in the Southwest, no stockade or wall surrounded Fort Union. The National Park Service is currently attempting to halt deterioration of the adobe walls of the fort's buildings. A visitor center contains exhibits and artifacts to assist in understanding the fort's history. Recorded messages and pictures are located along foot trails.

Facilities: Food and lodging are not available in the park. Las Vegas, New Mexico, contains overnight accommodations. Water and restrooms are provided in the visitor center, and picnic tables are available.

Camping: No camping is permitted at Fort Union, but Storrie Lake State Park, on State Road 518 (33 miles from Fort Union) offers campsites with sheltered tables, flush toilets, and showers.
Fishing: No fishing is available.

GILA CLIFF DWELLINGS NATIONAL MONUMENT
Route 11, Box 100
Silver City, NM 88061
(505) 534–9344

Gila Cliff Dwellings, which contains 533 acres, was established in 1907 to preserve some excellent cliff dwellings in natural cavities on the face of an overhanging cliff. The monument is located in southwestern New Mexico, approximately 44 miles north of Silver City via paved State Highway 15. The road is unsafe for trailers more than 20 feet long.

Ruins at Gila Cliff Dwellings date back to the second century. At that time, people constructed circular dwellings with floors below ground level. Variations of these pithouses were built in this area until around 1000, when square adobe or twig structures began to be built above ground. During this same period, Pueblo people began constructing cliff dwellings in natural caves. These people farmed the mesa tops and were skilled weavers and potters.

Seven natural caves are high on the southeast side of one cliff, and five of these contain cliff-dwelling ruins. About forty rooms are contained in these structures that probably housed ten to fifteen families at a time. Walls were made from stone and timbers, the latter being dated from the 1270s. By the early 1300s, for unknown reasons, the Pueblos had abandoned these dwellings. Approximately one hundred years later, the units were occupied by bands of Apaches.

A visitor center with exhibits and information to help interpret this historic area is open from 8:00 A.M. until 5:00 P.M. during summer and 8:00 A.M. to 4:30 P.M. in winter. The park is closed on Christmas and New Year's Day. From the visitor center, a short drive to a parking area at the end of the road provides access to the monument's main area. Guide leaflets with numbers keyed to trail markers are located in the contact station at the trail head. The 1-mile trail through the dwellings is steep in places and takes about one hour to walk the round trip. The dwellings are accessible 8:00 A.M. to 6:00 P.M. in summer, 9:00 A.M. to 4:00 P.M. the rest of the year.

Facilities: Food services and accommodations are not available at the monument, but a store at Gila Hot Springs offers groceries, snacks, soft drinks, gasoline, and ice. Drinking water and restrooms are located in the visitor center.

Camping: The U.S. Forest Service operates Lower Scorpion Corral Campground (seven spaces) and Upper Scorpion Corral Campground (thirteen spaces) between the visitor center and the cliff dwellings. Both are open all year and have tables, grills, water (May–October), and flush toilets. Two less-developed campgrounds with pit toilets and no water are located five miles east of the visitor center. A commercial campground is at Gila Hot Springs.

Fishing: Fishing with a New Mexico license is available in the Gila River.

PECOS NATIONAL HISTORICAL PARK
P.O. Drawer 11
Pecos, NM 87552
(505) 757–6414

Pecos National Historical Park was established in 1965 to preserve foundations of a seventeenth-century mission, ruins of an eighteenth-century church, and remains of ancient pueblos. The park is located in north-central New Mexico, 25 miles southeast of Santa Fe via Interstate 25 and State Route 63. When approaching from Las Vegas, New Mexico, exit Interstate 25 at the Rowe Interchange.

Pueblo Indians began settling in the Pecos Valley during the 1100s. By 1450, they had constructed a 660-room multistoried pueblo that served as living quarters and a storage area. The pueblo contained numerous ceremonial chambers ("kivas") and was built around a central plaza on a rocky ridge. The location of the village between the farmers to the west and the buffalo hunters to the east helped make the Pecos Indians relatively prosperous.

The first Spanish visitors to Pecos Pueblo were members of Coronado's 1540 expedition in search of riches. The Indians attempted to lure Coronado and his party onto the plains, hoping that they would die of starvation. Although the plan did not succeed, Coronado became disillusioned and returned to Mexico. Later expeditions were somewhat more successful, and by 1598, Franciscans had founded a mission at Pecos. A rebellion by the Indians in 1680 resulted in destruction of the missions and abandonment by the Spanish, although twelve years later the missions were reestablished. The decline of Pecos Pueblo began in the eighteenth century, and by 1838, seventeen remaining Pecos Indians emigrated to Jemez Pueblo, where their descendants live today.

A visitor center with exhibit room and a ten-minute introductory film is the start of a 1¼-mile self-guiding trail that leads through the ruins. Included along the walk are restored kivas, unexcavated mounds at the site of the old pueblo, and remnants of the two mission churches. The walls of the mission were a landmark for travelers along the Santa Fe Trail.

Facilities: Food and lodging are not available in the park, but both are located 1 mile north of the park in the town of Pecos. Restrooms and a picnic area are near the visitor center.

Camping: No camping is permitted at the park. Five campgrounds operated by the U.S. Forest Service are located from 5 to 21 miles north on State Highway 63. For information write Santa Fe National Forest, P.O. Box 1689, Santa Fe, NM 87501. Villanueva State Park, 30 miles south on State Highway 3, offers camping facilities, including flush toilets and showers. Two private campgrounds are 15 miles west on Interstate 25.

Fishing: No fishing is available in the park.

SALINAS PUEBLO MISSIONS NATIONAL MONUMENT
Box 496
Mountainair, NM 87036
(505) 847–2585

Salinas Pueblo Missions National Monument (formerly Gran Quivira National Monument) was established in 1980. It consists of 1,080 acres, including the ruins of four Franciscan seventeenth-century stone churches and three large Indian villages from an earlier Pueblo culture. The monument is located in central New Mexico in three separate units near the town of Mountainair, on U.S. 60 and New Mexico 55.

In the stones of Salinas Pueblo Missions National Monument are faint echoes of communities that existed there centuries ago. The first Indians began living in this area during the ninth century. As time passed and different cultures were introduced into the area, the inhabitants adapted a successful way of life in this marginal and frequently hostile environment. By the seventeenth century, Salinas had become an important trading center, with Gran Quivira being one of the larger villages in the region.

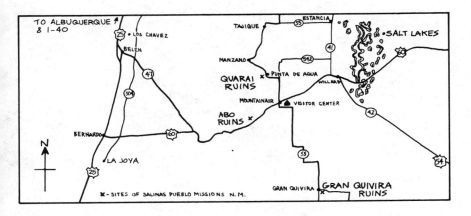

Salinas Pueblo Missions National Monument

Although the first Spanish expedition into what is now the south-western United States occurred in 1540, the first known visit to the Salinas area by any European was in 1598. Even though the Spanish were unable to find the expected mineral riches and crops were difficult to grow, they nevertheless attempted to settle the land and convert the Indians to Christianity. By the early 1670s, the area was vacated by both the Spanish and the Indians. Two of the primary factors that led to the abandonment were severe drought and raids by Apaches.

The monument's headquarters and visitor center is in the town of Mountainair. Here, one block west of the intersection of U.S. 60 and State Highway 55, visitors will find exhibits, an audio-visual program, and information on the history of this area. The three areas of ruins are:
Abo Ruins (9 miles west on U.S. 60, ½ mile north on New Mexico 513). This site contains sophisticated church architecture and a large unexcavated pueblo. A trail winds through unexcavated mounds, visible pueblo walls, and a limited number of excavated pueblo walls. Trail guides are provided. Telephone (505) 847–2400.
Quarai Ruins (8 miles north on New Mexico 55 and 1 mile west). This area contains the most complete Salinas church and has artifacts on display in a small museum. A trail leads past unexcavated mounds and excavated mission ruins. Trail guides are provided. Telephone (505) 847–2290.
Gran Quivira Ruins (26 miles south on New Mexico 55). Contains two churches and significant excavated pueblo ruins with excavated kivas. A contact station has exhibits, and an excellent forty-minute video is shown. A guide book is available to interpret the trail through the ruins.

Facilities: Food and lodging are available in Mountainair. Drinking water is provided at all sites. Restrooms are available at the visitor

center and at all three sites. A picnic area with tables is at each of the three sites. Grills are available only at Gran Quivira.

Camping: No camping is permitted at the monument. Manzano State Park (eighteen spaces) with tables (some sheltered), grills, flush toilets, and hot water (no showers) is fifteen miles north of Mountainair off Highway 55. Turn west at the south end of the town of Manzano and go 3 miles on a gravel and dirt road.

Fishing: Fishing is available in Manzano Lake, a small body of water located in the village of Manzano.

WHITE SANDS NATIONAL MONUMENT
P.O. Box 458
Alamogordo, NM 88310
(505) 437–1058

White Sands National Monument, which comprises 145,000 acres, was established in 1933 to preserve dunes of glistening white gypsum sand standing 10 to 60 feet high. The park is located in south-central New Mexico, approximately 54 miles northeast of Las Cruces and 15 miles southwest of Alamogordo via U.S. 70/82.

The features of this area were created millions of years ago (although the current dune field is only about several thousand years old) when a downfaulting of a portion of the earth's crust left surrounding mountains and highlands containing layers of gypsum rock. As rain and melting snow eroded the deposits, the dissolved gypsum washed into Lake Lucero and dried in the wind and sunshine of the basin. The encrusted lake bed is constantly scoured by a southwest wind, and sand-sized gypsum crystals are swept toward the white dunes. As each dune grows and moves farther from the lake, new ones form. Because of the harsh environment in the dunes area, plants and animals have developed unique features that permit their survival.

A visitor center at the park entrance has a sound-and-light program and exhibits to help visitors interpret this unique area. A paved road leading into the main part of the dunes (16 miles round trip) has numbered posts at pull-out spaces along the right-hand side that are keyed to a guide booklet that is available free at the entrance station. The best dunes for climbing are approximately 1½ miles from the picnic area. During summer, ranger-guided walks and evening programs are offered every night. Auto caravans to Lake Lucero are offered every month.

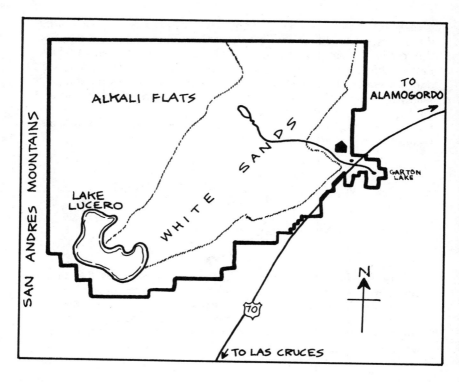

White Sands National Monument

Facilities: No lodging is offered at the park, but refreshments are sold at the visitor center. Water and modern restrooms are also available here. Additional restrooms (no water) are located in the picnic area.
Camping: No campground is located at the park. The nearest public camping facilities are in Lincoln National Forest, 35 miles east, and at Aquire Springs, 30 miles west. Oliver Lee Memorial State Park offers camping 10 miles south of Alamogordo on U.S. 54.
Fishing: No fishing is available at White Sands National Monument.

North Dakota

FORT UNION TRADING POST NATIONAL HISTORIC SITE
Buford Route
Williston, ND 58801
(701) 572–9083

*Fort Union Trading Post, which contains 434 acres, was author-
ized for inclusion into the National Park System in 1966 to
preserve the site of the principal fur-trading post in the Upper
Missouri River region from 1829 until 1867. The fort is located in
western North Dakota, 25 miles southwest of Williston via U.S. 2
and North Dakota 1804.*

In 1829, the construction of Fort Union was started by Kenneth
McKenzie, an executive and trader for the American Fur Company.
Four years later the structure was complete, and trade with Indian
tribes resulted in the fort's being surrounded by tepees during much of
the year. In 1843, McKenzie was replaced by Alexander Culbertson.

The fort's walls were constructed of cottonwood logs 18 feet high,
grounded on stone foundations. The walls were 220 feet wide on the
north and south sides and 240 feet long on the east and west. A
number of buildings were located inside the walls.

By the 1860s, civilization overtook the homelands of the Plains
Indians. A number of tribes had been subjected to smallpox epidemics
and tended to avoid the fort. In the late 1860s, Fort Union was
abandoned and gradually dismantled by the army for use at Fort
Buford, a short distance down the Missouri River.

The entire site was covered with grass when it was acquired by
the National Park Service in 1966. Since then, stone foundations of
some buildings have been excavated, and reconstruction work was
dedicated in 1989.

A visitor center contains exhibits and a short slide program. Park
personnel offer guided tours and living-history programs during sum-

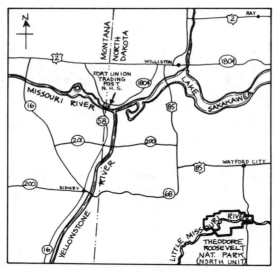

Fort Union Trading Post National Monument

mer months. Also in the historic confluence region of the Yellowstone and Missouri are Lewis-and-Clark sites, the ghost towns of Buford and Mon Dak, and the Fort Buford Military Post.

Facilities: The visitor center provides drinking water and restrooms. Food and lodging are available in Williston and Sidney, Montana.
Camping: Camping is not permitted at the site but is available at Fort Buford State Historic Site, a short distance to the east.
Fishing: The park is located on the Missouri River, and fishing is permitted with a North Dakota or Montana license.

INTERNATIONAL PEACE GARDEN
Route #1, Box 116
Dunseith, ND 58329
(701) 263–4390

International Peace Garden, an affiliated area of the National Park Service, contains approximately 2,330 acres. It was dedicated in 1932 to commemorate the peaceful relations between the United States and Canada. The garden is located in north-central North Dakota on U.S. 281 and State Route 3, between Dunseith, North Dakota, and Boissevain, Manitoba.

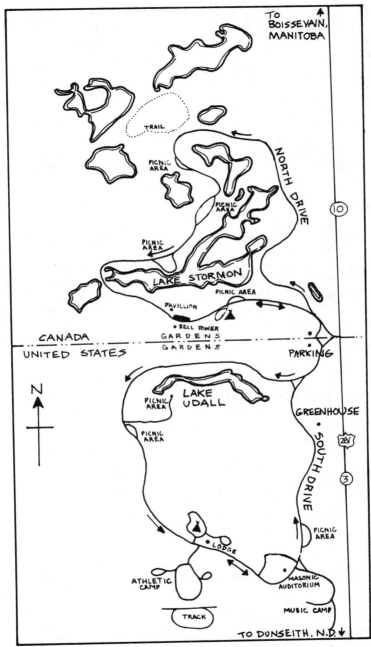

International Peace Garden

The International Peace Garden contains a variety of plant life on its beautifully landscaped grounds, which cross an international border. Wooded areas, flower gardens, and two man-made lakes provide visitors with a peaceful background for a leisurely stroll. Among other things, the garden contains a large floral clock, a sunken garden, an amphitheater, an auditorium, a chapel, and a pavilion. An arboretum identifies a large variety of trees and shrubs. Annual flowers in the park number 150,000.

Roads circle both the south and north sides of the park, and hiking trails into the wooded area around the lakes are available. Three different tours of the park—including the Canadian Natural Drive, the United States Cultural Drive, and the Formal Gardens walking tour—take a total of about two-and-one-half hours.

Facilities: Food service is available in the formal area. Overnight accommodations are not provided but can be found in nearby towns. Drinking water and modern restrooms are available in various locations. Picnic grounds are scattered throughout the park.

Camping: Campgrounds with tables, grills, water, and modern restrooms are provided on both sides of the park. The campground on the U.S. side has twenty sites with concrete pads and hookups. It also has a new bathhouse. Other public campgrounds are located near the park.

Fishing: No fishing is available at the park. Fishing areas are located nearby.

KNIFE RIVER INDIAN VILLAGES NATIONAL HISTORIC SITE
Rural Route #1, P.O. Box 168
Stanton, ND 58571
(701) 745–3309

Knife River Indian Villages, which comprises 1,293 acres, was authorized as part of the National Park Service in 1974 to preserve remnants of historic and prehistoric Indian villages containing an array of artifacts of Plains Indian culture. The park is located in central North Dakota, 3 miles north of the town of Stanton.

The Indians living along the Knife River were hunters and successful farmers. The Hidatsa, who lived here with their neighbors, the Mandan, built small villages with circular houses. By the early 1800s, the prosperity of this area on the Missouri River was enhanced by Knife River's being at the center of a trade network among various tribes and European-Americans.

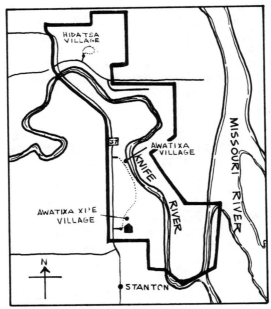

Knife River Indian Villages National Historic Site

Unfortunately, Europeans brought diseases that decimated the tribes around Knife River, and various smallpox epidemics broke out between the late 1700s and mid-1800s. By 1845, the Mandan and Hidatsa had banded together 40 miles northwest of Knife River at Fort Berthold. They were joined by the Arikara in 1863 to become the three affiliated tribes of today.

The park's new visitor center is a short distance east of Highway 37. Here, visitors will find exhibits and a theater that show the day-to-day life and customs of the Hidatsa, Mandan, and Arikara people. Crafts made by descendants of these Village Indians are sold here. There is hiking access, by trail, to each of the three major village sites. Awatixa Village and Awatixa XI'e Village are each near the visitor center and may be reached by trail from the center. Hidatsa Village is reached via a short trail that begins at a parking area in the north end of the park. Park personnel also give guided tours of village sites. Check the visitor center for a schedule of guided walks and other activities.

Facilities: Limited meals and lodging are in Stanton. Drinking water and restrooms are at the park's visitor contact station.
Camping: No camping is available at the site. Approximately 15 miles northwest of Knife River Villages, Lake Sakakawea provides a large

camping area with tables, grills, drinking water, flush toilets, and showers. The state park is 1 mile north of Pick City, off Highway 200. A U.S. Army Corps of Engineers' campground is 3 miles south of the town of Riverdale.

Fishing: Fishing is permitted along the Knife and Missouri rivers with a North Dakota license. Both camping areas noted provide opportunities for fishing.

THEODORE ROOSEVELT NATIONAL PARK
Medora, ND 58645
(701) 623–4466

Theodore Roosevelt National Park, established in 1947, comprises more than 70,000 acres, including scenic badlands along the Little Missouri River and part of Theodore Roosevelt's Elkhorn Ranch. The three separate units of the park are located in western North Dakota. The South Unit is along Interstate 94, west of Belfield, near Medora. The Elkhorn Ranch site is reached via a gravel and dirt road that begins in the South Unit; fording the Little Missouri River is necessary. The North Unit is intersected by U.S. 85, 53 miles north of Interstate 94.

The North Dakota Badlands are the result of erosion through ancient plains where waters had deposited materials from the Rocky Mountains. At one time, the area's lowlands were covered by a jungle whose vegetation decomposed under layers of sediment and eventually turned to coal. Later, volcanoes to the west spewed ash that drifted eastward and either landed in this region or was carried in by ancient streams. Finally, streams cut through the soft land areas and created the badlands.

The park is named for Theodore Roosevelt, who lived and vacationed in this area prior to being elected president of the United States. Roosevelt owned an open-range cattle ranch, the Elkhorn, and was a partner in another ranch, the Maltese Cross. The strenuous life of pioneer living and the rugged beauty of the badlands had a profound effect upon Roosevelt. Although the time he spent here was short, it had a strong influence on his later decisions concerning the nation's natural resources.

At the South Unit, the visitor center near the park's entrance includes a museum with the restored Maltese Cross Cabin located in the rear. From here, a 36-mile paved loop road provides access to some of this unit's highlights. Scoria Point allows the visitor to see

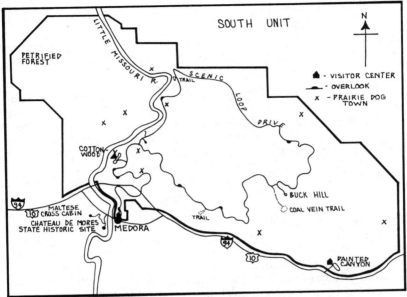

Theodore Roosevelt National Park—South Unit

where a vein of burning lignite coal baked the surrounding sand and clay to red brick. Farther down the road is a lignite vein that burned until 1977 and is thought to have been ignited by a lightning-caused prairie fire in 1951. Visitors may walk to Buck Hill, which at 2,855 feet is one of the highest points in the park. The nature trail at Wind Canyon provides an overlook of the Little Missouri River. Horses may be rented at Peaceful Valley Ranch. Seven miles east of Medora, off Interstate 94, Painted Canyon Overlook provides a view of the badlands.

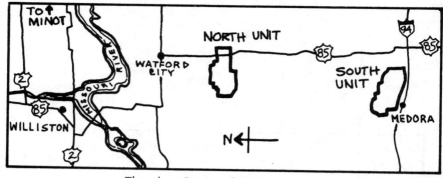

Theodore Roosevelt National Park

The park's North Unit is less crowded and more scenic. It contains a 15-mile scenic paved road to the vicinity of Sperati Point, the narrowest gateway in the badlands. The river once flowed north from here but was blocked during the ice age. At Squaw Creek, a ½-mile self-guiding trail begins at the southeast corner of Squaw Creek Campground. About 1½ miles west of here is the ¾-mile Caprock Coulee Self-Guiding Nature Trail, which is part of a 4-mile-loop hiking trail.

Facilities: Lodging and food are not available within the park. Near the South Unit, Medora has restaurants, motels, service stations, and supplies. Painted Canyon Overlook provides restrooms, picnic shelters, tables, water, and fireplaces. Fifteen miles north of the North Unit, Watford City has motels, restaurants, food stores, and service stations. Water and restrooms are available at various locations in both units.
Camping: Located in cottonwood groves near the Little Missouri River, campgrounds in both units are exceptional. In the South Unit, Cottonwood (eighty spaces) is open all year and has tables, grills, water, and flush toilets (pit toilets, October to May). Halliday Well (reservation-only group camp) is open from May through September and has tables, grills, water, and pit toilets. In the North Unit, Squaw Creek (fifty spaces) is open all year and has tables, grills, water, and flush toilets (pit toilets, October to May). No firewood is provided, and the gathering of firewood is prohibited in the park.
Fishing: The Little Missouri River flows through both the North and South units and provides catches of catfish and carp. Fishermen must have a North Dakota license.

Oklahoma

CHICKASAW NATIONAL RECREATION AREA
P.O. Box 201
Sulphur, OK 73086
(405) 622–3165

Chickasaw National Recreation Area, which contains approximately 10,000 acres, was established in 1976 by consolidating Platt National Park, Arbuckle National Recreation Area, and additional lands. The recreation area provides access to numerous outdoor activities. It is located in south-central Oklahoma, just east of Interstate 35, which connects Oklahoma City and Dallas.

Chickasaw National Recreation Area comprises two districts offering very different outdoor experiences. The smaller northeastern area (the former Platt National Park) is noted for its freshwater and mineral springs. On the east side, freshwater Buffalo and Antelope Springs are the source of Travertine Creek. A number of cold mineral-water springs are located in the central and western areas of this section, and both bromide and sulphur water are dispensed at Bromide Pavilion. Travertine Nature Center offers exhibits, a slide program, a daily children's nature program, and naturalist-conducted nature walks. Evening nature programs are held in the center's auditorium, and various nature trails lead from this area.

Eight miles southwest of this wooded area is the park's second unit (the former Arbuckle National Recreation Area). Here, Arbuckle Dam at the confluence of three creeks has resulted in the formation of a 2,350-acre lake that provides opportunities for fishing, boating, swimming, water-skiing, and scuba diving (with permit). Boat-launching ramps are located at Guy Sandy, The Point, and Buckhorn Rock.

Facilities: Food and lodging are not available in either unit. Both are provided in nearby towns. Drinking water and restrooms are located throughout both areas.

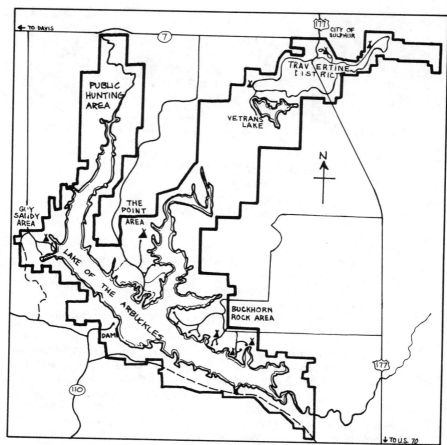

Chickasaw National Recreation Area

242 OKLAHOMA

Camping: In the smaller unit, tables, grills, water, and flush toilets are provided at Central (twenty-three group sites only), Cold Springs (sixty-three spaces), and Rock Creek (111 spaces, dump station). Of these, only Rock Creek is open year round. In the southwestern unit, Buckhorn (177 spaces, dump station), Guy Sandy (forty spaces), and The Point (fifty-two spaces) each offer tables, fireplaces, drinking water, and flush or chemical toilets. All units except Guy Sandy are open year round.

Fishing: Streams in the northeast unit contain sunfish, crappie, largemouth bass, and white bass. In the lake district, there is fishing for channel catfish, largemouth bass, sunfish, and crappie. An Oklahoma license is required to fish at the park.

Oregon

CRATER LAKE NATIONAL PARK
P.O. Box 7
Crater Lake, OR 97604
(503) 594–2211

Crater Lake National Park was established in 1902 to preserve a deep blue lake that resulted from the collapse of an ancient volcano. The lake is surrounded by lava walls of from 500 to 2,000 feet. The park contains 183,000 acres and is located in southern Oregon, 57 miles north of Klamath Falls. The major road into the park is Oregon Highway 62, which runs through the southwest corner. Only the south and west entrance roads to Rim Village are open during winter months.

Crater Lake is the remains of the 12,000-foot volcano, Mount Mazama, that was destroyed nearly 6,850 years ago after a series of eruptions drained its interior. Additional volcanic activity after the collapse produced a cinder cone now known as Wizard Island. Over a period of centuries the huge hole accumulated water from rain and snow. Only six lakes in the world are deeper than Crater Lake, which has been measured to a depth of 1,932 feet.

A variety of plant life can be found in the park, including mountain hemlock; Shasta, Douglas, and subalpine fir; and lodgepole, whitebark, and ponderosa pine. Wildflowers are abundant in July. Animals inhabiting the area include bears, deer, porcupines, bobcats, elk, coyotes, and many varieties of birds.

During summer a variety of activities are available. A thirty-three-mile paved road circles the lake and offers numerous scenic viewpoints. The visitor center at Rim Village provides information. A park ranger is on duty to answer questions. Talks on the origins of Crater Lake are presented throughout the day during summer months. Two nearby trails provide scenic views. Garfield Peak Trail (one and

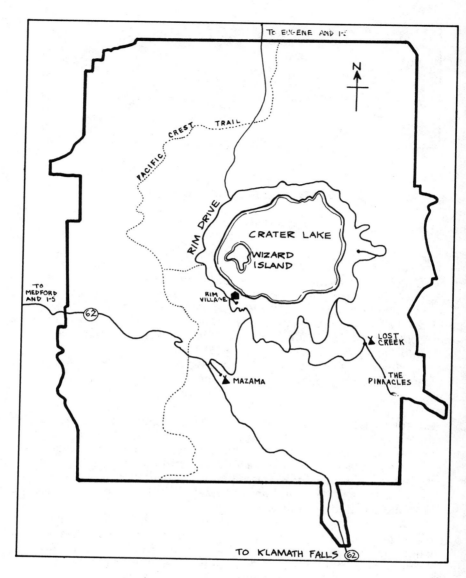

Crater Lake National Park

seven-tenths miles) begins behind the lodge and ends at a peak 1,900 feet above the lake. Discovery Point Trail (one and a half miles) begins at the opposite end of Rim Village and leads to a point where the lake was discovered in 1853. A number of other trails are located at various points around Rim Drive. Along the lake's north end, Cleetwood Trail (one and one-tenth miles) descends to Cleetwood Cove, the only access to the water. Launch trips around the lake and to Wizard Island originate here. A six-mile paved road off Rim Drive leads to the Pinnacles. Here spires of pumice and welded tuff rise 200 feet out of the Wheeler Creek Canyon.

Winter activities include cross-country ski trips around Crater Lake. Snowmobiling on a designated road is permitted when the snow depth is two feet or more. No downhill ski facilities are available.

Facilities: Lodging is available in the park from June through mid-October. Information and reservations can be obtained from Crater Lake Lodge, Inc., Crater Lake, OR 97604 (503–594–2511). A variety of food services are available from late May to early October. During winter, only light meals are served. Some groceries may be purchased at Mazama Campground, and a gasoline station is open during summer months. Modern restrooms are available at Rim Village, Park Headquarters, and the campground.

Camping: The park's single major campground, Mazama (198 sites), seven miles south of Rim Village, is one of the nicest in any of the major national park areas. It provides tables, grills, flush toilets, and a dump station. Sites are generally not squeezed together, and a few front on a canyon. G Loop offers the most secluded sites. A one-and-seven-tenths-mile trail behind the campground leads to the bottom of Annie Creek Canyon. Lost Creek Campground (sixteen spaces, tent camping only) is on the road to the Pinnacles and has pit toilets.

Fishing: The lake originally contained no fish but was stocked. Rainbow trout and kokanee salmon still survive in the lake. Numerous streams run through the park (Mazama Campground is near one) and no fishing license is required.

FORT CLATSOP NATIONAL MEMORIAL
Route 3, Box 604–FC
Astoria, OR 97103
(503) 861–2471

Fort Clatsop National Memorial became part of the National Park System in 1958. A replica of their fort marks the spot where the Lewis and Clark Expedition wintered in 1805–6 after their historic journey to the Pacific Ocean. The memorial is located in north-western Oregon, 5 miles southwest of Astoria off U.S. Highway 101.

After the expedition's party of thirty-three led by Meriwether Lewis and William Clark completed the journey from St. Louis to the Pacific, it needed a place to spend the winter before returning home. On December 8, 1805, construction began on a small fort they named Fort Clatsop after a friendly local Indian tribe. During the three and a half months they were here, the men consolidated their journals and maps, traded with the Indians, hunted and trapped, made buckskin clothing, and boiled salt water for salt to flavor and preserve meat for the trip home.

The memorial's visitor center contains exhibits, audio-visual programs, and reading material to enhance your understanding of the expedition and its conditions at Fort Clatsop. The reconstruction of the fort is nearby, and trails to the camp spring and canoe landing begin here. National Park Service rangers present living history programs during summer months, including flintlock rifle demonstrations, candle making, building canoes, making buckskin clothes, and dressing skins. Hours are 8:00 A.M. to 6:00 P.M. in summer, 8:00 A.M. to 5:00 P.M. the rest of the year. Closed Christmas.

Facilities: No food or lodging is available in the park. Both may be found nearby. A day-use lunch area is near the visitor center where water and modern restrooms are provided.

Camping: No camping is available in Fort Clatsop National Memorial. Eight miles northwest, Fort Stevens State Park provides camping for both tents (260 spaces) and trailers (343 spaces) with water, grills, tables, and 126 full hookups available. The state park offers fishing, hiking, and ocean beaches. For information call (503) 861–1671.

Fishing: Although few people fish in the memorial, fishing is permitted near the canoe landing in the Lewis and Clark River with an Oregon license. Fishing conditions are better in nearby streams outside Fort Clatsop National Memorial.

JOHN DAY FOSSIL BEDS NATIONAL MONUMENT
420 W. Main St.
John Day, OR 97845
(503) 575–0721

John Day Fossil Beds was incorporated into the National Park System in 1975 and contains 14,000 acres. The monument preserves a fossil record where scientists unearth evidence of land plants and animals extending back 50 million years. The park consists of three widely separated units in north-central Oregon. U.S. 26 runs in an east-west direction through the region, while

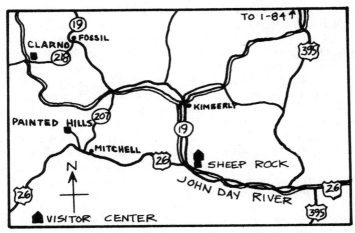

John Day Fossil Beds National Monument

U.S. 395 runs in a north-south direction. The Sheep Rock unit is 5 miles west of the city of Dayville via U.S. 26 and Oregon 19. To reach the Painted Hills unit, leave U.S. 26 near Mitchell and follow a marked country road for 6 miles. The Clarno unit is on Oregon 218, 20 miles west of Fossil and 15 miles east of Antelope.

The fossil record of John Day was recognized early by the State of Oregon, which began to purchase land in this area during the 1930s. Although rocks of the nearby highlands date from more than 250 million years ago, the record discovered in the monument begins with sea life of approximately 100 million years ago. Various geologic ages since that time have been marked by distinctive earth deposits containing outstanding fossil records. Fossil animals found here include several species of ancient horses, oreodonts, tapirs, titanotheres, camels, mastodons, rodents, cats, rhinoceroses, and dogs. In general, the formations are younger toward the south and east, so the oldest formation is in the Clarno unit and the youngest is in the Sheep Rock unit.

Animals inhabiting the park include bobcats, coyotes, badgers, mule deer, jack rabbits, and cottontail rabbits. Birds frequenting the river area and surrounding mountain slopes include Canada geese, ducks, great blue heron, bluebirds, black-billed magpies, green-tailed towhees, California quail, red-tailed hawks, and golden eagles. Visitors should watch for rattlesnakes.

Park headquarters, in the town of John Day, provides information and a display of fossils. The park's visitor center is in the Sheep Rock unit.

This unit includes outstanding examples of four of the five principal geological formations represented in the monument. The historic Cant Ranch includes a visitor facility at the former main ranch house containing exhibits on geology and local ranching history. This location is a nice resting place; a short trail to Sheeprock Overlook begins here. North of Cant Ranch at Blue Basin, two trails offer spectacular views of the basin and adjacent river valley. Farther north are a colorful rock formation at Cathedral Rock, and an area of eroded lava flows and impressive outcrops of the John Day Formation at Foree Deposits.

The Painted Hills area consists of an eroded landscape of volcanic ash deposits set within a vast picturesque valley. A half-mile trail near the overlook, a short quarter-mile loop trail at Painted Cove, and the three-quarters-of-a-mile Carroll Rim Trail provide opportunities to see the colorful formations at close range.

Clarno includes ancient mudslides with two quarter-mile trails to the base of the brown and black palisades that offer views of plant fossils preserved in mudstone.

Wayside exhibits at overlooks along roads interpret outstanding features of each area of the park. In addition, the John Day River offers recreational opportunities.

Facilities: Lodging, fuel, and food are available in nearby communities, but not within the park. Hospitals are located in John Day, Madras, and Prineville. Drinking water and restrooms can be found at the headquarters building, at the Cant Ranch, Painted Hills, and Clarno.

Camping: No camping is available within any of the three units of the park.

Fishing: The John Day River offers trout fishing in the summer and steelhead fishing in the winter with an Oregon license.

MCLOUGHLIN HOUSE NATIONAL HISTORIC SITE
713 Center Street
Oregon City, OR 97045
(503) 656–5146

McLoughlin House was designated a national historic site in 1941 to preserve the home of Dr. John McLoughlin, often called the "Father of Oregon." The house is one of the few remaining pioneer dwellings in the region once known as Oregon Country. McLoughlin House, an affiliated area of the National Park System, is located in Oregon City, 13 miles southeast of Portland on Interstate 205. In Oregon City it is in McLoughlin Park between Seventh and Eighth streets, less than four blocks east of Pacific Highway (U.S. 99).

John McLoughlin was born near Quebec, Canada, in 1784. When he came to the Oregon Country in 1824, McLoughlin was already in charge of the Columbia District of Hudson's Bay Company. This was later combined with another district to make up the Oregon Company. From Fort Vancouver, McLoughlin ruled an empire stretching from the Rocky Mountains to the Pacific Ocean and from Alaska to California. Although his primary responsibility was to facilitate activities associated with the fur-trading industry, he also helped to develop other economic pursuits of the Northwest and provided assistance to the increasing numbers of immigrants moving into the region.

In 1828, McLoughlin and Governor George Simpson chose the falls of the Willamette River as a site for development. This eventually evolved into Oregon City, capital of the provisional government and chief town of Oregon Country. In 1845, Dr. McLoughlin resigned from the Hudson's Bay Company. In 1846, he moved to Oregon City and into the house where he lived until his death in 1857.

In 1909, a movement to preserve the house was successful and the McLoughlin Memorial Association had the house moved from its original site at Third and Main streets to its present site in McLoughlin Park. Since 1935 the house has been restored as nearly as possible to its original appearance. It contains period furniture including some pieces that were at Fort Vancouver and many items that were owned by McLoughlin. In 1970, the remains of Mr. and Mrs. McLoughlin were moved next to the house.

The site was established by cooperative agreement among the McLoughlin Memorial Association, the municipality of Oregon City, and the National Park Service. The house is open Tuesday through Saturday (fee charged) from 10:00 A.M. to 4:00 P.M. and on Sunday from 1:00 P.M. to 4:00 P.M. Visitors may take either a self-guided or a conducted tour. National Park Service passes are not accepted. A tourist information center operated by the local chamber of commerce is at Abernathy Road and Washington Street.

Facilities: No facilities are at the site, but food and lodging are nearby in Oregon City.
Camping: No camping is permitted at the site. For those traveling south, Champoeg State Park (forty-eight spaces), approximately twenty-four miles southwest, provides full hookups, grills, and tables. From Oregon City take Interstate 205, Interstate 5 (south), and exit west on the Champoeg Park exit. For those traveling north, see the camping section under Fort Vancouver National Historic Site (Washington).
Fishing: No fishing is available at McLoughlin House National Historic Site.

OREGON CAVES NATIONAL MONUMENT
19000 Caves Highway
Cave Junction, OR 97523
(503) 592–2100

Oregon Caves National Monument was established in 1909 to protect eleven small caves and a 3-mile cave that has rare bats, endemic insects, and all of the earth's six main rock types. Transferred to the National Park Service in 1934, the monument contains 480 acres of old growth, including part of the most diverse conifer forest in the world. The monument is located in southwestern Oregon, 20 miles east of Cave Junction via Oregon Highway 46. The last 8 miles are very winding and are not recommended for trailers.

Collision of North America and the Pacific Ocean destroyed an ocean basin and metamorphosed limestone into marble 153 million years ago. Uplift formed faults, joints, and other cracks. Underwater and stream enlargement of cracks dissolved out the caves about a million years ago. Extensive formations include rimstone, stalagmites, stalactites, coralloids, flowstones, helictites, moonmilk, vermiculations, bell canopies, columns, cave "ghosts," scallops, domepits, pendants, and natural bridges.

After a hunter discovered the main cave in 1874, commercialization damaged the fragile cave. Through airlocks, rubble removal, etc., restoration of the cave to its original state started in 1985. Annual precipitation, mostly snow during winter, is about 55 inches, and the average surface temperature is in the mid-40s. Many plants are at their range limit or are endemic to the Siskiyou/Klamath Mountains.

Most visitors take a seventy-five-minute, concession-guided tour (fee charged) that covers ½ mile of the caves. Over 500 damp steps must be climbed to a manmade exit that is 240 feet above the entrance. Rubber- or vibram-soled shoes and warm clothing should be worn. Waiting for a summer tour can exceed one and a half hours. Tours are given during the winter several times a day. Annual visitation is about one hundred thousand with 75 percent taking place in the summer. Many visitors also stop at the visitor center in Cave Junction. The national monument also has five miles of outdoor trails, with scenic views, waterfalls, and meadows. These trails are maintained only in the summer.

Facilities: There is handicap access to restrooms, phones, and the first room in the caves. A restaurant and National Historic Landmark hotel are open from mid-June to early September. A snackbar is open year round. For rates or reservations, write Oregon Caves Chateau, Box 128, Cave Junction, OR 97523 (503–592–3400).

Camping: There is no camping, fishing, or fires in the monument. The U.S. Forest Service operates two campgrounds in the adjoining Siskiyou National Forest from about the end of May to early September. Cave Creek Campground is four miles from the park on Oregon 46. It has tables, grills, water, and pit toilets. Trailers are permitted only in Grayback Campground, located eight miles down Oregon 46 from the park. Grayback has grills, water, a picnic area, flush toilets, and a phone. Campsites in both areas are secluded and many are alongside a fishing stream.

Fishing: Fishing is available along the road to the monument but not in the monument itself.

South Dakota

BADLANDS NATIONAL PARK
P.O. Box 6
Interior, SD 57750
(605) 433–5361

Badlands National Monument, authorized in 1929 (changed to a national park in 1978), comprises 243,000 acres of prairie grassland and a scenic eroded landscape, with animal fossils that are between 23 and 38 million years old. The park is located in southwestern South Dakota. The Pinnacles entrance is 57 miles southeast of Rapid City, off Interstate 90, and the "main" entrance at Cactus Flats is off Interstate 90, 71 miles east of Rapid City. Don't miss Wall Drug in the town of Wall. It is unique.

Today's badlands are the remains of what was a plain with slow-moving streams 23 to 38 million years ago. On this land roamed such animals as a sabre-toothed cat and a camel the size of a dog. After dying, they were sometimes buried in mud washed down from the Black Hills. This, in turn, was buried under additional layers. Periodically, volcanic activity to the west produced layers of ash, which today appear as gray or white layers in the badlands formations. As the climate became warm and dry, the jungles turned into grassland. Today, White River and its tributaries erode the soft sedimentary layers and leave the strange formations that give the park its name.

Badlands National Park has two visitor centers. Cedar Pass Visitor Center, located 8 miles south of Interstate 90 via the northeast entrance, has exhibits and a slide program to help interpret the badlands. White River Visitor Center, in the south end of the park, has Indian cultural exhibits and a videotape program on the history of the Oglala Sioux. Wayside exhibits are along the main park road, and self-guiding nature trails are located near the Cedar Pass Visitor Center and along the park road. Ranger-conducted hikes and evening slide programs are available during summer.

◄ **Fossil Exhibit Trail at Badlands National Park**   **SOUTH DAKOTA   255**

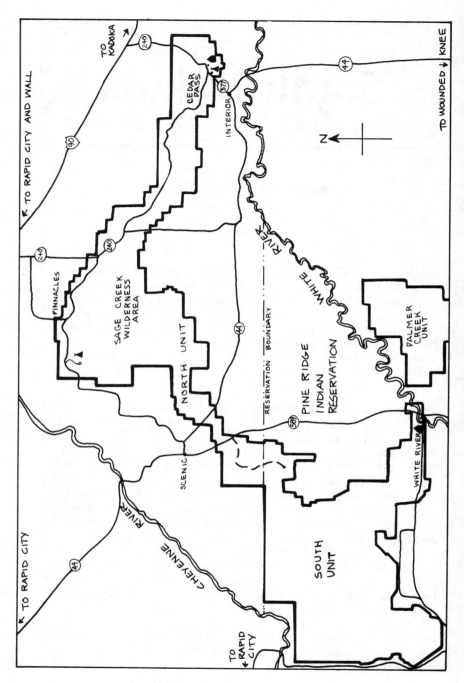

Badlands National Park

Facilities: Cedar Pass Lodge offers twenty-three cabins, as well as meals from May 1 to October 15. For information and reservations, write Oglala Sioux Park and Recreation Authority, P.O. Box 5, Interior, SD 57750 (605–433–5460). Drinking water and restrooms are located in the visitor center and the lodge.

Camping: Cedar Pass Campground (136 spaces, one group site) provides sheltered tables, water, flush toilets, and a dump station. Sage Creek Campground (six spaces) has vault toilets but no water. Both campgrounds are open year round.

Fishing: No fishing is available at the park.

JEWEL CAVE NATIONAL MONUMENT
RR 1, Box 60AA
Custer, SD 57730
(605) 673–2288

Jewel Cave National Monument, which comprises 1,275 acres, was established in 1908 to preserve a series of underground chambers, connected by narrow passageways, with many side galleries and fine calcite crystal encrustations in the second longest cave in the United States. The monument is located in southwestern South Dakota, 13 miles west of Custer via U.S. 16. For a map of the Black Hills region, see the map under Mount Rushmore National Memorial.

The caves in this region lie in a limestone layer that was deposited about 300 million years ago in an ancient sea. Later, after being covered with layers of sediment, an uplifting associated with the formation of the Rocky Mountains exposed the interior of the hills. As acidic water seeped into cracks in the limestone, the rock dissolved and caves were formed. Decorating began after the water table fell and additional acidic water, combined with carbon dioxide, percolated into the voids. The cave was named after the many jewellike calcite crystals that form when calcite crystalizes out of standing water.

Jewel Cave was discovered in 1900 by two prospectors who recorded it as a mining claim. After failing to find valuable minerals, they attempted to turn it into a tourist attraction. In 1908, President Theodore Roosevelt proclaimed the cave a national monument.

The monument's visitor center is open daily year round. It contains exhibits and an information counter. Naturalist-guided tours (fee charged) are conducted through portions of the cave on a daily basis from Memorial Day through Labor Day. Three types of tours are

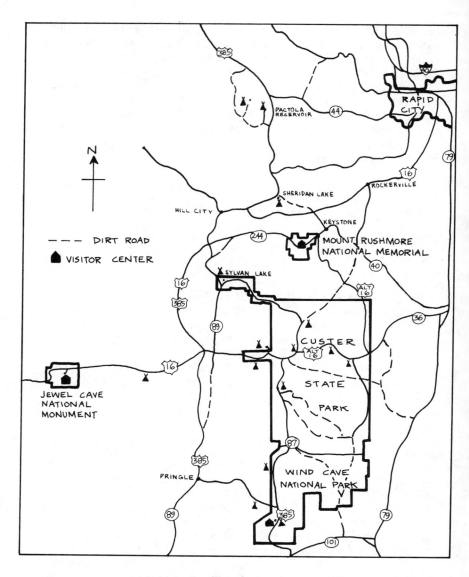

Mount Rushmore National Memorial

available. The scenic tour enters and leaves the cave by elevator in the visitor center; the historic tour uses the natural entrance found by the cave's discoverers. This latter trip is quite strenuous and uses an unimproved trail. For those desiring an even more demanding trip, the spelunking tour (reservations required) is made to order.

Facilities: Food and lodging are not available in the park. Motels, restaurants, and service stations are in Custer, South Dakota, and Newcastle, Wyoming. Drinking water and restrooms are located in the visitor center.

Camping: No camping is permitted in the park. Public camping facilities are available nearby in Wind Cave National Park, Custer State Park, and Black Hills National Forest.

Fishing: No fishing is available at the monument.

MOUNT RUSHMORE NATIONAL MEMORIAL
P.O. Box 268
Keystone, SD 57751
(605) 574–2523

Mount Rushmore, which comprises 1,278 acres, was dedicated on August 10, 1927, the same day work commenced on sculpting the heads of George Washington, Abraham Lincoln, Thomas Jefferson, and Theodore Roosevelt on the face of this granite mountain. The memorial is located in southwestern South Dakota, 25 miles southwest of Rapid City and 2 miles from the town of Keystone.

The idea of a large sculpture in the Black Hills region was first conceived in 1923. Although the project initially received little public support, opinion gradually changed, and authorization and funding eventually were obtained. In the fall of 1924, Gutzon Borglum, a sculptor then at work on Stone Mountain in Georgia, was invited to study the proposal. Borglum suggested that United States presidents be used as subjects and that the sculpture be on the smooth granite of Mount Rushmore. The original proposal had called for the figures of famous western heroes on another granite formation known as the Needles.

Borglum worked on the project from 1927 until his death in 1941. His son continued the work until funds were exhausted later that year. Although private donations supported the project in its early years, the federal government contributed most of the nearly $1 million the project consumed between 1927 and 1941.

The sixty-foot-tall faces are best viewed under morning light. During summer evenings, floodlights illuminate the faces, and programs are presented in the amphitheater. The visitor center, with exhibits explaining the history of the memorial, is open year round.

Facilities: Meals, souvenirs, and handicrafts are available at the concession. Overnight accommodations are located in nearby communities.

Camping: No camping is permitted in the park. Public camping facilities are provided in a number of campgrounds in Black Hills National Forest and in Custer State Park and Wind Cave National Park.

Fishing: No fishing is available at the memorial.

WIND CAVE NATIONAL PARK
Hot Springs, SD 57747
(605) 745–4600

Wind Cave National Park, which comprises more than 28,000 acres, was established in 1903 to preserve a part of the prairie ecosystem and a unique type of limestone cavern that is the third longest cave in the United States. The park is located in southwestern South Dakota, approximately 60 miles south of Rapid City via U.S. 16 and 385. Vehicles more than 10½ feet high or 10 feet wide should avoid U.S. 16A. Those more than 11½ feet high or 9 feet wide should avoid Route 87.

The 300- to 630-foot-thick limestone bed containing Wind Cave was deposited at the bottom of a great sea about 300 million years ago. Later, the region was covered with many layers of sediment before being uplifted approximately 60 million years ago. During the uplift, the limestone was fractured, allowing ground water to dissolve the limestone and deposit the calcite that now decorates the cave.

The cave is most noted for its "boxwork" formations, but other interesting decorations also may be seen. Unlike many caverns, stalactites and stalagmites are uncommon in Wind Cave. The strong winds that blow in and out of the cave (hence, its name) are apparently caused by changes in atmospheric pressure on the outside. Although more than 57 miles of passages have been explored, the regular tours (fee charged) cover from ½ to 1 mile of hard-surfaced trails with stairways and electric lighting. Rubber-soled shoes (low-heeled) and a light jacket (53 degrees Fahrenheit inside) are recommended for visitors desiring to tour the cave.

One of the park's most popular attractions is the bison herd that roams this wildlife sanctuary. A number of prairie dog towns are located in the park, as are herds of elk, pronghorn, and mule and white-tailed deer. During summer months, park personnel conduct guided outdoor activities mornings and evenings. Schedules are posted at the visitor center, which also contains exhibits on the area's history.

Facilities: No overnight accommodations are available in the park, but motels, hotels, trailer courts, camping supplies, and service stations are in Custer and Hot Springs. In the visitor center a lunchroom with sandwiches and light lunches and a gift shop are open during the summer.

Camping: Elk Mountain Campground (one hundred spaces), located 1 mile north of the visitor center, is open year round. Tables, grills, water, and flush toilets are provided. During the off-season (October 1 to May 15) pit toilets are available, but water is available only at the visitor center. Camping also is available in Custer State Park and Black Hills National Forest, to the north.

Fishing: Fishing for brown trout and lake trout is available adjacent to the park.

Texas

ALIBATES FLINT QUARRIES NATIONAL MONUMENT
Box 1438
Fritch, TX 79036
(806) 857–3151

Alibates Flint Quarries was authorized as a national monument in 1965. It contains 1,333 acres in an area where, for nearly 12,000 years, pre-Columbian Indians dug agatized dolomite from quarries to make knives, projectile points, scrapers, and other tools. The monument is in northern Texas, 40 miles northeast of Amarillo. From Texas Highway 136, take Alibates Road, 6 miles south of Fritch, and drive 5 miles to the information station.

Tools made from flint dug in the Lake Meredith area of the Texas Panhandle have been found in many places in the Great Plains and the American Southwest. Evidence from archeological excavations indicates almost continuous use of the flint quarries at Alibates from 10,000 B.C. to the late 1800s. Alibates flint is a hard sharp-edged rock that, unlike most other flint, has a multitude of bright colors.

Although much of the mining at Alibates was done by nomads, some Indians did settle this area briefly from about A.D. 1200 to A.D.1450 These Indians farmed in addition to mining and bartering flint.

A small information station at Bates Canyon contains a few exhibits, and park personnel are on duty to answer questions. During summer months free guided walking tours of the quarry pits leave the information station at 10:00 A.M. and 2:00 P.M. daily. The rest of the year tours are available with advance reservation.

Facilities: The monument is undeveloped, and no visitor facilities other than the information station are available. Meals and lodging are available in Fritch and Borger.

◄ **Santa Elena Canyon in Big Bend National Park**   **TEXAS 263**

Camping: No camping is permitted at the monument. Developed campsites are available in the Bates Canyon area of Lake Meredith National Recreation Area.

Fishing: No fishing is available in Alibates, but quite a lot of good fishing is nearby in Lake Meredith.

AMISTAD NATIONAL RECREATION AREA
P.O. Box 420367
Del Rio, TX 78842
(512) 775–7491

Amistad, established in 1965, contains 62,000 acres that provide numerous outdoor recreation opportunities, including boating, fishing, swimming, water-skiing, and hunting. The park is located along the Rio Grande River in southwest Texas, near Del Rio. It is accessible via U.S. 90.

Lake Amistad, the main attraction at Amistad National Recreation Area, is a result of the 1968 completion of Amistad Dam, 12 miles upstream from Del Rio. The dam, a cooperative undertaking between the United States and Mexico, was developed for flood control, water conservation, hydroelectric power, and recreation. It is constructed of a 254-foot-high concrete section in the Rio Grande channel connecting flanking earth embankments. Near the center of the dam is a customs station, an international monument, and the International Boundary and Water Commission Visitor Center.

The area's most popular activity is boating, and major boat ramps are at Pecos River, Diablo East, and Rough Canyon. Boat rentals, rental slips, bait, and gasoline are available at the latter two locations. Voluntary boat registration at launch ramps is requested. From spring to fall, water in the coves is pleasantly warm for swimming and water-skiing. The beaches are not protected by lifeguards. Swimming is not permitted in the harbor areas. Certain areas of the park are designated for hunting dove, duck, and quail with shotgun; deer, wild turkey, and javelina may be hunted with bow and arrow only. Interested individuals should inquire at the National Park Service headquarters.

Facilities: Concessioner-operated snack bars are located at Diablo East and Rough Canyon. No lodging is available at the park, but motels, travel trailer parks, restaurants, and service stations are in Del Rio, at Rough Canyon area, and along U.S. 90 West, near the lake. A

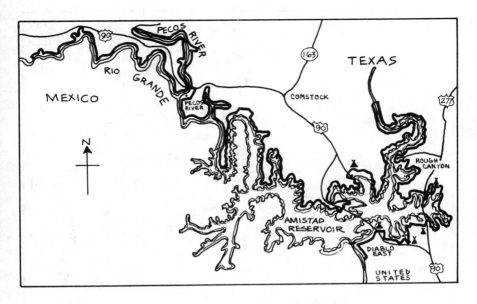

Amistad National Recreation Area

marina with a swimming beach and launching ramp is located near
the west end of the dam in Mexico.

Camping: Primitive campsites with chemical toilets but no drinking
water are in various locations in the park. Commercial campgrounds
are near Diablo East, Rough Canyon, and Pecos.

Fishing: Principal sport fishing is for bass, channel catfish, yellow
catfish, striped bass, crappie, and sunfish. There is no closed season,
and a Texas license is required. Fishing is not permitted in the harbor
areas.

BIG BEND NATIONAL PARK
Big Bend National Park, TX 79834
(915) 477–2251

*Big Bend, established in 1944, comprises more than 801,000
acres of desert, mountain ranges, steep-walled canyons, and
ribbons of green plant life along the Rio Grande River. The park is
located in southwestern Texas on the Mexican border. Access
from the north is via U.S. 385 from Marathon or State Highway
118 from Alpine. Enter from the west on Texas Ranch Road 170
from Presidio.*

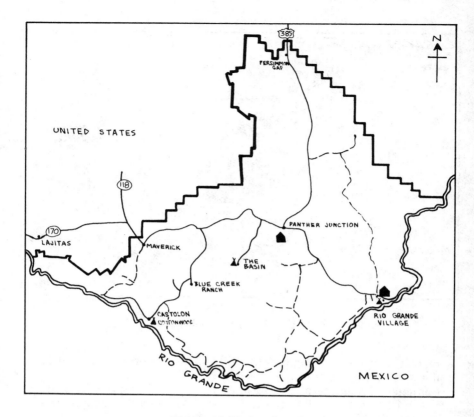

Big Bend National Park

The land of Big Bend is one of vastness and adventure. Its remoteness makes it less heavily used than better-known parks, even though it offers a wide variety of outdoor activities. Big Bend is especially pleasant to visit during the long spring and fall seasons when the weather is mild.

Visitor centers are located at Panther Junction (park head-quarters), Persimmon Gap, The Basin, Rio Grande Village, and Castolon. These centers provide information and sell publications concerning the park. Park naturalists present evening programs at The Basin amphitheater all year and at Rio Grande Village during fall, winter, and spring. A movie is often presented at Panther Junction in the afternoon. Ranger-conducted hikes and special programs are available, and schedules are posted at various locations. Self-guiding nature trails are at Rio Grande Village, Santa Elena Canyon, Panther

266 TEXAS

Junction, Dagger Flat Road, and the Lost Mine and Window View Trail in The Basin.

The 37-mile drive from Panther Junction to Santa Elena Canyon ends at a shaded picnic area, where high cliffs overhang the Rio Grande River. A foot trail to the base of the cliff leads upward to a panoramic viewpoint. From there, the trail wanders three quarters of a mile along the river. On the other side of the park, Boquillas Canyon is the longest (25 miles) of Big Bend's famous gorges. The path into the canyon descends gently after a short, steep climb.

Primitive roads offer access to scenery not available elsewhere in the park. These roads are patrolled infrequently, so those planning such trips should obtain current road information and register at park headquarters.

River trips on the Rio Grande are offered by outfitters outside the park. A permit is required to run the river, but no equipment rentals are available inside the park. The visitor centers sell a river guide and can supply a list of river outfitters.

Facilities: Chisos Mountains Lodge in The Basin provides a total of seventy-two rooms in motel-type units, stone cottages, and frame cottages, with reservations available from National Park Concessions, Inc., Big Bend National Park, TX 79834 (915–477–2291). The lodge has a dining room and coffee shop. Groceries and camping supplies are available at The Basin, Rio Grande Village, and Castolon. Minor auto repair and gas are available at Panther Junction. Gasoline is also at Rio Grande Village and Castolon. Diesel fuel is not available in the park.

Camping: Campgrounds with tables, grills, water, and flush toilets are at The Basin (sixty-two spaces, eight group sites, dump station), Cottonwood (thirty-four spaces, one group site, pit toilets only), and Rio Grande Village (ninety-nine spaces, four group sites, dump station). A concessioner-operated trailer village with hookups is at Rio Grande Village (twenty-five sites, pay showers). The road into The Basin is steep and winding. Trailers longer than 20 feet are not permitted, and recreational vehicles longer than 23 feet are advised to avoid the road.

Fishing: The Rio Grande provides catches of catfish. No license is required.

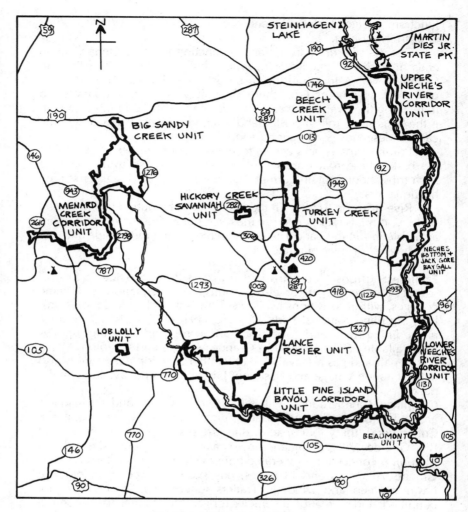

Big Thicket National Preserve

BIG THICKET NATIONAL PRESERVE
3785 Milam
Beaumont, TX 77701
(409) 839–2689

Big Thicket National Preserve contains 86,000 acres and was authorized in 1974 to preserve a unique ecosystem of great diversity. Plants and animals from southwestern deserts, central plains, eastern forests, Appalachian Mountains, and southeastern swamps can be found coexisting in close proximity. The preserve comprises twelve widely separated units north and northeast of the city of Beaumont, Texas. The Information Station is on FM 420, 2½ miles east of U.S. 69, 7 miles north of Kountze. Big Thicket is also designated a Man and the Biosphere Reserve by the United Nations Educational, Scientific, and Cultural Organization (UNESCO).

Big Thicket is unique because of the abundance of diverse plant life coexisting in a small remnant of what was once a combination of virgin pine and cypress forest, hardwood forest, meadow, and black-water swamp. The area contains eighty-five tree species, more than sixty species of shrubs, and nearly 1,000 other flowering plants including twenty orchids and four carnivorous plants. Wildlife thrives in the diverse habitats, although many animals are seen only at night. During annual migrations nearly 300 kinds of birds have been sighted. Big Thicket is home to a few threatened or endangered species, including the red-cockaded woodpecker, American alligator, and paddlefish.

The Information Station is open daily from 9:00 A.M. to 5:00 P.M. All twelve units of the preserve are open to the public, and several have developed hiking trails. Two trails are handicapped accessible. The only way to explore the Big Thicket is to hike a trail or boat or canoe into a back slough. Few roads enter the preserve, limiting visitors from seeing the woods from their cars. Ranger-led programs for groups and individuals are available by reservation only. Contact the Information Station at (409) 246–2337 for information and reservations.

Facilities: No lodging or food service is available in the park, but both are in the nearby communities of Woodville, Kountze, Silsbee, and Beaumont. Restrooms and drinking water are at the Information Station.

Camping: There are no developed camping facilities, although back-country camping is permitted in designated areas of the preserve. A backcountry permit is required. A campground with flush toilets and showers is at Martin Dies State Park, 13 miles west of Jasper on U.S.

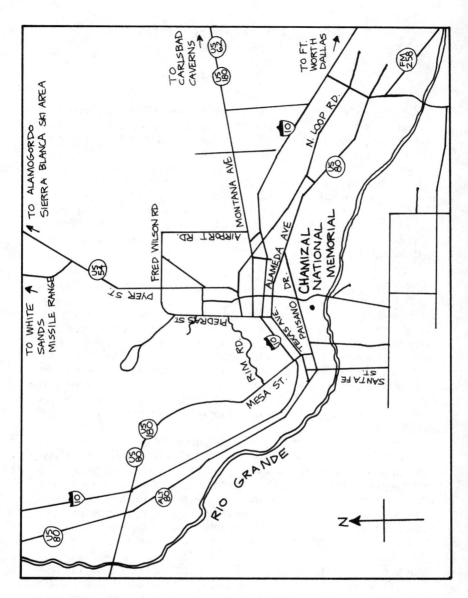

Chamizal National Memorial

190. Another campground, operated by the U.S. Army Corps of Engineers, is nearby on B.A. Steinhagen Lake. Contact the preserve for a listing of nearby private campgrounds.

Fishing: Opportunities for bass, catfish, and carp are available in the preserve. A valid Texas fishing license is required.

Hunting: Hunting is allowed in certain units of the preserve with an annual permit. These free permits are issued during July on a first-come, first-served basis. Contact the preserve for permit information.

CHAMIZAL NATIONAL MEMORIAL
800 South San Marcial Street
El Paso, TX 79905
(915) 534–6668

Chamizal, which comprises fifty-five acres, was authorized in 1966 to memorialize the peaceful settlement of a ninety-nine-year boundary dispute between the United States and Mexico. The park is located in south-central metropolitan El Paso, next to the international border. Entrances to the park are from San Marcial Street and Delta Drive.

The first commission to survey the international boundary between the United States and Mexico was established in 1849. The survey disclosed that 1,248 miles of the border was formed by the Rio Grande River and an additional 23 miles was defined by the Colorado River. These river boundaries created difficulties because they tended to change courses with each flood season. In an 1884 treaty, both nations agreed to the principle that if a river changed course by a slow process of erosion, then the boundary moved with the deepest channel. Conversely, if the river changed its course suddenly, then the boundary remained in the old bed.

The Chamizal problem developed when changes in the river channel in the area between El Paso and Juarez could not definitely be ascribed to either process. Because a detached part of Mexico was projecting into El Paso, development in both cities became difficult. In 1963, the two sides agreed to the construction of a concrete channel through the disputed area.

The park, established on a portion of the land acquired in the agreement, is open daily from 10:00 A.M. until 5:00 P.M. (11:00 P.M. on days of scheduled activities). There is a museum that has exhibits and shows a film to help visitors understand the history of this disputed area. Special programs take place throughout the year, with a Border Folk Festival scheduled during the first weekend of each October. The Republic of Mexico has established a 700-acre park directly across the

Rio Grande River. This park contains gardens, unique architectural structures, and statuary.

Facilities: No food or lodging is available at the memorial, but both are nearby.
Camping: No camping is permitted. Private campgrounds are near the park.
Fishing: No fishing is available.

FORT DAVIS NATIONAL HISTORIC SITE
P.O. Box 1456
Fort Davis, TX 79734
(915) 426–3225

Fort Davis, which contains 460 acres, was authorized in 1961 to preserve the site of an important fort of the late 1800s whose remains are more extensive and impressive than any other of that period in the southwest. The site is located in western Texas on the northern edge of the town of Fort Davis. It is reached from Interstate 10 via Texas Highways 17 and 118 or from U.S. 90 via Texas Highways 505, 166, and 17.

Fort Davis, named in honor of Secretary of War Jefferson Davis, was constructed in the mid-1850s to protect travelers and settlers in the West Texas region. The original fort consisted of pine structures. By 1856, six stone barracks had been built to house enlisted men. During this period, the soldiers of Fort Davis spent most of their time escorting mail and freight trains and patrolling this sector of the Southwest.

With the beginning of the Civil War, Union troops abandoned the fort, which then became occupied by Confederate forces for nearly a year. After Fort Davis was in turn abandoned by the Southern troops, it was wrecked by Apaches and lay deserted for five years. In 1867, federal troops returned to rebuild the fort, and by the 1880s more than fifty stone and adobe structures housed both companies of cavalry and infantry. As the Indian menace to West Texas declined, the fort became an unnecessary expense and was finally abandoned in 1891.

The visitor center, open daily from 8:00 A.M. until 5:00 P.M., offers a slide show and audio programs. Of the more than fifty buildings that the second fort comprised, visitors may view fifteen restored residences on officers' row, two sets of troop barracks, warehouses, and the hospital. Stone foundations mark the sites of other buildings. A number of foundations to buildings of the original fort have been uncovered.

Park personnel dressed in 1880 period dress present living-history interpretations during June, July, and August in the commanding officer's quarters, an officers' kitchen, servants' quarters, the commissary, and an enlisted men's barracks.

Facilities: Food and lodging are not available at the site but can be found in the town of Fort Davis. Water and restrooms are located in the visitor center. A picnic area is located on the grounds. Many of the buildings are equipped with ramps for wheelchair visitors.
Camping: No camping is permitted in the park. Camping facilities are available in Davis Mountains State Park, 4 miles to the north.
Fishing: No fishing is available at the park.

GUADALUPE MOUNTAINS NATIONAL PARK
HC 60, Box 400
Salt Flat, TX 79847
(915) 828–3251

Guadalupe Mountains National Park, established in 1972, contains 76,293 acres of mountain landscape, including the most extensive exposed fossil reef on earth. The park is located in western Texas, 55 miles southwest of Carlsbad, New Mexico, and 110 miles east of El Paso via U.S. 62/180.

The Guadalupe Mountains began to form nearly 250 million years ago, when this region was covered by a great inland sea. Near the shoreline, a reef grew from lime-secreting organisms and precipitates from the water. At the end of the Permian period the reef died, and layers of sediment buried the entire area. Much later, a general uplifting raised the region several thousand feet and allowed the shaping of today's mountain range through erosion by wind and water. Today, only a small portion of the 350-mile horseshoe-shaped reef is not buried beneath the ground. The most outstanding stretch is that which is included in this park.

A variety of people have passed through and lived in this arid region. Spanish conquistadors passed the range on their explorations north from Mexico; later, military surveyors rode just south of El Capitan. In the mid-1850s, the Butterfield Overland Mail Line carried mail and passengers through Guadalupe Pass. Pine Springs ("The Pinery") was a regular stop for changing horses.

The area is entered via U.S. 62/180, which connects Carlsbad and El Paso. A visitor center at Pine Springs is open daily from 8:00 A.M. to

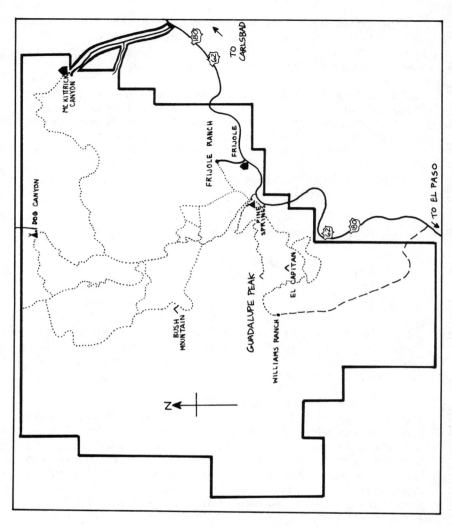

Guadalupe Mountains National Park

4:30 p.m. in winter and 7:00 a.m. to 6:00 p.m. in summer. Here visitors will find exhibits, literature, and maps. One and one-half miles north of the Pine Springs Visitor Center, Frijole Historic Site has the most complete and substantial buildings of early ranching in the region. Just northeast of the Pine Springs Visitor Center are the ruins of a stagecoach station built on the Butterfield Stage Line in 1858. In the southern end of the park, Williams Ranch Historic Site is at the end of an 8-mile four-wheel-drive road.

The primary activity in the park is hiking over the 80 miles of trails. Overnight permits and information are available at the Frijole Visitor Center.

Facilities: Food and lodging are not available in the park. Water and restrooms are provided at the visitor centers and campground.
Camping: Pine Springs Canyon Campground (twenty tent spaces, nineteen recreational-vehicle spaces, two group sites, no hookups), one-eighth mile northwest of the Pine Springs Visitor Center, is open all year and provides tables, water, and flush toilets. Dog Canyon Campground (twenty-three spaces) is in the Dog Canyon area in the northern part of the park. This campground has tables, grills, drinking water, flush toilets, and is reached via New Mexico Highway 137, north of Carlsbad. Back-country campsites are available at various locations throughout the park.
Fishing: No fishing is available at the park.

LAKE MEREDITH NATIONAL RECREATION AREA
P.O. Box 1438
Fritch, TX 79036
(806) 857–3151

Lake Meredith National Recreation Area (formerly Sanford Recreation Area) has been administered under a cooperative agreement with the Bureau of Reclamation since 1965. The area covers nearly 45,000 acres. The park is a popular spot for all types of water activities. It is located in the Texas Panhandle, 33 miles northeast of Amarillo via State Highway 136.

Lake Meredith is an oasis located on the high, flat, and dry plains area of North Texas. Formed by Sanford Dam on the Canadian River, the resulting body of water is used by eleven cities as a municipal water supply. As the lake continues to rise to its planned level, the 200-foot canyon walls with white limestone caps and red-brown coves present

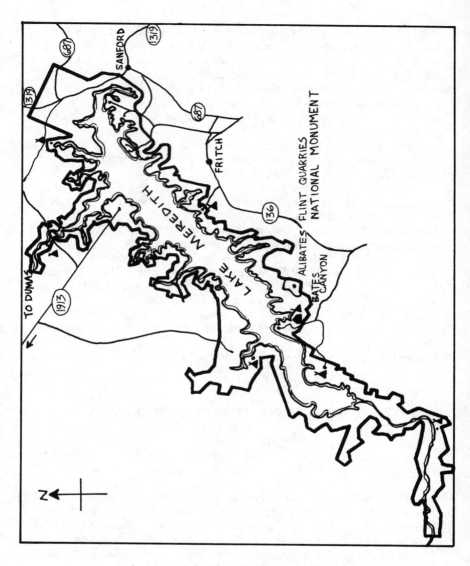

Lake Meredith National Recreation Area

an attractive contrast to the blue waters. A variety of wildlife inhabits the area, including bald eagles, golden eagles, hawks, and pronghorn antelope.

Typical activities at Lake Meredith National Recreation Area include water-skiing, sailing, swimming, scuba-diving, fishing, and hunting. Boat-launching ramps are located at Plum Creek, Harbor Bay, Blue West, Sanford-Yake, Cedar Canyon, Fritch Fortress, and Bates Canyon. A marina is at Sanford-Yake. Off-road vehicle trails are available at Rosita and Blue Creek Bridge. The only supervised swimming area is at Spring Canyon, below Sanford Dam (summer only).

Facilities: At Sanford-Yake, a concessioner provides a snack bar, marina and related services, and an enclosed fish house for year-round fishing. Lodging and food are available in nearby towns. Drinking water and restrooms are located at Fritch Fortress and Sanford-Yake. Chemical toilets are provided in most of the other areas.

Camping: Campgrounds with tables, grills, water, and flush toilets are located at Sanford-Yake (fifty-three spaces, dump station) and Fritch Fortress (ten spaces). Campgrounds with chemical toilets but no water are at Blue West (forty spaces), McBride Canyon (ten spaces), Plum Creek (fifteen spaces), and Spring Canyon (six spaces). These sites are open year round. No camping is permitted at the launching areas or the parking lots.

Fishing: The lake provides opportunities to fish for largemouth, smallmouth, and white bass, four species of catfish, crappie, sunfish, carp, and the only naturally reproducing walleye in Texas. A Texas license is required.

LYNDON B. JOHNSON NATIONAL HISTORICAL PARK
P.O. Box 329
Johnson City, TX 78636
(512) 868–7128

Lyndon B. Johnson National Historical Park, which comprises 235 acres, was authorized in 1969 to preserve the birthplace, boyhood home, and ranch of the thirty-sixth president of the United States. Johnson's grandparents' ranch is also included in the park. The site is made up of two areas. One section is in Johnson City, Texas, 45 miles west of Austin via U.S. 290. The park's main section is 14 miles west of Johnson City, on the same highway.

Lyndon Baines Johnson was born and raised in the Hill Country of Texas. After serving as U.S. congressman from 1937 to 1948, U.S. senator from 1948 to 1960, vice-president from 1960 to 1963, and U.S. president from 1963 to 1968, Johnson returned to Texas and lived there from 1969 until his death in 1973. Lyndon Johnson is buried in the family cemetery near his birthplace on the Pedernales River.

The historical park is a cooperative effort between the state and federal governments. The area south of the Pedernales River is operated by the Texas Parks and Wildlife Department, and north of the river, where the Johnson home is located, the National Park Service manages the area.

When visiting the LBJ Ranch area of the park, first go to the LBJ State Park visitor center, located just north of U.S. 290. Along with exhibits concerning the president's life, scheduled shuttle buses leave here for a ranch tour. Included on this National Park Service tour are the one-room school attended by LBJ, his birthplace, the family cemetery, and views of the ranch and ranch house. The tour is well worth the time and allows one to get a feel for the man and the land. The state park operates the Sauer-Beckman living historical farm and provides facilities for outdoor recreation, including a swimming pool.

The second area of the national park in Johnson City includes a visitor center, LBJ's boyhood home, and the early Johnson settlement. Visitors may walk from the boyhood home to the settlement. This area contains a complex of restored historic structures tracing the agricultural evolution of the Hill Country. An exhibit center contains pictures and artifacts.

Facilities: No food or lodging is available in either section of the park. Both can be found nearby. Drinking water and restrooms are provided in both visitor centers.

Camping: No camping is permitted in the park. Pedernales Falls State Park provides camping facilities east of Johnson City. Lady Bird Johnson Park in the town of Fredericksburg has an attractive campground.

Fishing: Fishing is permitted in the Pedernales River with a Texas license.

PADRE ISLAND NATIONAL SEASHORE
9405 South Padre Island Drive
Corpus Christi, TX 78418
(512) 937–2621

*Padre Island National Seashore, established in 1962, contains
134,000 acres of wide sand beaches on a grass-covered barrier
island that stretches for 110 miles. The park is located along the
Gulf Coast in southern Texas. It is accessible via State Highway
358 and Park Road 22 from Corpus Christi or by ferry to Port
Aransas.*

Padre Island has been built by a combination of wave action and
winds off the Gulf of Mexico. This long barrier island, from a few
hundred yards to 3 miles in width, is continually changing as grassy
interior sections are gradually covered by windblown sand. In some
areas the sands have become stabilized by grasses and shrubs that
have binding long roots. Between the island and the mainland lies
Laguna Madre, a shallow body of water with a maximum width of 10
miles.

Life on the island is difficult for plant life, which must constantly
battle the sand and wind to gain a foothold. Mammals living here
include coyotes, gophers, and jack rabbits. There are also more than
350 species of birds that are year-round residents or seasonal visitors
passing through on their migration routes. Reptiles that may be seen in
the area include garter snakes, bull snakes, and lizards.

Visitor information is available at park headquarters in Corpus
Christi, at Malaquite Visitor Center, and at the ranger station. A short
self-guiding nature trail begins near the entrance station. Nearly all of
the park is open to hikers and four-wheel-drive vehicles. Conventional
cars may be driven 14 miles south of the park's northern boundary.
Even four-wheel-drive vehicles cannot be driven the entire length of
the island because of the Mansfield Channel. The gradual slope and
warm water along the Gulf beach make swimming a popular activity.
During the summer months, lifeguards are on duty at Malaquite Beach.

Facilities: A snack bar, free showers, and rental equipment for beach
use are available at Malaquite Beach during summer months. Motels
and restaurants are at both ends of the island and in Corpus Christi and
Port Isabel. Boating supplies and launching ramps are along the John
F. Kennedy Memorial Causeway.

Camping: Malaquite Beach Campground (forty-two spaces) provides
tables, water, flush toilets, and a dump station. Primitive camping

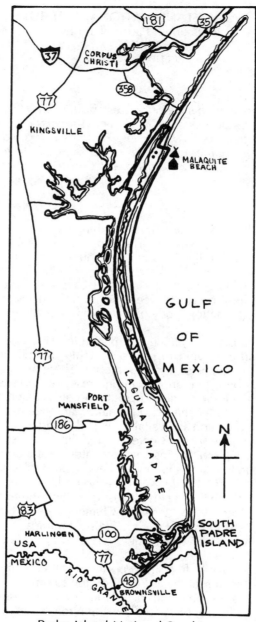

Padre Island National Seashore

is permitted on the beaches. Public campgrounds with hook-ups are in Nueces County Park north of the seashore boundary and in Cameron County Park at the south end of the island near Port Isabel. **Fishing:** Fishing is available year round in Laguna Madre and the Gulf. Some fish, with the respective best seasons, that may be caught are pompano (April and October), redfish (fall), drum (December to April), red snapper (October to March), and tarpon (October and November). Sharks, rays, and sawfish are occasionally caught in the surf. A Texas license is required, as well as a saltwater stamp.

SAN ANTONIO MISSIONS NATIONAL HISTORICAL PARK
2202 Roosevelt Avenue
San Antonio, TX 78210
(512) 229–5701

San Antonio Missions National Historical Park comprises 835 acres and was authorized in 1978 to commemorate four Spanish frontier missions that were part of a colonization system stretching across the Spanish Southwest in the eighteenth century. The park also includes a historic dam and aqueduct. The missions are in south San Antonio along the San Antonio River.

To extend the Spanish culture and propagate the Catholic faith, in the seventeenth, eighteenth, and nineteenth centuries Spain introduced missions from California to Florida. Included in this expansion was a chain of missions established in the eighteenth century along the San Antonio River. These missions provided a link between the missions of East Texas and other Franciscan missions in Mexico. The missions served primarily as religious centers and training grounds for Indians to learn the Spanish culture. Indians who lived at the missions came from a number of hunting and gathering bands. These missions flourished in the mid-1700s, but Indian hostilities and a lack of military support eventually sapped the missions' ability to carry out their tasks. In 1824, Texas missions had their lands distributed among the mission Indians and the churches transferred to the secular clergy.

The historical park includes four missions along the San Antonio River, south of the city of San Antonio. Except for Mission Espada, which lies just south of Interstate 410, the missions are located between city center and Interstate 410, which loops San Antonio. A marked driving trail to all of the areas begins in downtown San Antonio at Mission San Antonio de Valero ("the Alamo"). Public buses provide service near Mission Concepcion and Mission San Jose. The

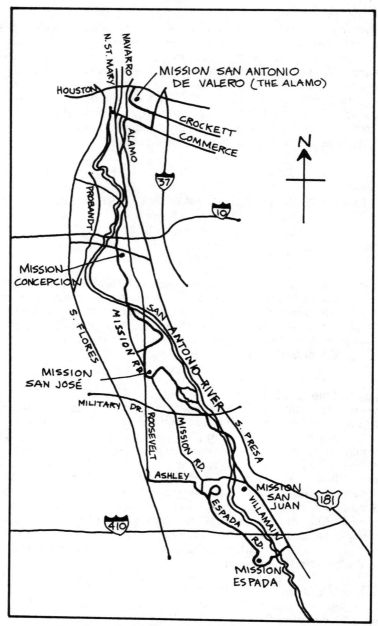

San Antonio Missions National Historical Park

missions are closed on Christmas and New Year's Day. A wheelchair is available at each mission, but mobility-impaired visitors may have some difficulty with accessibility at Mission San Juan and Mission Espada.

North of Mission Espada is an acequia system that provided irrigation water to crops that were grown at the mission. The system consists of a dam, gravity-flow ditches, and one of the oldest arched Spanish aqueducts in the United States. The system continues to provide water to nearby farms.

Facilities: Restaurants, lodging, and picnic facilities are near the historical park. Restrooms and drinking water are in the missions.
Camping: No camping is available in the park, although commercial camping facilities are nearby.
Fishing: No fishing is available in the park.

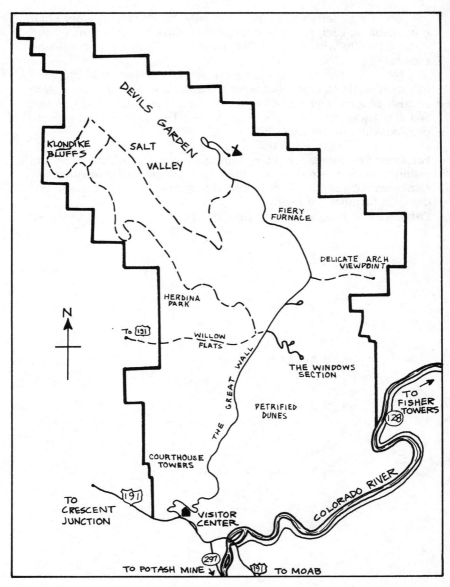

Arches National Park

Utah

ARCHES NATIONAL PARK
P.O. Box 907
Moab, UT 84532
(801) 259–8161

Arches National Park was established as a national monument in 1929, and now as a park preserves 73,000 acres encompassing the country's largest collection of brilliantly colored natural stone arches, spires, windows, and pinnacles. The park is in southeast Utah on U.S. 191, 5 miles northwest of Moab or 28 miles southeast of Interstate 70.

The rock that now presents such beautiful scenery was originally deposited as sand nearly 150 million years ago. This 300-foot layer was eventually formed into rock after being buried by even more sand. Later, the hardened layers of rock were uplifted and cracked. The top sand and stone eroded away and Entrada sandstone began to form into shapes that can be seen today. Carved out of red rock by years of rain, frost, running water, and wind, the resulting shapes resemble nearly any fantasy a visitor can imagine. In some areas the stone is softer and the weathering is more rapid. This results in shallow canyons and fins. Arches is particularly spectacular after a summer shower, when streams turn into waterfalls.

The visitor center, located at the main entrance in the southern end of the park, is a recommended stop before continuing on. The visitor center provides a museum and slide program. In addition, visitors may obtain information on activities such as guided walks, sightseeing, and hiking. A road guide is available.

Twenty-one miles of paved roads permit visitors to see much of Arches by car. A paved road begins at the visitor center and ends in the north part of the park. An eight-mile dirt road then continues to Klondike Bluffs in the northwest corner. Klondike Bluffs offers a moderate half-day hike into a remote backcountry area of fins, which contains the massive Tower Arch. Paved roads run to the Windows Section in the east-central part of the park and to Panorama Point. The Windows Section is an amazing spectacle of arches, offering close-up views from the road and easy half-mile round trip walks for closer viewing. A few unimproved roads for four-wheel drive vehicles are located throughout the park.

Outside the park, State Highway 128, between the park entrance and Moab, takes the motorist in a northeasterly direction along the Colorado River toward Interstate 70. If there is time, the drive is worthwhile and presents some of the most beautiful scenery found anywhere in the United States.

Trails for hiking leave from various points along the main road. The most popular for visitors with only a short time to spare is the leisurely one-mile walk (each way) through Park Avenue. This worthwhile hike goes through a narrow corridor surrounded by high red-rock walls. Parking lots are located at each end of the trail. The Devils Garden Trail provides access to Landscape Arch, one of the longest natural arches in the world. This trail is a well-maintained gravel path for one mile and then becomes primitive for a moderate five-mile round trip hike through a fin canyon. Hikers should be aware that daytime temperatures during the summer may reach over 100 degrees F. High temperatures and low humidity make it necessary for hikers to carry a minimum of one gallon of water per person for the full hike.

Perhaps the single most scenic and best-known feature of Arches National Park is Delicate Arch. This isolated formation is located amid bowls and domes. Also within view are the canyon walls of the Colorado River and the peaks of the La Sal Mountains. Delicate Arch is reached by means of a 1.8-mile graded road and a 1.5-mile foot trail. A drive to Delicate Arch Viewpoint provides a look across a canyon for a distant view of the arch.

Naturalist-guided walks are made regularly through the Fiery Furnace area (two hours, two miles) during summer months when nightly campfire programs are also presented. The Fiery Furnace walk takes hikers through a labyrinth of red-rock fins leading deep into the Furnace where a surprise arch may wait. On these walks the park naturalists share their knowledge of the wildlife and natural features that make Arches a unique national park. Visitors should also be prepared with good walking shoes, a hat, and water. Reservations are now required for joining the guided walks and can be made at the visitor center.

Facilities: No food service or lodging is available within the park. Grocery stores, restaurants, service stations, and motels are a few miles south of the park in Moab. Modern restrooms and drinking water are available at both the visitor center (year round) and the campground (mid-March through October).

Camping: A single improved campground (fifty-three spaces) is located 18 miles north of the park entrance in the Devils Garden area. Tables, grills, and flush toilets (no dump station) are available. Both short and longer hiking trails originate at the campground.

Fishing: No fishing is available within Arches National Park.

BRYCE CANYON NATIONAL PARK
Bryce Canyon, UT 84717
(801) 834–5322

Bryce Canyon contains 36,010 acres and was authorized as a national monument in 1923 and changed to national park in 1928. Bryce contains numerous alcoves cut into cliffs along the eastern edge of the Paunsaugunt Plateau. Bordering this winding cliff line is a badlands of vivid colors and fragile forms. The park is located in southwestern Utah and is most easily reached via U.S. 89. 7 miles south of Panguitch turn east on Utah 12 for 17 miles to the park entrance.

Bryce Canyon is a high section of the Colorado Plateau containing rock strata from the most recent chapter of geologic history. Formed from compacted sediments, this area caps a sequence of rock layers— the most ancient of which are seen in the Grand Canyon. The massive sandstone boulders that represent the middle history may be seen in nearby Zion National Park. At Bryce these rock formations remain buried.

The cliffs in the park are the result of an accumulation of sand, silt, and lime washed into inland lakes and compacted into layers of rock. Later, the lands were uplifted to mountainous heights and persistent erosion widened gaps and fractures. The resulting color and shapes of the rock formations are Bryce's most outstanding sights.

A visitor center near the entrance provides a slide program and exhibits to help explain the history and geology of the area. A schedule of the park's various programs is posted here. Tickets for a concessioner-operated tour to various points in the park can be purchased at the lodge.

For those with a limited amount of time, a short tour presenting four of the best viewpoints may be seen within one hour. Sunset Point, Inspiration Point, Bryce Point, and Paria View form a scenic concentration of sculptured red rocks. Trailers should be unhooked and

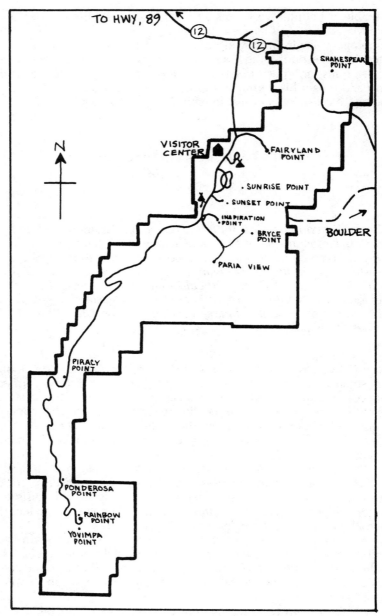

Bryce Canyon National Park

parked at the visitor center parking lot or at Sunset Point prior to the tour.

A variety of hiking trails is available for visitors. These include the Navajo Loop Trail (1.5 miles, one and a half hours) and the Navajo and Peekaboo Loops combined (5.5 miles, four to five hours) starting at Sunset Point, the Queens Garden Trail (1½ miles, one and a half hours) beginning at Sunrise Point, Tower Bridge Trail (3 miles, three hours) starting north of Sunrise Point, and the Fairyland Loop Trail (8 miles, four to five hours) beginning at Fairyland or north of Sunrise Point. For the hardy, the Under-the-Rim Trail extends from Bryce Point to Rainbow Point (22 miles). During the summer, ranger-guided walks are given daily on the Navajo or Queen's trails and periodically at other points in the park. Morning and afternoon horseback trips are available from a concessioner and begin at the corral near the lodge. Other activities include a geology talk at Sunset Point and a rim walk near the lodge.

Facilities: The park is open year round. Bryce Canyon Lodge, near the rim of Bryce amphitheater, has sleeping accommodations and is open from late April through mid-October. The lodge has a dining room and gift shop. For information or reservations write TW Services, Inc., P.O. Box 400, Cedar City, UT 84721 (801–586–7686, individuals; 801–586–7624, groups). A store near the Sunrise Point parking area provides groceries, pay showers, and a laundromat. A nearby service station is open year round. The nearest hospital is located at Panguitch, 26 miles away.

Camping: North Campground (109 spaces) is immediately east of the visitor center, and Sunset Campground (109 spaces, one group camp) is 2 miles south. Both provide tables, grills, and flush toilets. The North Campground has a dump station, is closer to the park's developed facilities, and generally fills first.

Fishing: No fishing is available in Bryce Canyon National Park. Trout fishing can be found 22 miles north of the park entrance at Pine Lake and 12 miles west at Tropic Reservoir. The trout are larger and more difficult to catch in Pine Lake.

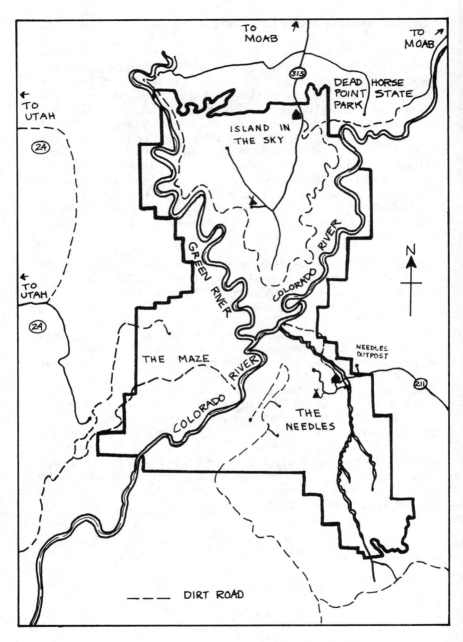

Canyonlands National Park

CANYONLANDS NATIONAL PARK
125 West Second, South
Moab, UT 84532
(801) 259–7164

Canyonlands National Park contains 338,000 acres and was established in 1964 to protect a geological wonderland of rocks, spires, and mesas. The park is located in east-central Utah and is reached via Utah 191 and its paved extensions. Park headquarters is located in Moab.

Canyonlands is an outstanding and unique national park. Its incredible sandstone landscape has been shaped over a period of 300 million years by oceans, winds, and floods. A portion of the park is built on a 1 mile-thick layer of rock and sand covering 3,000 feet of pure salt. The salt was left after the outlet of an inland salt sea was blocked by mountains, and evaporation concentrated the brine into layers of salt. As the salt dissolved and was carried away by underground water, the surface sandstone slowly settled and formed long, narrow, straight canyons (the Needles district).

One of the many spectacular sights in the park is the merging of the Colorado and Green rivers at the confluence. Commercially operated float trips, led by licensed guides, are available down either river. Private groups with proper equipment and experience may attempt the trip upon obtaining a permit from the superintendent.

The Needles district in the southern portion of the park contains a forest of rock spires. Within the district, Salt Creek and Horse Canyon expose graceful walls and glimpses of past Indian history in the form of rock art and ruins. Visitors will travel thirty-five miles through magnificent canyon country to reach this area. All passenger cars must stop at Elephant Hill, a 40-percent grade traversed only by four-wheel-drive vehicles. Tours can be obtained at nearby towns, or jeeps may be rented immediately outside the park at Needles Outpost. Be sure to stop at Newspaper Rock State Historical Monument when entering this area on Highway 211.

The Maze district, lying west of the Green and lower Colorado rivers, is the least accessible portion of the park. Two-wheel-drive vehicles can reach the ranger station at Hans Flat most of the time, but the backcountry must be approached by four-wheel-drive vehicles. The Maze itself is accessible only by foot. This area contains sheer-walled canyons that twist and wind in a wild manner. Some outstanding pictograph panels are found here.

In the north district of the park, Island in the Sky overlooks the remarkable array of landforms to the south that encompass the

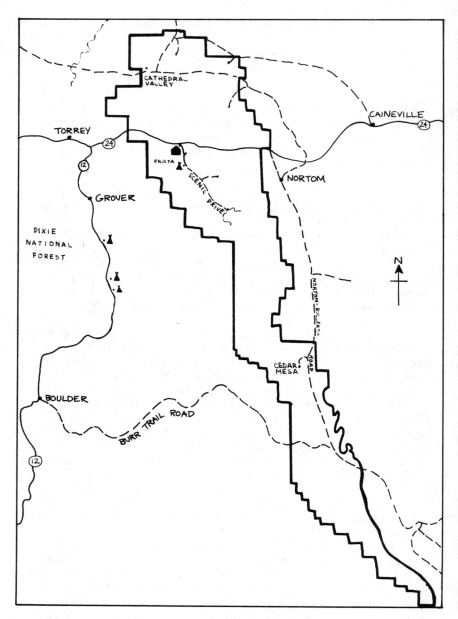

Capitol Reef National Park

forty-mile wide erosional basin of the Green and Colorado rivers. A new paved road makes this area completely accessible year round. From overlooks, visitors can view White Rim, 1,000 feet below, and catch glimpses of the Colorado and Green rivers 1,000 feet below White Rim. The White Rim Trail offers more than one hundred miles of four-wheel-drive travel to the backcountry. Shafer Trail, for which a four-wheel-drive vehicle is advised, is a thrilling route involving some "testy" driving.

Facilities: No overnight accommodations or food services are available within the park. Monticello, Moab, and Hanksville are the nearest towns providing a full range of services. Needles Outpost, near the Needles entrance, offers fuel, snacks, limited supplies, and scenic flights over the park. Pit toilets (but no modern restrooms) are located in the park.
Camping: Squaw Flat Campground (twenty-six spaces, three group sites) near the main entrance provides tables, grills, pit toilets, and treated trucked-in water. Primitive campsites without water are located in four-wheel-drive areas.
Fishing: Ninety miles of the Colorado and Green rivers flow through the park and contain channel catfish and other sport fishes. The waters are generally inaccessible except by boat.

CAPITOL REEF NATIONAL PARK
Torrey, UT 84775
(801) 425–3871

Capitol Reef National Park contains 240,000 acres and was established to protect an area where narrow high-walled gorges cut through a 75-mile uplift of sandstone cliffs with highly colored sedimentary formations. Capitol Reef is relatively lightly used and, for most travelers, remains one of the undiscovered treasures of the National Park System. The park is located in south-central Utah, with the visitor center 37 miles west of Hanksville on Utah 24.

The geology of this high-desert land is derived from thousands of centuries of wind and water erosion. Millions of years ago this part of the country was covered by a shallow sea. As the sea gradually retreated the land changed to a flood plain and then a desert. The alternation between shallow sea and desert occurred many times during ensuing centuries. Water and wind-borne sediments deposited during these periods slowly hardened into rock layers of varying color, composition, and thickness. Immense geological forces next buckled and tilted the rocks into an upwarp called the Waterpocket Fold, the geologic structure that is Capitol Reef National Park. Erosional forces have subsequently dissected and sculptured the Fold and revealed its inner structure. Steeply pitching rock layers plunge into or spring out of the ground across the breadth of the Fold. The normally horizontal geologic column has been tipped nearly on end, allowing park visitors to literally drive through 200 million years of geologic history.

Perhaps the biggest surprise a visitor will encounter after driving for hundreds of miles in an area devoid of most forms of plant life is the oasis nature of the park's headquarters area. The sagebrush plains and desert stand in stark contrast to the lush vegetation made possible by irrigation from the Fremont River and Sulphur Creek. Away from the rivers and other sparse water areas, the park's land returns to its true desert state.

Capitol Reef National Park was named, in part, because of the resemblance of its rounded sandstone Capitol Dome to the Capitol Building in Washington. The second half of the name originates from a word used by miners to describe a natural rock barrier to travel. The area was home for Indians and later for Mormon settlers. The first permanent settlement here occurred in Fruita in 1880. Orchards surrounding this small community at one time supported up to ten families.

Most of the activity at Capitol Reef is located along or near Highway 24, which cuts through the park in an east-west direction. The visitor center, next to the highway on the south side, contains a slide program and exhibits to help interpret the area. Just east of here, the old Fruita schoolhouse has been restored and is open to the public on a limited basis. Ancient Fremont Indian petroglyphs can be found close by the school and also about ten miles south of the visitor center in Capitol Gorge. Ranger-guided hikes and interpretive programs take place daily during spring, summer, and fall. These generally begin near the campground. Visitors may pick fruit from orchards maintained by the Park Service. Depending upon the season, cherries, apricots, apples, pears, and peaches are available. A paved ten-mile scenic drive heads south from the visitor center. A guidebook is provided at the visitor center.

Facilities: No food or lodging is available in the park. Both may be found in the town of Torrey, eleven miles west of the visitor center on Utah 24. A beautiful shaded picnic area with picnic tables and drinking water (and cherry trees) is located just north of the campground. Modern restroom facilities are available at the visitor center, the campground, and the picnic area.

Camping: The park's single developed campground (seventy-one spaces) is one and a half miles south of the visitor center. The campground is surrounded by fruit trees and backs up to the Fremont River. Staying there is one of life's great pleasures. The campsites generally fill early on holidays and weekends. Primitive campgrounds (no water) are approximately twenty-three-miles south of the park's east entrance on the dirt Notom-Bullfrog Road and twenty-five miles north on the Hartnet Road.

Fishing: No fishing is available at Capitol Reef National Park.

CEDAR BREAKS NATIONAL MONUMENT
P.O. Box 749
Cedar City, UT 84720
(801) 586–9451

Cedar Breaks is a 6,155-acre monument that was established in 1933 to preserve a huge multicolored amphitheater that has eroded into the 2,000-foot thick Pink Cliffs. The park is located in southwestern Utah and can be reached via Utah 14, 27 miles from U.S. 89 at Long Valley Junction, and 23 miles from Interstate 15 at Cedar City. It can also be reached from the north via Utah 143 and Parowan (22 miles) or from U.S. 89 at Panguitch via Utah 143 (36 miles). Zion National Park and Bryce Canyon National Park are 73 and 65 miles away, respectively.

The rock layers that form the amphitheater walls at Cedar Breaks were deposited nearly 55 million years ago as a limy ooze in shallow freshwater lakes. Later, as the area was uplifted from near sea level to over 10,000 feet, the westward-facing limestone wall was exposed to the elements. The softer parts of the limestone have been eroded by centuries of rain, wind, snow, and ice, leaving spires and ridges of spectacular shapes. The period of uplifting was accompanied by volcanic eruptions, and lava may be seen along the road between Cedar Breaks and U.S. 89. The colors of the breaks stem from oxidation of impurities (mainly iron and manganese) contained in the white limestone.

Wildlife in the monument includes mule deer, marmots, pikas, red squirrels, and chipmunks. Birds include the Clark's nutcracker, violet-green swallow, white-throated swift, blue grouse, and golden eagle. Wildflowers begin blooming as the snow melts and the blooms

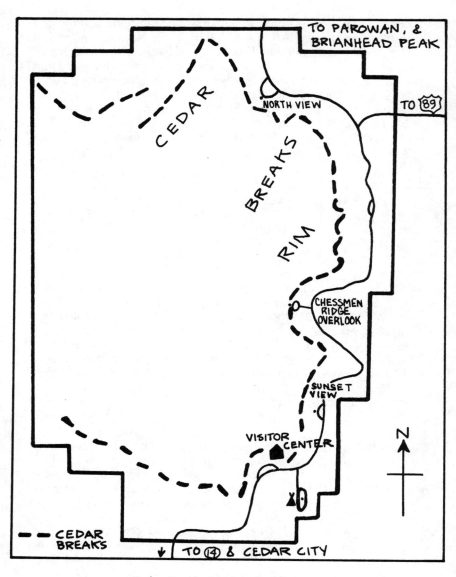

TO PAROWAN, &
BRIANHEAD PEAK

TO 89

CEDAR

NORTH VIEW

BREAKS

RIM

CHESSMEN
RIDGE
OVERLOOK

SUNSET
VIEW

VISITOR CENTER

N

CEDAR
BREAKS

TO ⑭ & CEDAR CITY

Cedar Breaks National Monument

reach a peak during late July. Bristlecone pines up to 1,650 years old grow within the monument.

Depending upon the weather, the season at Cedar Breaks extends from early June to late October. The visitor center, one mile inside the south entrance, contains exhibits on geology and life within the park. The visitor center is open from early June through September and into October depending on the weather. Much of the monument may be seen from a 5-mile paved road running north and south along Cedar Breaks Rim. Viewpoints with parking areas are located along the road. A number of trails are scattered along 6-mile Rim Drive. Wasatch Ramparts Trail (two miles) begins near the visitor center and leads through forests and meadows to a stand of bristlecone pine on Spectra Point (one mile from the visitor center). Alpine Pond Trail, a self-guided nature trail, leads to an area containing a pond and many wildflowers. Bristlecone Pine Trail is a short walk at Chessmen Ridge Overlook that takes visitors to a stand of bristlecone and limber pine on the rim. Brianhead Peak, two and a half miles north of the north entrance in Dixie National Forest, offers an impressive view of the area. Interpretive presentations are offered daily from late June to Labor Day.

Facilities: No food service or overnight lodging is available in the park, but both are in Cedar City (23 miles southwest), Parowan (19 miles north), and Brian Head (8 miles north). Drinking water and flush toilets are available at the visitor center and the campground.

Camping: Point Supreme Campground (thirty spaces) provides tables, grills, water, and flush toilets. The campground is usually open from June 15 to September 15. A number of Forest Service campgrounds are located southeast of Cedar City along Utah Highway 14. One Forest Service campground is four miles south of Parowan off Highway 143.

Fishing: Fishing is permitted at Alpine Pond with a valid Utah fishing license.

GOLDEN SPIKE NATIONAL HISTORIC SITE
P.O. Box W
Brigham City, UT 84302
(801) 471–2209

Golden Spike National Historic Site contains 2,200 acres and was authorized by Congress in 1965 to commemorate the Union Pacific and Central Pacific railroads joining on May 10, 1869, to form the first transcontinental railroad. The historic site is located 84 miles northwest of Salt Lake City via Brigham City. To reach

Golden Spike, drive 23 miles west from Brigham City to the Promontory Junction on Utah 83. Turn left and go 2 miles to the next junction. At this last junction turn right and drive 6 miles.

Although many individuals saw the benefits of a railroad from the Atlantic to the Pacific soon after the development of the steam locomotive, years of debate over the amount of federal financing and the location of an eastern terminus kept the project from commencing. Finally, in 1862, a bill was signed by President Lincoln under which the Union Pacific was to build from Omaha westward and the Central Pacific eastward from Sacramento. The railroads were given a 400-foot right-of-way through the public domain, twenty sections of land for each mile of completed track, and the loan of government bonds to use as collateral for issuing their own bonds.

The Central Pacific broke ground in January 1863 with a serious manpower shortage that was resolved by hiring imported Chinese laborers. The Union Pacific began in Omaha in December 1863 with Civil War veterans and European immigrants as laborers. Because the intent of Congress was that the two railroads were to build until they met, the junction point was not spelled out and both roads built as fast as possible. This resulted in considerable duplication once the roads began approaching each other and it was decided in the spring of 1869 that Ogden, Utah, would be the final junction point. Although the actual joining would be at Promontory Summit, the Central Pacific would buy the section of track from there to Ogden. On May 10, 1869, the final section of track was laid and precious-metal spikes from California, Nevada, and Arizona were symbolically driven with a silver-plated spike maul.

By 1904, a shorter route was completed across Great Salt Lake by Southern Pacific (which had absorbed Central Pacific) and little traffic was routed through Promontory. In 1942, the rails were pulled and contributed as scrap to the war effort.

A visitor center at the park offers exhibits, slide presentations, and films. Nearly two miles of track have been relaid on the original roadbed where the rails were joined in 1869. Two operating replica steam locomotives are on site.

Facilities: No overnight accommodations or food services are available in the park, but both are found in Brigham City and Tremonton. Water and modern restrooms are located in the visitor center.
Camping: No camping is permitted at the site. Hyrum Lake State Park (thirty-five spaces with flush toilets) is located approximately fourteen miles northeast of Brigham City on U.S highways 89 and 91. U.S. Forest Service Box Elder campground (pit toilets) is one mile east of

Brigham City on U.S. 89. Numerous commercial campgrounds are available in Brigham City.

Fishing: No fishing is available at Golden Spike.

NATURAL BRIDGES NATIONAL MONUMENT
Box 1 Natural Bridges
Lake Powell, UT 84533
(801) 259–5174

Natural Bridges National Monument contains approximately 7,800 acres. It was established in 1908 to protect three natural bridges carved from sandstone. The monument is in the southeastern corner of Utah, approximately 5 miles off State Highway 95. Natural Bridges is approached from the east via Highway 95 from Blanding or from the south via Mexican Hat and Highway 261 or from the west via Highway 95 from Hanksville and Hite Crossing.

The making of a natural bridge requires a proper stone with joints or fractures and a desert-type stream with a head of water and sand. In the United States such conditions are most favorable in the Four Corners region of the Southwest. As streams gradually entrench themselves in deep meandering channels and canyons, they constantly attempt to straighten their courses. During heavy rainstorms, the sand-filled waters batter against the walls in the streambeds. In several places the rock around which a stream winds is so thin that over many centuries a hole is gradually bored through. The result is a natural bridge.

Three natural bridges are highlighted in the monument. Sipapu Bridge (220 feet high, 268-foot span, 31-foot width, 53-foot thickness) has a graceful and symmetrical span with its abutments now far enough from the streambed that the river has little or no cutting effect. Kachina Bridge (210 feet high, 204-foot span, 44-foot width, 93-foot thickness) is the youngest of the three. Its bulk is still being eroded by flood waters in White Canyon. Numerous prehistoric pictographs may be seen on one of its abutments. Owachomo Bridge (106 feet high, 180-foot span, 27-foot width, 9-foot thickness) is the oldest bridge and is no longer eroded by a stream.

A visitor center is located just inside the monument's boundary. A ranger is on duty to answer questions, and a slide program is presented upon request. Ranger talks are given at the campground during the

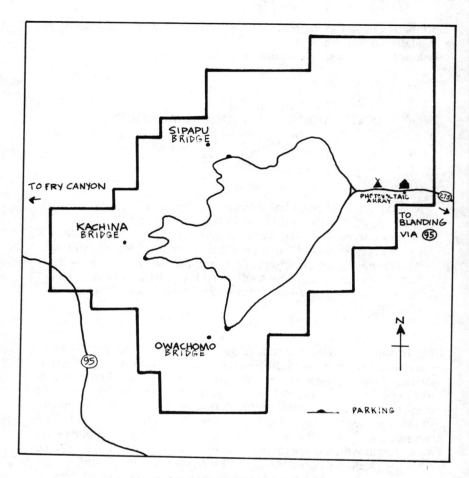

SIPAPU
BRIDGE

TO FRY CANYON

KACHINA
BRIDGE

PHOTOVOLTAIC
ARRAY

TO
BLANDING
VIA 95

275

95

OWACHOMO
BRIDGE

N

PARKING

Natural Bridges National Monument

summer when staff permits. A paved nine-mile loop road links the trailheads to the three bridges.

Facilities: No food service or lodging is available at the monument. Drinking water and modern bathrooms are located at the visitor center. The nearest source of gasoline and food is at Blanding, forty miles away. The nearest overnight accommodations and year-round services are at Blanding (40 miles) and Mexican Hat (45 miles).

Camping: A single campground (thirteen sites) is located near the visitor center. There is a length limit of twenty-one feet, and only one vehicle per site is permitted. Grills, tables, and pit toilets are available and modern bathrooms at the visitor center remain unlocked at night. The campground usually fills in the early afternoon during summer months.

Fishing: No fishing is available.

RAINBOW BRIDGE NATIONAL MONUMENT
c/o Glen Canyon National Recreation Area
Box 1507
Page, AZ 86040
(602) 645–2471

Rainbow Bridge National Monument was established in 1910 and contains 160 acres, including the world's largest-known natural bridge. Rainbow Bridge is as high as the nation's Capitol and thicker at the top than a three-story building is tall. The monument is located in south-central Utah on the south edge of Glen Canyon National Recreation Area. It is reached only by a 24-mile trail from Navajo Mountain Trading Post, a 13-mile trail from abandoned Rainbow Lodge, or by boat on Lake Powell. This hiking trail is located on Navajo Reservation land. Permits are required from the Navajo Tribe and may be obtained at P.O. Box 308, Window Rock, AZ 86515.

Millions of years ago slow streams flowed south and west across a broad floodplain in this region. Sand and mud were deposited in thin beds that eventually consolidated to form the reddish-brown layer that is now exposed beneath Rainbow Bridge. Much later, a change in the climate brought winds that deposited great quantities of sand. The resulting pale orange to reddish-brown rock called Navajo Sandstone is the material in which Rainbow Bridge and Bridge Canyon have been carved.

Following this period, the next 100 million years saw the area change from desert to swamp to lakes, and the Navajo Sandstone was buried under more than 5,000 feet of strata. Approximately 60 million years ago the region was gradually uplifted and streams began cutting into the rock layers. Rainbow Bridge was formed during this period by Bridge Creek, which flows today from Navajo Mountain northwest to Lake Powell. For a short description of the formation of a natural bridge, see the narrative on Natural Bridges National Monument.

Water dripping into pools near the bottom of Rainbow Bridge Canyon is from rainwater seeping through the porous Navajo Sandstone. Once it reaches the underlying impervious rock layers, it accumulates and eventually seeps out along the walls of the canyon as springs. Rainwater also causes dark streaks on the side of the arch by washing iron oxide down from the top.

Most visitors to Rainbow Bridge National Monument take the water route of approximately fifty miles from Wahweap, Bullfrog, or Halls Crossing to the landing in Bridge Canyon, and then walk about one half mile up the canyon to the bridge. For visitors bringing their own boats, launching ramps are available at Wahweap, Halls Crossing, Bullfrog, and Hite. For visitors interested in the trail trip, inquiry should be made as to trail conditions and availability of water and supplies before beginning. This is a difficult hike and the roadway leading to the trail is only accessed by a high-clearance vehicle.

Facilities: There are no facilities within the monument. The nearest town with complete facilities is Page, Arizona, on U.S. 89. Concessioners at Wahweap, Halls Crossing, Bullfrog, Dangling Rope, and Hite sell boating and camping supplies. Tour boat trips are provided at Halls Crossing, Bullfrog, and Wahweap. A floating complex anchored in Dangling Rope Canyon contains a refueling station, a small store for camping supplies, and a ranger station.

Camping: Although picnicking is permitted at Rainbow Bridge, there is no camping within the monument and no picnic area located within the monument boundary. No water is available. Modern National Park Service campgrounds are located at Wahweap, Bullfrog, and Halls Crossing as part of the Glen Canyon National Recreation Area.

Fishing: Striped, largemouth, and smallmouth bass, black crappie, and catfish are caught in Lake Powell. A Utah and/or Arizona fishing license is required.

TIMPANOGOS CAVE NATIONAL MONUMENT
RR #3, Box 200
American Fork, UT 84003
(801) 756–5238

Timpanogos Cave was set aside as a national monument in 1922 to preserve a series of small underground limestone caverns ornamented with white translucent crystals. The monument is located in north-central Utah. From Salt Lake City, Timpanogos is south on Interstate 15 and then east on Utah 92, a few miles south of "The Point of the Mountain." From Provo, turn east at Pleasant Grove or American Fork. Timpanogos Cave is 7 miles by paved road from either town.

Timpanogos Cave began forming when underground pressures elevated the rock in the region during formation of the Wasatch Range. The strain produced a break with pulverized rock through which water could pass. As the water drained and carried away pulverized rock and dissolved limestone, a tunnel was formed. This was eventually enlarged to form a cavern. During this period it is thought the American

Fork River was flowing at the approximate level of the cave. As the river cut deeper into the canyon, the water left in the cave commenced a period of cave decorating.

A one-and-a-half-mile trail winds up the steep side of Mount Timpanogos from park headquarters to the cave entrance. The entrance is 1,000 feet above the canyon floor and the three-hour round trip presents some outstanding views of the Wasatch Mountains, Utah Valley, and American Fork Canyon. The cave system consists of three caves connected by manmade tunnels. The first, Hansen Cave, was discovered by Martin Hansen in 1887 as he followed cougar tracks to its entrance. The two remaining caves, Timpanogos and Middle, were not discovered until 1921.

Much of the cave glows with white crystals that sparkle like jewels. Flowstone, helictites, and sodastraw stalactites culminate in larger forms such as Chocolate Falls, Father Time Jewel Box, and the Great Heart of Timpanogos. Tiny pools of water reflect the beauty of the cave.

A visitor center near the parking area presents exhibits explaining the formation and history of the cave. The center and cave are open daily from mid-May through mid-October. Visitors to the cave must be accompanied by a guide and a nominal fee is charged.

Facilities: A picnic area with water, tables, and grills is near the visitor center. Modern restrooms and drinking water are located at the visitor center. Lunches and supplies are available at a nearby store from Memorial Day to Labor Day.

Camping: No camping facilities are available in the monument, but the U.S. Forest Service provides a number of campgrounds nearby in Uinta National Forest.

Fishing: The campgrounds are near the American Fork River where fishing is permitted with a Utah license.

ZION NATIONAL PARK
Springdale, UT 84767
(801) 722–3256

Zion National Park contains nearly 147,000 acres of colorful canyons and mesas that create phenomenal shapes and landscapes. Zion is located in southwestern Utah, with the southwest entrance approximately 60 miles northeast of Las Vegas, Nevada, via Interstate 15 and Utah 9. The southern section of the park is bisected by Utah Highway 9, while access to the northern section is by paved road (exit 40) off Interstate 15.

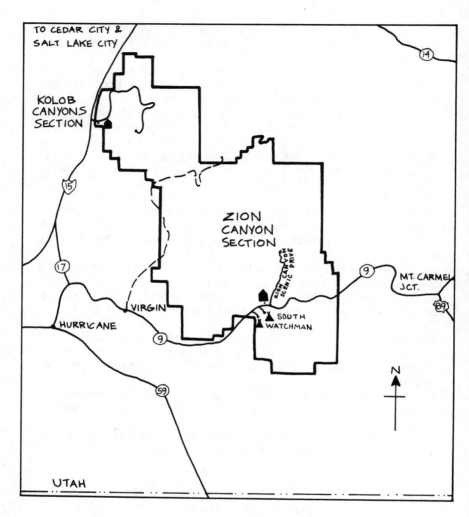

Zion National Park

Zion National Park formed through thousands of years of erosion from wind, rain, freezing, and the persistent force of the Virgin River. Scenic drives and trails provide spectacular vistas of canyons, sculptured rocks, cliffs, and rivers. The park is one of the most beautiful in the National Park System and will remind many visitors of an uncluttered Yosemite.

In addition to Utah 9, there are three roads in the park. A seven-mile paved road leads from near the visitor center through Zion Canyon and past Zion Lodge. Scenic points from the road are The Sentinel, Court of the Patriarchs, Mountain of the Sun, and Great White Throne. In the park's northwest section, Kolob Canyons Road is a 5.2-mile paved road originating from Interstate 15. This road is open all year. A partially paved road connects the town of Virgin with Cedar City to the north. The narrow road leads to Lava Point fire lookout on the Kolob Terrace highlands and includes steep grades.

A great variety of hiking trails wander through Zion. The most popular (round trip: 2 miles, two hours) begins at the Temple of Sinawava and winds near a canyon wall to Gateway to the Narrows. On this walk visitors can view the Hanging Gardens of Zion. Self-guided trails to Weeping Rock (round trip: ½-mile, half hour) and to Canyon Overlook (round trip: 1 mile, one hour) are open during most of the year, and trails to Emerald Pools (beginning near the lodge with round trip: two miles, two hours) and Hidden Canyon (round trip: 3 miles, three hours) provide scenic points for observing the park. West Rim Trail (round trip: 12½ miles, eight hours), leading to views of the Great West Canyon, and East Rim Trail (round trip: 7 miles, five hours), with a view of Zion Canyon, are more strenuous. In the park's northwest section, the trail beginning at Lee Pass leads down Timber Creek and up La Verkin Creek to Kolob Arch, perhaps the world's largest natural span, at 310 feet. Check at the Kolob Canyons Visitor Center for trail conditions.

The Zion Canyon Visitor Center, near the south entrance, contains exhibits and information on the park's history and geology. In addition, a schedule of events and orientation programs is available. Evening talks are given spring through fall at the lodge and campgrounds. A nature center for children six through twelve years of age operates during June and July. Ranger-guided walks and hikes originate at various points around the park. A concessioner-operated tram system provides tours of the park during summer months. Information may be obtained at the lodge. Reservations for horseback trips within the park may be made at Zion Lodge.

Facilities: Zion Lodge has cabin and motel accommodations and is open all year. Write Utah Parks Division of TW Services, 451 N. Main St., Cedar City, UT 84720 (801–586–7686) for reservations. A dining room and a snack bar are also available at the lodge. Additional food service and accommodations are located in nearby communities. Modern restrooms and drinking water are available at the lodge, visitor centers, and both campgrounds. Picnic sites are located at the Grotto in Zion Canyon and at the end of the Kolob Canyons Road in the northwest section of the park. A physician is located in Hurricane, twenty-four miles west of the park. A physician's assistant is at Zion Clinic in Springdale during summer.

Camping: The two major campgrounds at Zion are near the south entrance. Watchman (228 spaces and seven group campsites) and South (145 spaces) each have tables, grills, flush toilets, and dump stations. Both border the Virgin River, which offers tubing and small beach areas. In addition, both are near a private store lying just outside the park. Lava Point (six spaces) is a primitive campground off the Kolob Terrace Road and near the West Rim Trail that has pit toilets and no water.

Fishing: Fishing is allowed all year in the Virgin River below Zion Narrows, but is poor because of frequent flooding and seasonal fluctuations in water levels. A Utah license is required.

Washington

COULEE DAM NATIONAL RECREATION AREA
P.O. Box 37
Coulee Dam, WA 99116
(509) 633–9441

Coulee Dam was added to the National Park System in 1946. It contains 100,000 acres of blue water and rolling hills. The area's principal feature is 151-mile-long Franklin D. Roosevelt Lake, which was formed by Grand Coulee Dam. The park is located in northeastern Washington, and its eastern side is bordered by Washington Highway 25.

Millions of years ago, this region was the scene of successive volcanic lava floods that filled the Columbia Basin and pressed against the granite mountains to the north. As the Columbia River was forced into new channels by each additional flow, it eventually made a large westward bend. About 10,000 years ago, a glacier blocked the river in the vicinity of Grand Coulee Dam and a natural lake larger than that which presently exists was formed. As the lake overflowed, the lava was cut and the Grand Coulee was excavated.

Grand Coulee Dam is the largest hydroelectric dam on the Columbia River. Excellent views of the structure may be obtained from the canal headworks, above the west end, or from Crown Point, two and a half miles north on Washington 174. Behind the dam, Roosevelt Lake stretches nearly to the Canadian border.

Driving northward by way of Fort Spokane, the road passes through the rolling wheatlands of eastern Washington before nearing the lake and plunging into evergreen forests. A museum and self-guided trail at Fort Spokane tell the story of the frontier period of the American West. From Fort Spokane, Highway 25 winds northward in the narrow valley between the Huckleberry and Kettle River mountains. The Gifford ferry (summer months only) provides access to the

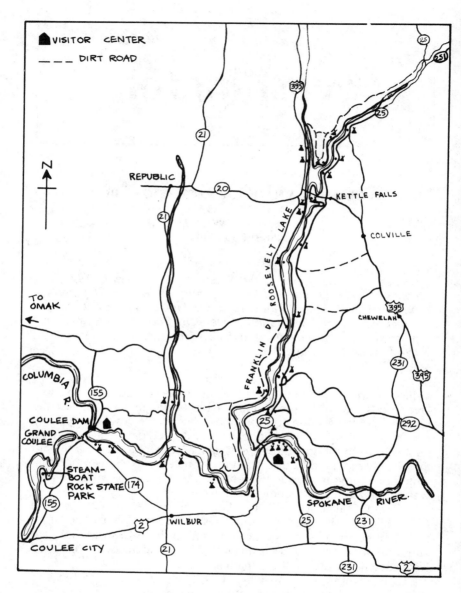

Coulee Dam National Recreation Area

lake's west side and a different type of scenery. Another scenic drive is to cross the lake on the Keller ferry and follow the Sanpoil River north to the old mining town of Republic. From there a drive east over Sherman Pass goes past numerous spots for camping, fishing, picnicking, or relaxing.

Most of the activity in Coulee Dam NRA is water-related. Waterskiing is popular within the shelter of larger tributaries such as the Spokane, Kettle, and Colville rivers and Sanpoil Bay. Sailing is excellent because a breeze usually blows on the lake from the surrounding hills. The lake reaches its maximum level in late June or early July.

Facilities: Food, lodging, groceries, gasoline, and other services are available in Grand Coulee, Coulee Dam, and other nearby towns. Similar services are at Colville, Kettle Falls, and Northport on the northern portion of the lake. Small stores with groceries are at Seven Bays and McCoys marinas, and at marinas at Keller Ferry, Kettle Falls, and Daisy. Snack bars are at Keller Ferry, Kettle Falls, Porcupine Bay, and Spring Canyon. Smaller towns and nearby Indian reservations usually sell gasoline, groceries, and snacks.

Camping: Thirty-two campgrounds surround Lake Roosevelt. Those with tables, grills, water, and flush toilets are Spring Canyon (seventy-eight spaces, one group camp, dump station), Keller Ferry (fifty-five spaces, dump station), Fort Spokane (sixty-seven spaces, one group camp, dump station), Porcupine Bay (thirty- one spaces, dump station), Hunters (thirty-nine spaces), Kettle Falls (eighty-nine spaces, one group camp, dump station), and Evans (forty-six spaces). Other campgrounds shown on the map are less developed but can be reached by auto. A number of campgrounds have access by boat only and are not included on the map. All campgrounds are open during summer months except Hunters and Porcupine Bay, which have a season of May through October. Campgrounds on the west arm of the lake are on open terraces where shade is limited, while those on the north arm are generally in forested areas.

Fishing: Over thirty species of fish make fishing one of the most popular activities in the park. Common catches include walleye (1 to 4 pounds), rainbow trout (1 to 3 pounds), white sturgeon (100 to 300 pounds), yellow perch (3 to 5 pounds), lake whitefish (2 to 3 pounds), and Kokanee salmon (1 to 3 pounds). Other fish present are cutthroat trout, bass, carp, pike, white perch, and sunfish. Trolling is a popular method of fishing these waters, with dawn and dusk being the best times.

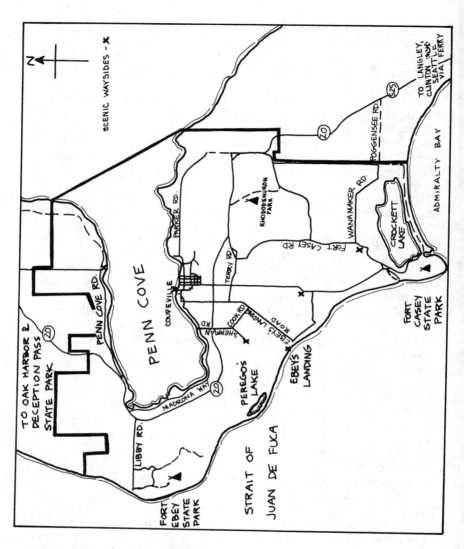

Ebey's Landing National Historical Reserve

EBEY'S LANDING NATIONAL HISTORICAL RESERVE
P.O. Box 774
Coupeville, WA 98239
(206) 442–4590

Ebey's Landing contains 17,000 acres, including the waters of Penn Cove. It was established as the first national historical reserve in 1978 to preserve a rural community providing a historical record of Puget Sound from its nineteenth-century exploration and settlement to the present. The reserve is located in northwestern Washington on Whidbey Island, about a two-hour drive from Seattle. It is reached from Mount Vernon via the town of Oak Harbor and State Highway 20. The reserve may also be reached by ferry from either Port Townsend or Mukilteo (via Highway 525).

Whidbey Island is the largest of over 600 islands in Puget Sound. The island was named by Captain George Vancouver who, while exploring this region in 1792, wrote of the beautiful, open, fertile lands. Subsequent years saw the Hudson's Bay Company established near present-day Olympia, but English rule came to an end with the Treaty of 1846, which gave the Oregon Territory to the United States. This treaty opened the Pacific Northwest to settlement. Settlers in wagon trains soon followed the Oregon Trail west and established homesteads, and then farms and communities around Puget Sound. People also arrived by sailing ship, as did most early settlers of Central Whidbey Island.

Ebey's Landing National Historical Reserve provides a glimpse of this early settlement. The town of Coupeville was settled by New England sea captains. There are forty-eight historic structures, including many of the sea captains' homes, in the town. The Historical Society maintains a museum of settler life, and there is a National Park Service information kiosk at the foot of the Coupeville wharf.

Ebey's Landing, where the island's first American settler landed, is across the island from Coupeville. The beach and a bluff hiking trail are part of the Washington state park system. There are spectacular views of the Olympic Mountains and Puget Sound from the beach and the trail. Several scenic waysides offer beautiful views of open waters, farmland, and historic structures.

The open fields between Coupeville and Ebey's Landing are natural prairies that have been farmed continuously since the 1850s. The farmers who live here today, many themselves descendants of early settlers, continue to plow land claims established by their families in the 1800s. Many of the farmhouses that dot the prairie are the original homes or are homes built on the foundations of the homes of the first settlers.

There are two state parks within the reserve. Fort Casey, a turn-of-the-century coastal-defense fort, has a lighthouse, gun emplacements, and a beach to explore. Fort Ebey, established during World War II, offers beach hiking, picnicking, and exploration of World War II gun emplacements.

Facilities: Food and lodging are available in Coupeville.
Camping: Campgrounds are at Fort Ebey State Park, Fort Casey State Park, and Rhododendron Park.
Fishing: Surf fishing and a boat ramp are available at Fort Casey State Park.

FORT VANCOUVER NATIONAL HISTORIC SITE
612 East Reserve Street
Vancouver, WA 98661
(206) 696–7655

Fort Vancouver was authorized as part of the National Park Service in 1948. It contains 165 acres commemorating what was the economic, political, social, and cultural hub of the Pacific Northwest. Fort Vancouver is located within the city limits of Vancouver, Washington, and is reached by exiting from Interstate 5 at the East Mill Plain Boulevard Interchange (exit 1C). From Interstate 205, exit on Washington 14, drive west 5 miles, and turn right on Grand Boulevard. The visitor center is on East Evergreen Boulevard.

After 1800, traders from Canada, England, the United States, and several European countries were competing for the fur resources of the Pacific Northwest. After years of struggle a British firm, Hudson's Bay Company, gained supremacy in the region. In an attempt to strengthen its claim to the territory, in 1824 the company decided to move its western headquarters from a location at the mouth of the Columbia River to a site about one hundred miles upstream. It was here that Fort Vancouver was built.

The fort became the center of activity in the Pacific Northwest. Not only did it serve as the headquarters to a huge commercial empire, it was also the center of a farming and manufacturing community, and provided much of the cultural and social life for the Oregon Country. At the height of its importance (1844–46), the fort included twenty-two major structures within a stockade of upright logs. In addition, thirty to fifty wooden dwellings were located on the plain to the west and southwest of the stockade.

The Treaty of 1846 between the United States and Great Britain established the 49th parallel as the southern boundary of Canada and placed Fort Vancouver on American soil. A U.S. Army camp was established nearby in 1849, and in 1860 the fort was abandoned by the Hudson's Bay Company. Six years later, the old stockade was destroyed by fire.

The park's visitor center contains exhibits, a small store, and an audio-visual presentation depicting the fort's early history. The National Park Service has reconstructed the stockade and some of the buildings in the stockade. Guides are available to take visitors through the reconstructed Chief Factor's house, kitchen, bakery, blacksmith shop, Indian trade store, and dispensary.

Facilities: No food or lodging is provided by the Park Service but both are available nearby. Restrooms and drinking water are available in both the visitor center and the fort. A picnic shelter lies next to the visitor center.

Camping: No camping is permitted at the site. Battleground Lake State Park (thirty-five regular sites, fifteen walk-in tent sites) provides tables, grills, flush toilets, showers, swimming, and fishing, but no hookups. To reach the state park, drive twenty miles northwest of Vancouver via Interstate 5 and State Highway 502. Directions are available at the Fort Vancouver visitor center.

Fishing: No fishing is available within the park.

KLONDIKE GOLD RUSH NATIONAL HISTORICAL PARK
117 S. Main Street
Seattle, WA 98104
(206) 553-7220

Klondike Gold Rush was established in 1979 to commemorate the 1898 gold rush to the Yukon. The park is divided into two sections, with the main area located in Skagway, Alaska (see Klondike Gold Rush National Historical Park in the Alaska section of this book), and an interpretative center in Seattle. The Seattle center is in the Union Trust Annex at 117 South Main Street, two blocks north of the Kingdome.

The city of Seattle was the focal point through which thousands of goldseekers poured on their way to riches in the Yukon. Seattle advertised itself as the place where miners could outfit themselves before setting off by steamer for the gold fields. It was the people and money brought by the Klondike gold rush that made Seattle the trade and financial center of the Northwest.

The park's visitor center in the Union Trust Annex contains exhibits and a variety of films and slide presentations explaining the gold rush and Seattle's role in the historic event. Interpretive programs are offered on an unscheduled basis. The center is open daily from 9:00 A.M. to 5:00 P.M. except on Thanksgiving, Christmas, and New Year's Day. Union Trust Annex is within Pioneer Square Historic District, an area of the city that has been restored. Pioneer Square contains a number of gold rush–era buildings and many unique shops, restaurants, and antique dealers.

Facilities: Restrooms and drinking water are available at the visitor center. Restaurants and lodging are nearby.
Camping: No camping is permitted at the park. The nearest public camping is at Saltwater State Park (fifty-two spaces), two miles south of Des Moines on Highway 509. The park has hiking trails and a concession stand.
Fishing: No fishing is available at the park.

LAKE CHELAN NATIONAL RECREATION AREA;
NORTH CASCADES NATIONAL PARK;
ROSS LAKE NATIONAL RECREATION AREA
2105 Highway 20
Sedro Woolley, WA 98284
(206) 856–5700

This group of parks, established in 1968, contains 1,049 square miles of magnificent scenery. Here, high peaks intercept moisture-laden winds, producing glaciers, icefalls, and waterfalls in a wild alpine region where lush forests and meadows thrive. The park is located in northern Washington—the north boundary borders on Canada. Access to the area is gained via Washington Highway 20, which bisects the park through a portion of the Ross Lake section. Hiking access and roadside views of the northwest corner are available from Washington 542 east from Bellingham. Access to Stehekin Valley is by boat, float plane, or trail. Vehicle access to Ross Lake is by unimproved road from Canada.

The North Cascades group contains alpine scenery unmatched in the continental United States. Some visitors believe that this is the most

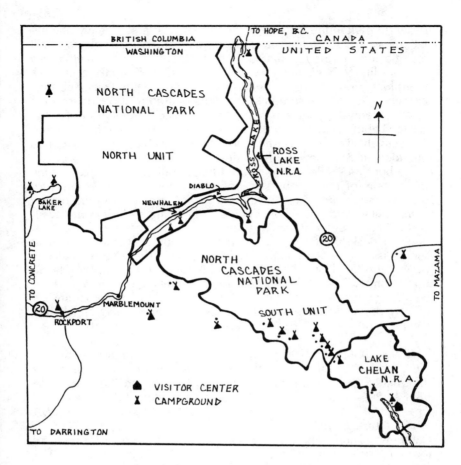

Lake Chelan National Recreation Area
North Cascades National Park
Ross Lake National Recreation Area

beautiful park in the National Park System. The area's heavy precipitation has produced alpine lakes, ice caps, more than 300 glaciers (half the glaciers in the contiguous United States), and glacier-carved canyons like Stehekin at the head of Lake Chelan. This lake is fifty-five miles long, from one to two miles wide, and occupies a glacial trough exceeding 8,500 feet in depth from lake bottom to valley crest. Ross Lake is twenty-four miles long and two miles across at its widest point, while Diablo Lake and Gorge Lake occupy 910 acres and 210 acres, respectively. Three dams impounding Ross, Diablo, and Gorge lakes provide electrical power for Seattle.

About 345 miles of hiking and horse trails exist throughout the three areas of the North Cascades group. Permits are required for back-country camping. Horses and mules are for rent in nearby communities and professional guide and packtrain services are available. Cross-country skiing is popular during winter months but no developed ski areas are in the park. Scheduled commercial boat service is available on Diablo and Chelan lakes. The latter is an all day (round) trip that leaves Chelan around 8:30 A.M. Call the Lake Chelan Boat Company (509–682–2224) for schedule information and for details on a new express boat. Guided walks and evening programs are offered during summer months at Colonial Creek and Newhalem campgrounds and at Hozomeen and Stehekin.

Facilities: Guest accommodations are available in the recreation areas and in smaller communities within or near the park. For information or reservations write Diablo Lake Resort, Rockport, WA 98283 (206–386–4429); North Cascades Lodge, P.O. Box 1779, Chelan, WA 98816 (509–682–4711); Ross Lake Resort, Rockport, WA 98283 (206–386–4437).

Camping: Three developed campgrounds with vehicle access are located along Highway 20 in Ross Lake NRA. Colonial Creek (164 spaces) has tables, grills, flush toilets, and a dump station. Goodell Creek (twenty-two sites and two group camps) provides tables, grills, water, and pit toilets, and is open all year. Newhalem Creek (129 spaces) offers flush toilets and a dump station. The other camp in Ross Lake with highway access is less developed and has pit toilets. Hozomeen (122 spaces) is reached via Canada 3.

Purple Point (seventeen sites) at Stehekin is within walking distance of the boat landing. It has drinking water and pit toilets. Access to all campgrounds in North Cascades National Park is by boat, shuttle bus, or trail only.

Fishing: The principal game fish are trout—rainbow, brook, golden, and Dolly Varden. Lake Chelan offers fishing for Kokanee salmon. In addition to the two big lakes, there are many small mountain and valley lakes and countless streams. A Washington license is required.

MOUNT RAINIER NATIONAL PARK
Tahoma Woods Star Route
Ashford, WA 94304
(206) 569–2211

Mount Rainier National Park was established in 1899 and contains 368 square miles including the greatest single-peak glacial system in the contiguous United States. The summit and slopes of the ancient volcano are surrounded with snow, dense forests, and subalpine flowered meadows. The park is located in southwestern Washington, 80 miles south of Seattle via Interstate 15 and Highways 161, 7, and 706 or Interstate 5 and Highways 161, 7, and 706, and 64 miles west of Yakima via U.S. 12.

Mount Rainier National Park was named after what has become one of the most-photographed mountains in the United States. The 14,410-foot peak collects snowfall in large quantities as the wet Pacific air flows eastward; it is not unusual to have the three-story Paradise Inn on the park's south side covered up to its roofline during winter. The mountain's two craters and general shape betray its earlier life as an active volcano. Some experts believe Rainier is still a likely candidate for an eruption because steam from within the mountain continues to carve tunnels in the summit ice cap.

Mount Rainier is best known for the numerous glaciers that flow down its slopes. Thirty-five square miles of ice are contained in twenty-six named glaciers. These ice flows have carved deep valleys into the mountain's sides. The huge quantities of ice and snow create dangers that are unique to this type of mountain. These include mudflows, snow and ice avalanches, and rock slides.

The most popular activities at Rainier are climbing and hiking. The ultimate is a climb to the summit of Mount Rainier. A guide service at Paradise offers one-day snow-and-ice climbing seminars and rents climbing equipment. The summit trip is a two-day affair. Three hundred miles of trails, both short and long, begin at various locations around the mountain. Trail guides and maps are sold at visitor centers. The center at Longmire is open all year; those at Sunrise and Ohanapecosh are open in summer only. Paradise is open year round but only on weekends from mid-October through April.

Self-guided nature trails are at Carbon River, Sunrise, Longmire, Ohanapecosh, and Paradise. Naturalist-guided walks and evening programs are available during summer months. Weekly schedules are posted at campgrounds and visitor centers.

During winter, food, lodging, gifts, and recreation equipment are available at Longmire. Inner tubes and platters may be used only in

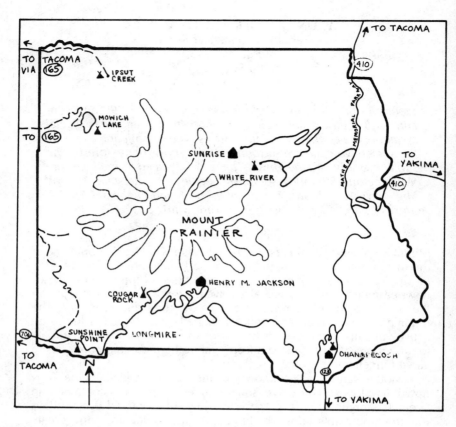

Mount Rainier National Park

constructed runs near the Paradise ranger station. Information about cross-country ski routes and snow conditions are available from rangers. Snowmobiles are permitted on designated roads only. Except for the roads from Nisqually Entrance to Paradise, park roads are usually closed from late November to June.

Facilities: As one of the country's older and more popular areas administered by the National Park Service, Mount Rainier National Park contains a wide variety of facilities for visitors. Overnight accommodations are available at the National Park Inn at Longmire (year round) and Paradise Inn (late May to early October). For reservations and rates write Mount Rainier Guest Services, Star Route, Ashford, WA 94304 (206–569–2275). Outside the park, accommodations are at Ashford, Packwood, White Pass, Crystal Mountain, and Enumclaw.

Fast food service is available in the visitor center at Paradise; restaurant service is provided all year at Longmire and at Paradise Inn during its season of operation. A snack bar is available only at Sunrise. Groceries are sold at Sunrise during summer and at Longmire year round. Gas is sold at Longmire all year.

Camping: Improved campgrounds with grills, tables, flush toilets, and drinking water are at Cougar Rock (200 spaces, dump station), Ohanapecosh (205 spaces, dump station), and White River (117 spaces). Campgrounds without flush toilets are at Ipsut Creek (twenty-nine spaces) and Sunshine Point (eighteen spaces). The latter is the only campground open all year.

Fishing: Fishing is permitted all year without a license. Most lakes melt by early to mid-July. Fishing through ice is not permitted but alpine lakes and streams contain cutthroat, rainbow, brown, and brook trout. The Ohanapecosh River and its tributaries are open to fly fishing only.

OLYMPIC NATIONAL PARK
600 East Park Ave.
Port Angeles, WA 98362
(206) 452–9235

Olympic is a 1,442-square-mile mountain wilderness containing active glaciers, rare Roosevelt elk, 57 miles of wild scenic ocean shore, and the finest remnant of Pacific Northwest rain forest. The park's two sections are located in the northwestern corner of Washington. Main access is via U.S. 101 and its numerous side roads. Roads penetrate only the perimeter of the park.

The Olympic Mountains are composed mostly of sedimentary rocks, such as sandstone and shale, formed from sand and silt deposited in the shallow sea that covered this region millions of years ago. These rocks were later uplifted and carved by erosion and glaciers. There are currently about sixty glaciers in the Olympic Mountains; the three largest are found on 7,965-foot Mount Olympus.

The strip of park along the Pacific contains some of the most primitive coastline to be found in the continental U.S. The rocky shoreline is the home of birds, seals, and other marine wildlife.

The park has two visitor centers—Pioneer Memorial Museum near Port Angeles (open all year) and the Hoh Rain Forest Visitor Center. Each contains exhibits, slide programs, and park personnel to answer visitor questions. Self-guided nature trails are available at both locations (two at Hoh) and also at Ozette, Staircase, Elwha, Quinault, and at Hurricane Hill. During summer months park rangers lead guided walks and present evening campfire programs. Six hundred miles of trails wander throughout the park.

The west side of the Olympic Peninsula has the wettest winter climate in the continental United States, with annual precipitation of more than 140 inches in some sections. Easy access to the rain forest is available at Hoh. Many visitors consider this to be the single best place to visit in the entire park. Additional rain forest access can be found via the Quinault River and Queets River roads.

The park's high country is reached from the north side at Heart O' The Hills. Hurricane Ridge provides excellent views of Mount Olympus and subalpine meadows.

Winter activities at Olympic National Park include cross-country skiing along open subalpine ridge tops and snowmobiling on five designated roads when they are infrequently closed to wheeled vehicles. Downhill skiing is available at Hurricane Ridge Winter Use Area (road open on weekends and holidays) where three tow ropes, rental shop, and a ski school are located.

Facilities: Lodging is available throughout the park. For information or reservations write Kalaloch Lodge, HC 80, Box 1100, Forks, WA 98331 (206–962–2271); Lake Crescent Lodge, HC 62, Box 11, Port Angeles, WA 98362 (206–928–3211); Log Cabin Resort, 6540 East Beach Road, Port Angeles, WA 98362 (206–928–3245); Sol Duc Hot Springs Resort, P.O. Box 2169, Port Angeles, WA 98362 (206–327–3583).

Restaurants are at each of the four lodges while light meals are provided at Hurricane Ridge Lodge (no rooms) during summer months and on weekends in winter. A snack bar is at Fairholm General Store.

Groceries and gasoline are sold at Fairholm Visitor Service Area and Kalaloch Lodge. Groceries only are at Sol Duc Hot Springs and

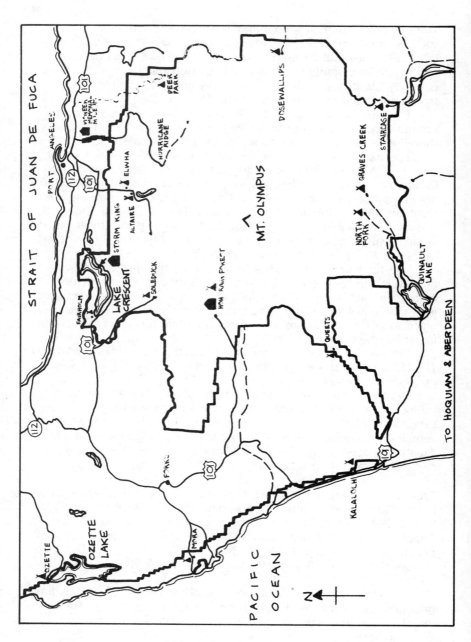

Olympic National Park

Log Cabin Resort. Boat rentals are provided at Fairholm, Lake Crescent Lodge, and Log Cabin Resort.

Camping: Campgrounds with tables, grills, water, and flush toilets include Altaire (thirty spaces, summer only, no large trailers), Dosewallips (thirty-two spaces, summer only, no trailers), Elwha (forty-one spaces, no large trailers), Fairholm (eighty-seven spaces, dump station), Graves Creek (thirty spaces, summer only), Heart O' The Hills (105 spaces), Hoh (eighty-nine spaces, dump station), Kalaloch (177 spaces, dump station), Mora (ninety-four spaces; dump station), Soleduck (eighty-four spaces, summer only, dump station), and Staircase (fifty-nine spaces). There are limited spaces at each of these campgrounds that will accommodate larger RVs. All other sites are recommended to a maximum of twenty-one feet.

Campgrounds with tables, grills, and pit toilets include Deer Park (eighteen spaces, summer only, no trailers), Erickson Bay (fifteen spaces, access only by boat or trail), July Creek (twenty-nine spaces, walk-in, water available), North Fork Quinault (seven spaces, summer only, no trailers), Ozette (fourteen spaces, dirt road access), Queets (twenty spaces, no trailers).

Fishing: Olympic's streams and lakes contain cutthroat, rainbow, and brook trout, Dolly Varden, and several species of salmon. Large rivers are noted for steelhead trout. No license is required, but steelhead and salmon punchcards are required.

SAN JUAN ISLAND NATIONAL HISTORICAL PARK
P.O. Box 429
Friday Harbor, WA 98250
(206) 378–2240

San Juan Island contains 1,752 acres and was authorized as part of the National Park System in 1966 to commemorate the peaceful relations maintained by the United States, Great Britain, and Canada since an 1846 to 1872 boundary dispute. British and American military campsites are included. San Juan Island is reached by Washington State ferries from Anacortes, Washington, about 83 miles north of Seattle and by ferry from Sydney, British Columbia, 15 miles north of Victoria. For private boats, good docking facilities are available at Friday and Roche harbors.

San Juan Island was the scene of a confrontation and then relatively peaceful coexistence between American and English forces during the

1800s. The Oregon Treaty of 1846 between Great Britain and the United States settled the larger land disputes by giving the U.S. undisputed possession of the Pacific Northwest below the 49th parallel, extending the boundary to the middle of the channel separating the mainland from Vancouver Island. The treaty's wording left unclear who owned San Juan Island. Both sides declared the island as their possession, and in 1859 an insignificant event caused a confrontation between the two powers. After a series of threats, both sides agreed to withdraw all but token military forces and negotiate a settlement. The British landed a detachment of Royal Marines at what is now called British Camp, and San Juan Island remained under joint military occupation for the next twelve years. In 1871, the two sides signed the Treaty of Washington and submitted the San Juan question to Kaiser Wilhelm I of Germany for settlement. In 1872, the Kaiser ruled in favor of the United States.

Park headquarters at First and Spring streets in Friday Harbor serves as an information station. It is open from 8:00 A.M. to 4:30 P.M. with extended hours in spring and summer. At British Camp, four historic buildings and a small British formal garden have been restored. The buildings are open from 9:00 A.M. to 6:00 P.M. in summer and the barracks contains an exhibit explaining the territorial dispute. At American Camp, two historic buildings and the remains of an earthwork gun emplacement survive. An exhibit center and self-guided foot trail are located here. South Beach offers a nice area for walking and observing wildlife.

Facilities: A number of motels, lodges, and bed and breakfast facilities are available on the island. A listing is at the visitor center. Picnic areas, restrooms, and drinking water are at both American Camp and British Camp.

Camping: No camping is provided by the National Park Service. Limited camping facilities (with flush toilets) are available at San Juan County Park (eleven sites). For reservations write 380 West Side Road No., Friday Harbor, WA 98250 (206–378–2992). A small commercial trailer park (twenty-four sites, hookups) is one mile from the ferry landing on Roche Harbor Road (206–378–4717), and two private campgrounds are available on the island.

Fishing: Fishing in bays surrounding the island and in San Juan Channel is available at various locations.

WHITMAN MISSION NATIONAL HISTORIC SITE
Route 2, Box 247
Walla Walla, WA 99362
(509) 522–6360

Whitman Mission was authorized in 1936 to commemorate a landmark on the Oregon Trail where Dr. and Mrs. Marcus Whitman ministered to the spiritual and physical needs of Indians. The site is located in southeastern Washington near Walla Walla. It is 7 miles west of Walla Walla and 4 miles west of College Place. A short connecting road leads south from U.S. 12 to the park.

Marcus Whitman was sent west in 1835 by a Protestant church society to carry out missionary work among the Indians. After returning east to recruit workers, Whitman and his wife crossed the continent in 1836 via steamboat, wagon, two-wheeled cart, and horseback. His mission was established among the Cayuse Indians at Waiilatpu. The Indians remained nomadic and were generally apathetic to spiritual matters, so the society considered closing the mission in 1842. Whitman was able to convince his superiors of the mission's value, and it continued to provide shelter to both the Indians and emigrants traveling the Oregon Trail. In 1847, a wagon train brought measles to the area, creating an epidemic that killed half of the Cayuse tribe. In the same year, a small group of Cayuse attacked the mission and killed Marcus Whitman, his wife, and eleven others. The mission buildings were also destroyed. The tragedy spurred Congress to create the Territory of Oregon in August 1848.

The visitor center contains exhibits on Whitman Mission and the Oregon Trail, and a slide show on the establishment of the mission is presented hourly. Self-guided walks lead past the Whitman Memorial and the Great Grave where the remains of those killed in the massacre are buried. Visitors may also walk around the old mission grounds where recorded messages and building outlines help interpret the site. A restored section of the old Oregon Trail is available to walk. The mission is open daily except for Thanksgiving, Christmas, and New Year's Day.

Facilities: No food service or lodging is available at the site. Water and restrooms are provided at the visitor center. A shaded picnic area with tables and drinking water (no grills) is located north of the visitor center near the parking area. Full facilities are seven miles east in Walla Walla.

Camping: No camping is permitted in the park. A county-operated campground with hookups is located seven miles east in Walla Walla at Fort Walla Walla Park. The park is on Dalles Military Road and a map showing directions to the campground may be obtained at the visitor center of Whitman Mission National Historic Site.

Fishing: No fishing is available at Whitman Mission National Historic Site.

Wyoming

DEVILS TOWER NATIONAL MONUMENT
Devils Tower, WY 82714
(307) 467–5370

Devils Tower contains nearly 1,350 acres and was established in 1906 as the country's first national monument. The monument contains a spectacular stump-shaped cluster of rock columns rising 856 feet above its base (featured in the movie "Close Encounters"). Devils Tower is located in extreme northeastern Wyoming, 29 miles northwest of Sundance. The entrance is off Wyoming Highway 24, 7 miles north of U.S. 14. The drive over paved Wyoming Highway 24 (South Dakota Highway 34) connecting Belle Fourche, South Dakota, and the monument is quite scenic.

Devils Tower was formed millions of years ago when molten materials originating from within the earth cooled and crystallized. Joints in the columns were established when the hot rock cooled and contracted. Some of the columns have since fallen as the joints enlarged by the freezing and thawing of water. These broken columns may be seen piled around the base of the tower. The remainder of the monument is composed of rocks formed through the accumulation of materials on the floors of ancient seas. The prominence of Devils Tower is due to the more rapid erosion of the surrounding rock and to the color difference between the tower's core and base.

For centuries the rock was an important focus of Indian legends. As explorers and pioneers moved westward it became one of their landmarks. The naming of Devils Tower is generally credited to Col. Richard Dodge, who was the commander of a military escort for a U.S. geological survey party.

The monument's visitor center contains exhibits explaining the history and geology of the area. The 3-mile paved road to the visitor

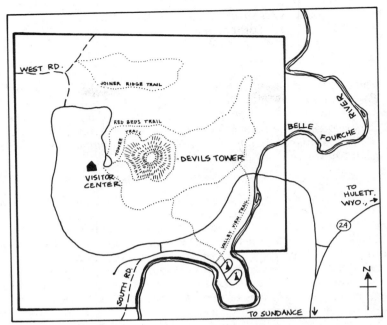

Devils Tower National Monument

center passes through a prairie dog town approximately ½ mile from the east entrance. A number of trails are provided for hiking, including an easy self-guided nature trail (1¼ miles, one hour) that circles the tower and begins at the visitor center. Here the visitor may see a wide variety of animals and birds. A longer 2¾-mile Red Beds Trail is quite scenic and is easiest to hike in a clockwise fashion. A picnic area is near the campground.

Facilities: Three general stores, restaurants, and a post office are located just outside the monument, approximately 2 miles from the campground. Modern restrooms and drinking water are available at the visitor center and at the campground.

Camping: A pleasant campground (fifty-one spaces) located in a grove of cottonwood trees, provides tables, grills, water, and flush toilets. Depending upon the weather, the campground is open with water and restrooms available from approximately May 1 through October. A private campground with hookups and showers is just outside the park entrance.

Fishing: Fishing is permitted in the Belle Fourche River, which cuts through the park and borders the campground. Catches include catfish, bass, and carp. A Wyoming license is required.

FORT LARAMIE NATIONAL HISTORIC SITE
Fort Laramie, WY 82212
(307) 837–2221

Fort Laramie contains 856 acres and was added to the National Park System in 1938 to preserve the site and remaining buildings of an important fur trading and military post of the 1800s. The park is located in eastern Wyoming, 3 miles southwest of the town of Fort Laramie on County Road 160. It is approximately 95 miles from Cheyenne.

The original stockade called Fort William was constructed by two traders in 1834. Two years later it was purchased by a large fur company and soon became one of the major trading centers in the Rockies. By the 1840s, the fur trade had declined but the fort's location on one of the main routes west gave it renewed importance.

In 1849, the post was purchased by the U.S. Government for use as an Army post to protect travelers along the Oregon Trail. Subsequently, Fort Laramie was used as a station for the Pony Express and the Cheyenne–Deadwood Stagecoach and as a staging area for military campaigns against the Plains Indians. By the late 1800s, the importance of the fort had waned, and, by 1890, it was abandoned.

The National Park Service has restored a number of the fort's standing buildings—eight have been refurbished and are open to visitors. A visitor center in the commissary storehouse is open from 7:00 A.M. until 7:00 P.M. during summer. Exhibits on the post's history are provided and park personnel are on hand to answer visitor questions. This park presents an excellent living history program.

Facilities: No food service or lodging is available in the park. Both can be found in the town of Fort Laramie. Water and restrooms are located in the visitor center.

Camping: No camping is permitted in the historic site. The town of Fort Laramie has camping facilities with tables, grills, water, and flush toilets at a small but nice municipal park. Thirteen miles west of Fort Laramie on Highway 26, the town of Gurnsey provides campsites in a city park south of town. Water, electrical hookups, grills, tables, and hot showers are available. Fishing access is provided to the North Platte River which flows through the park.

Fishing: Fishing is permitted in the Laramie River outside the fort's historic zone with a Wyoming License. Catches include catfish, carp, and some trout.

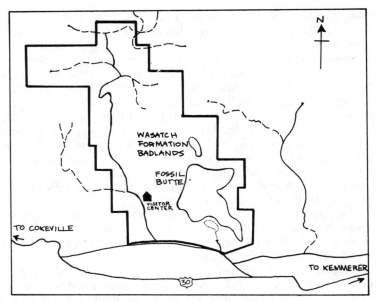

Fossil Butte National Monument

FOSSIL BUTTE NATIONAL MONUMENT
P.O. Box 592
Kemmerer, WY 83101
(307) 877–4455

Fossil Butte contains nearly 8,200 acres. It was established as part of the National Park System in 1972 to preserve the nation's most extensive concentration of fossilized fresh-water fish. Fossil Butte is located in southwestern Wyoming, 11 miles west of Kemmerer via U.S. 30.

For nearly 500 million years, much of the western United States was covered by a huge sea. Then, 70 to 80 million years ago, mountains rose above the sea and immediately began to erode, with sediment filling the surrounding basins. A subsequent uplifting and additional weathering caused red conglomerate, sandstone, and mudstone to be deposited in streambeds.

Fifty-million-year-old fossil specimens found at the butte indicate that the higher elevations were covered with pine, spruce, and fir, while lower parts of surrounding mountains were covered with oak, maple, and hickory. Palms, ferns, and reeds were along the shores. Fossils also show the forests were inhabited by monkeys and horses the size of dogs, while the streams contained crocodiles and turtles.

Several theories are advanced for the pristine fossilization conditions over the life of the lake. One theory attributes the abundance of fish fossils, which are actually found in several layers of sediments, to the stratified nature of the large lakes. The temperate climate created surface waters that were warmer and lighter than the deeper waters. Winds blowing across the lakes created well-oxygenated surface layers that acted as seals for the dense bottom waters that became stagnant and void of oxygen. When the fish that thrived in the warm surface water died and sank to the lake bottoms, there were no scavengers to bother their remains, and the fish were rapidly buried by limestone precipitating out of the water.

The new visitor center, located one mile north on the park road, provides numerous examples of fossils and information about them. Two videos are offered. One presents an orientation to the Fossil Lake deposits and a second displays how fossils are quarried and prepared. A preparation lab permits the visitor to observe and sometimes participate in preparing fossils. A Junior Ranger program that takes about an hour to complete is offered for children. Personnel in the visitor center provide assistance, give hiking information, and lead occasional guided walks. A trail from the visitor center leads to a historic quarry on Fossil Butte. Wayside exhibits describe some of the natural and cultural features of the area. The one-mile Fossil Lake Trail begins at the picnic area and winds through aspen groves and meadows.

Facilities: No food or lodging is available at the monument, but both are at Kemmerer and Cokeville. Restrooms and drinking water are at the visitor center. A picnic area is located three and three-quarter miles beyond the visitor center.
Camping: No camping is permitted in the park.
Fishing: No fishing is available at Fossil Butte.

GRAND TETON NATIONAL PARK;
JOHN D. ROCKEFELLER, JR., MEMORIAL PARKWAY
P.O. Drawer 170
Moose, WY 83012
(307) 733–2880

Grand Teton National Park was established in 1929 and contains more than 310,521 acres of some of America's most impressive mountain landscape. The John D. Rockefeller, Jr., Memorial Parkway contains nearly 24,000 acres and provides a scenic link between Grand Teton and Yellowstone. The parks are located in

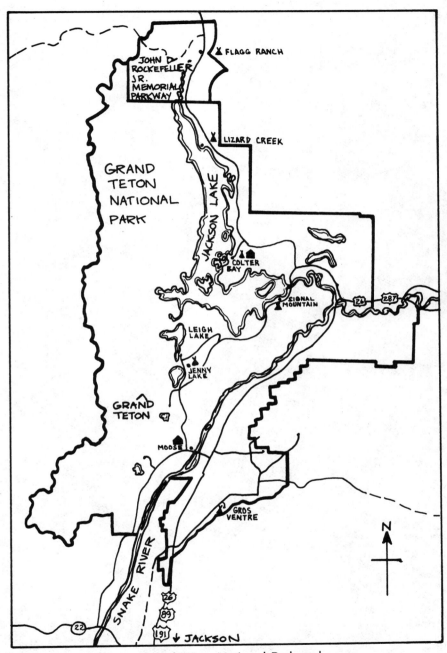

Grand Teton National Park and
John D. Rockefeller, Jr., Memorial Parkway

Grand Teton National Park ▶

*northwestern Wyoming. From Yellowstone and the north, access
is via U.S. 89/287 and from the south via U.S. 26/89. This road
parallels the Teton Range. From the east (Casper and Riverton) the
park is entered on U.S. 26/287.*

The Teton Range rises nearly 7,000 feet above the valley called
Jackson Hole. The steep eastern front is the result of an uplifting that
occurred along a fault zone in the earth's crust. As the uplifting
progressed, the mountains were eroded by wind and water. Later,
glaciers carved the gullies into U-shaped valleys. The rock debris
carried down by the glaciers (now melted) has resulted in natural dams
for lakes at the base of the range.

This spectacular park offers visitors a wide variety of outdoor
activities. Moose Visitor Center (307–733–2880) at the park's south
end is open all year and park personnel are on duty to answer
questions. At the north end of the park, the Colter Bay Visitor Center
(307–543–2467) is open from mid-May through September and offers
audio-visual presentations, map and publication sales, and an Indian
art collection.

Some of the more popular activities are boating, fishing, hiking,
and mountaineering. The Snake River diagonally bisects the valley
portion of the park. A float trip with your own boat (permit required) or
on one of the many concessioner-operated rafts is an exciting experience. No motors are allowed on the Snake. Hand-propelled boats are
permitted on Emma Matilda, Two Ocean, Bradley, Taggart, Leigh,
Bearpaw, and String lakes. Motors of up to 7½ h.p. are allowed on
Jenny Lake, where boat transportation across the lake is available. All
types of boats are permitted on Jackson Lake and concessioner boat
tours operate daily during the summer.

Grand Teton contains more than 200 miles of trails (horses
allowed on many miles of these) including access to the high country.
One of the more popular hikes near Jenny Lake is a half-day trip to
Hidden Falls. Self-guided trails are located at Cascade Canyon, Colter
Bay, Cunningham Cabin, and Menors Ferry. Frequent ranger-guided
hikes are available in the summer, with schedules posted in the park
newspaper. For visitors interested in mountaineering, instruction and
guide service are available during summer months. Climbers must
register with a back-country ranger at Jenny Lake.

Two other relatively popular activities are horse riding and
swimming. Horses may be rented at Colter Bay, Jackson Lake Lodge,
and Jenny Lake. Swimming is possible during late summer in shallow
areas of String, Leigh, and Jackson lakes. Most lakes are quite cold.

During winter months ranger-conducted snowshoe hikes are
available (snowshoes provided) and snowmobiles may be operated in
designated areas. An annual permit is required. Although no downhill

skiing is available in the park, two private ski developments are nearby.

Facilities: A wide assortment of facilities may be found throughout Grand Teton and Rockefeller Parkway. A summary by location is:

Colter Bay: Lodging (cabins, tent village), food (grill, restaurant, snack bar), laundry, showers, service stations, general store, groceries, and marina. Write Grand Teton Lodge Co., Box 240, Moran, WY 83013 (307–543–2811, 307–543–2855).

Flagg Ranch (Rockefeller Parkway): Lodging (motel, cabins), food (cafeteria, snack bar, steak house), package store, service station, gift shop, grocery, float trips, cross-country skiing, and snowmobile rentals. Write Flagg Ranch Village, Box 187, Moran, WY 83013 (800–443–2311, 307–543–2861, or 307–733–8761).

Jackson Lake: Lodging, food, beauty shop, package store, service station, gift shop. Write Grand Teton Lodge Co., Box 240, Moran, WY 83013 (307–543–2811, 307–543–2855).

Jenny Lake: Lodging, food, boat rentals and cruises, grocery. Write Grand Teton Lodge Co., Box 240, Moran, WY 83013 (307–543–2811, 307–543–2855).

Moose: Housekeeping cabins, food (restaurant, snack bar), package store, laundry, service station, canoe rental, grocery store. Write Dornan's, Box 39, Moose, WY 83012 (307–733–2415).

Signal Mountain: Lodging (log cabins, motel unit, housekeeping apartments), food (coffee shop, restaurant), service station, gift shop, marina, grocery store, float trips. Write Signal Mountain Lodge, Box 50, Moran, WY 83013 (307–543–2831, 307–733–5470).

Camping: In Grand Teton, campgrounds with tables, grills, water, and flush toilets are Colter Bay (350 spaces, nine group camps, a concessioner-operated 111-site trailer village, showers, laundry, dump station), Gros Ventre (360 spaces, dump station), Jenny Lake (forty-four spaces for small units and tents only), Lizard Creek (sixty spaces), and Signal Mountain (eighty-six spaces, dump station). Jenny Lake and Signal Mountain generally fill first; Gros Ventre fills last.

In Rockefeller Memorial Parkway, a concessioner trailer village with 175 spaces is located at Flagg Ranch.

Fishing: Jackson Lake offers cutthroat and lake trout. A number of other lakes and many streams contain whitefish, and cutthroat, brook, and rainbow trout. Ice fishing is permitted on Jackson, Leigh, and Jenny lakes and the Snake River is open only for whitefish in winter. A Wyoming fishing license is required.

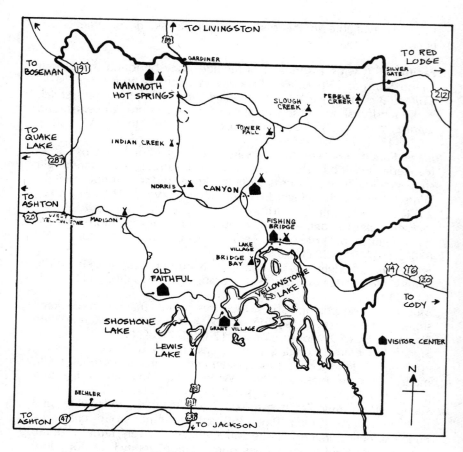

Yellowstone National Park

YELLOWSTONE NATIONAL PARK
P.O. Box 168
Yellowstone National Park, WY 82190
(307) 344–7381

Yellowstone was established in 1872 as America's first national park. It contains nearly 3,400 square miles of lakes, waterfalls, mountains, and some 10,000 geysers and hot springs. The majority of the park is located in the northwestern corner of Wyoming, with overlapping areas in Montana and Idaho. Access is available from all four major directions.

The central portion of Yellowstone is a volcanic plateau with an average elevation of approximately 8,000 feet. On the northwest, north, east, and south this table is surrounded by mountain ranges rising from 2,000 to 4,000 feet above the plateau. The region has been shaped by volcanoes and ice. The volcanic activity began 50 to 55 million years ago and is still evident by the geysers and hot springs drawing heat from the earth's interior. Ice has moved through the park at least three times. In each case, permanent ice on mountains to the north and east quarried rocks and debris as it flowed into the valleys. As the climate warmed and ice melted, lakes and piles of debris were left.

The park contains nearly 300 miles of public roads leading to a seemingly endless supply of scenic areas. Many major attractions are found near the Grand Loop Road, which makes a figure eight in the park's central area. The road's east side provides access to canyons, mountains, and waterfalls, while the west side leads to areas of thermal activity. The most popular of these latter attractions is Old Faithful. Numerous other geysers have predictable eruption times that are posted at Old Faithful Visitor Center and Norris Museum. Norris Geyser Basin is the park's most active thermal area—it has numerous steam vents and hot springs. At Mammoth Hot Springs, hot waters cascade over colored limestone pools. In Lower Geyser Basin, Fountain Paint Pots Trail provides access to more varied hot water phenomena in a concentrated area than any other trail in the park.

Some of Yellowstone's most scenic areas lie along the Yellowstone River. Near Canyon, there are spectacular views of the Grand Canyon of the Yellowstone from Artist Point and Inspiration Point. North of here, a hike to the top of Mt. Washburn ends with a view of the entire park.

Other activities in Yellowstone include horseback trips from Canyon, Tower-Roosevelt, and Mammoth, and stagecoach rides on a regular schedule at Roosevelt. Bus tours leave from hotels and lodges,

and boat tours leave regularly from Bridge Bay. Power boating is permitted only on open areas of Yellowstone Lake and on Lewis Lake (includes boat launch). All boaters are required to purchase permits for motorized and non-motorized boats. For most, swimming is an uncomfortable experience because of Yellowstone's cold lakes and streams.

Winter activities are concentrated at Mammoth and Old Faithful, and U.S. 89 to the north entrance is open year round for automobiles. The north entrance to Cooke City, Montana, is also open to automobiles year round. Several trails are available for cross-country skiing, and major roadways are open to snowmobiles from December through mid-March. Snowmobiles may be rented at Mammoth, Gardiner, West Yellowstone, and Flagg Ranch, and tours in enclosed snowmobiles are available via TW Services, Inc. No downhill skiing is possible in the park, but several ski developments are located nearby.

Facilities: Yellowstone is one of the more developed parks administered by the National Park Service. As such, visitors can find nearly anything at some location inside its borders. For lodging information and reservations write TW Services, Inc., Yellowstone National Park, WY 82190 (307–344–7311).

Bridge Bay: Boat rental.

Canyon: Food service, gasoline station, grocery, laundry, lodging, photo shop, post office, visitor center, nurse on duty.

Fishing Bridge/Lake Area: Food service, gasoline station, grocery, hospital, laundry, lodging, marina, photo shop, post office, propane service, visitor center.

Grant: Food service, gasoline station, laundry, lodging, post office, propane service, visitor center, nurse on duty.

Mammoth: Food service, gasoline station, grocery, lodging, medical clinic, photo shop, post office, visitor center.

Old Faithful: Food service, gasoline station, grocery, lodging, photo shop, medical clinic, post office, propane service, visitor center.

Tower-Roosevelt: Food service, gasoline, grocery, lodging.

Camping: Campgrounds with tables, fireplaces, dump stations, and flush toilets are located at Bridge Bay (420 spaces, showers), Canyon (280 spaces, hard-sided units only, showers), Grant Village (403 spaces, showers), Madison (292 spaces, no showers), Mammoth (eighty-seven spaces, no dump station, no showers), and Norris (116 spaces, no dump station, no showers). Less developed campgrounds are located at Indian Creek (seventy-five spaces), Lewis Lake (eighty-five spaces), Pebble Creek (thirty-six spaces), Slough Creek (twenty-nine spaces, no water), and Tower Falls (thirty-two spaces). Only Mammoth is open all year. All campgrounds are first come, first served except for Bridge Bay, which has a partial reservation system. Write Ticketron, P.O. Box 617516, Chicago, IL 60661 (800–452–1111).

A concessioner-operated trailer park at Fishing Bridge offers hook-ups and is open from mid-June to early September. For information or reservations use the address and phone number to TW Services under facilities section.

Fishing: Yellowstone Lake is noted for its native Yellowstone cutthroat trout. Other park streams and lakes contain rainbow, brook, brown, cutthroat, and lake trout and grayling and whitefish. Fishing regulations vary widely throughout the park—some waters are closed, others are restricted to fly fishing, and some are open only for catch and release. No license is required, but a free permit with regulations is necessary.

National Park Areas
Facilities and Activities Chart

This chart presents current information on visitor services in the areas described in this book. Generally, the services listed are those in the parks themselves. Additional services are usually available in nearby cities. Parks permitting activities such as horseback riding or boating do not necessarily rent equipment. Many parks curtail service in their off-season. A few park areas are not listed here because they do not have visitor services.

Facilities and Activities

Column headings (left to right):
Entrance Fee · Visitor Center · Museum/Exhibit · NPS Guided Tour · Self-guiding Tour/Trail · Guide for Hire · Picnic Area · Campground · Group Campsite · Backcountry Use Permits · Hiking · Mountain Climbing · Horseback Riding · Swimming · Bathhouse · Boating · Boat Rental · Boat Ramp · Fishing · Hunting · Off-road Vehicle Trail · Bicycle Trail · Snowmobile Route · Cross-country Ski Trail · Cabin Rental · Hotel, Motel, Lodge · Groceries, Ice · Restaurant, Snacks · Campsites · Handicap Access Restrooms · Handicap Access Visitor Center

Park	EF	VC	M/E	NPS	SG	GfH	PA	CG	GC	BUP	Hik	MC	HR	Sw	BH	Bo	BR	BRa	Fi	Hu	ORV	BT	SR	XC	CR	HML	GI	RS	Cmp	HA-R	HA-VC
ALASKA																															
Aniakchak Natl. Monument and Preserve, P.O. Box 7, King Salmon, AK 99613										●									●	●											
Bering Land Bridge Natl. Preserve, P.O. Box 220, Nome, AK 99762										●									●	●											
Cape Krusenstern Natl. Monument, P.O. Box 1029, Kotzebue, AK 99752			●							●									●	●			●								
Denali Natl. Park and Preserve, P.O. Box 9, McKinley Park, AK 99755	●	●	●	●	●		●	●		●	●	●				●			●	●					●	●	●	●	●	●	●
Gates of the Arctic Natl. Park and Preserve, P.O. Box 74680, Fairbanks, AK 99707										●	●	●							●	●											
Glacier Bay Natl. Park and Preserve, Gustavus, AK 99826		●	●	●		●	●	●		●	●					●			●							●	●	●			
Katmai Natl. Park and Preserve, P.O. Box 7, King Salmon, AK 99613		●	●	●	●	●		●		●	●					●	●	●	●						●	●	●	●		●	●
Kenai Fjords Natl. Park, P.O. Box 1727, Seward, AK 99664		●	●		●		●	●		●	●	●				●			●						●					●	●
Klondike Gold Rush Natl. Historical Park, P.O. Box 517, Skagway, AK 99840 (See also Wash.)		●	●		●						●																			●	●
Kobuk Valley Natl. Park, P.O. Box 1029, Kotzebue, AK 99752		●								●	●					●			●	●											
Lake Clark Natl. Park and Preserve, 701 C St., P.O. Box 61, Anchorage, AK 99513										●	●	●				●			●	●					●	●					
Noatak Natl. Preserve, P.O. Box 1029, Kotzebue, AK 99752		●			●					●	●					●			●	●											
Sitka Natl. Historical Park, P.O. Box 738, Sitka, AK 99835		●	●	●	●		●				●											●								●	●
Wrangell-St. Elias Natl. Park and Preserve, P.O. Box 29, Glennallen, AK 99588		●	●		●		●		●	●	●	●				●			●	●		●			●	●	●	●		●	●
Yukon-Charley Rivers Natl. Preserve, P.O. Box 64, Eagle, AK 99738		●								●	●					●			●	●					●						
ARIZONA																															
Canyon de Chelly Natl. Monument, P.O. Box 588, Chinle, AZ 86503		●	●	●	●	●	●	●	●	●	●															●	●	●	●	●	●
Casa Grande Ruins Natl. Monument, P.O. Box 518, Coolidge, AZ 85228	●	●	●	●	●		●																							●	●
Chiricahua Natl. Monument, Dos Cabezas Route, Box 6500, Wilcox, AZ 85643	●	●	●	●	●		●	●	●	●	●																		●	●	●
Coronado Natl. Memorial, R.R. 2, Box 126, Hereford, AZ 85615		●	●		●		●			●	●																			●	●
Fort Bowie Natl. Historic Site, P.O. Box 158, Bowie, AZ 85605		●	●		●		●				●																				
Grand Canyon Natl. Park, P.O. Box 129, Grand Canyon, AZ 86023	●	●	●	●	●	●	●	●	●	●	●		●						●					●		●	●	●	●	●	●
Hubbell Trading Post Natl. Historic Site, P.O. Box 150, Ganado, AZ 86505		●	●	●	●		●																							●	●

ARIZONA *(continued)*

Montezuma Castle Natl. Monument, P.O. Box 219, Camp Verde, AZ 86322

Navajo Natl. Monument, H.C. 71, Box 3, Tonalea, AZ 86044-9704

Organ Pipe Cactus Natl. Monument, Rt. 1, Box 100, Ajo, AZ 85321

Petrified Forest Natl. Park, Petrified Forest Natl. Park, AZ 86028

Pipe Spring Natl. Monument, Moccasin, AZ 86022

Saguaro Natl. Monument, 3693 S. Old Spanish Trail, Tucson, AZ 85730-5699

Sunset Crater Volcano Natl. Monument, Rt. 3, Box 149, Flagstaff, AZ 86004

Tonto Natl. Monument, P.O. Box 707, Roosevelt, AZ 85545

Tumacacori Natl. Historical Park, P.O. Box 67, Tumacacori, AZ 85640

Tuzigoot Natl. Monument, Clarkdale, AZ 86324

Walnut Canyon Natl. Monument, Walnut Canyon Rd., Flagstaff, AZ 86004-9705

Wupatki Natl. Monument, H.C. 33, Box 444A, Flagstaff, AZ 86004

ARKANSAS

Arkansas Post Natl. Memorial, Rt. 1, Box 16, Gillett, AR 72055

Buffalo Natl. River, P.O. Box 1173, Harrison, AR 72601

Fort Smith Natl. Historic Site, P.O. Box 1406, Fort Smith, AR 72902

Hot Springs Natl. Park, P.O. Box 1860, Hot Springs, AR 71902

Pea Ridge Natl. Military Park, Pea Ridge, AR 72751

CALIFORNIA

Cabrillo Natl. Monument, P.O. Box 6670, San Diego, CA 92106

Channel Islands Natl. Park, 1901 Spinnaker Dr., Ventura, CA 93001

Death Valley Natl. Monument (Calif., Nev.), Death Valley, CA 92328

Devils Postpile Natl. Monument, c/o Sequoia and Kings Canyon Natl. Parks, Three Rivers, CA 93271

Fort Point Natl. Historic Site, P.O. Box 29333, Presidio of San Francisco, CA 94129

Golden Gate Natl. Recreation Area, Fort Mason, Bldg. 201, San Francisco, CA 94123

John Muir Natl. Historic Site, 4202 Alhambra Ave., Martinez, CA 94553

CALIFORNIA (continued)

Park	Entrance Fee	Visitor Center	Museum/Exhibit	NPS Guided Tour	Self-guiding Tour/Trail	Guide for Hire	Picnic Area	Campground	Group Campsite	Backcountry Use Permits	Hiking	Mountain Climbing	Horseback Riding	Swimming	Bathhouse	Boating	Boat Rental	Boat Ramp	Fishing	Hunting	Off-road Vehicle Trail	Bicycle Trail	Snowmobile Route	Cross-country Ski Trail	Cabin Rental	Hotel, Motel, Lodge	Groceries, Ice	Restaurant, Snacks	Campsites	Restrooms	Visitor Center
Joshua Tree Natl. Monument, 74485 National Monument Dr., Twentynine Palms, CA 92277	●	●	●		●		●	●	●	●	●	●																	●	●	●
Kings Canyon Natl. Park, Three Rivers, CA 93271	●	●	●	●	●		●	●	●	●	●	●	●						●				●	●		●	●	●	●	●	●
Lassen Volcanic Natl. Park, P.O. Box 100, Mineral, CA 96063	●	●	●	●	●		●	●	●	●	●	●	●			●			●				●	●		●	●	●	●	●	●
Lava Beds Natl. Monument, P.O. Box 867, Tulelake, CA 96134	●	●	●	●	●		●	●		●	●	●														●			●	●	●
Muir Woods Natl. Monument, Mill Valley, CA 94941		●	●		●						●																	●		●	●
Pinnacles Natl. Monument, Paicines, CA 95043	●	●	●		●		●	●	●	●	●	●																	●	●	●
Point Reyes Natl. Seashore, Point Reyes, CA 94956		●	●	●	●		●	●	●	●	●		●						●			●							●	●	●
Redwood Natl. Park, 1111 Second St., Crescent City, CA 95531		●	●		●		●	●	●	●	●		●	●					●		●								●	●	●
Santa Monica Mountains Natl. Recreation Area, 22900 Ventura Blvd., Suite 140, Woodland Hills, CA 91364		●	●	●	●		●	●			●		●	●					●										●	●	●
Sequoia Natl. Park, Three Rivers, CA 93271	●	●	●	●	●		●	●	●	●	●	●	●						●				●	●	●	●	●	●	●	●	●
Whiskeytown-Shasta-Trinity Natl. Recreation Area, P.O. Box 188, Whiskeytown, CA 96095		●	●		●		●	●	●		●		●	●		●	●	●	●	●					●		●	●	●	●	●
Yosemite Natl. Park, P.O. Box 577, Yosemite Natl. Park, CA 95389	●	●	●	●	●		●	●	●	●	●	●	●	●			●		●				●	●	●	●	●	●	●	●	●

COLORADO

Park	Entrance Fee	Visitor Center	Museum/Exhibit	NPS Guided Tour	Self-guiding Tour/Trail	Guide for Hire	Picnic Area	Campground	Group Campsite	Backcountry Use Permits	Hiking	Mountain Climbing	Horseback Riding	Swimming	Bathhouse	Boating	Boat Rental	Boat Ramp	Fishing	Hunting	Off-road Vehicle Trail	Bicycle Trail	Snowmobile Route	Cross-country Ski Trail	Cabin Rental	Hotel, Motel, Lodge	Groceries, Ice	Restaurant, Snacks	Campsites	Restrooms	Visitor Center
Bent's Old Fort Natl. Historic Site, 35110 Highway 194 East, La Junta, CO 81050-9523	●	●	●	●	●		●				●																	●		●	●
Black Canyon of the Gunnison Natl. Monument, P.O. Box 1648, Montrose, CO 81402	●	●	●		●		●	●		●	●	●										●							●	●	●
Colorado Natl. Monument, Fruita, CO 81521	●	●	●		●		●	●		●	●											●							●	●	●
Curecanti Natl. Recreation Area, 102 Elk Creek, Gunnison, CO 81230		●	●	●	●		●	●			●			●		●	●	●	●								●		●	●	●
Dinosaur Natl. Monument (Colo., Utah), P.O. Box 210, Dinosaur, CO 81610	●	●	●	●	●		●	●		●	●		●			●		●	●										●	●	●
Florissant Fossil Beds Natl. Monument, P.O. Box 185, Florissant, CO 80816	●	●	●	●	●		●				●													●						●	●
Great Sand Dunes Natl. Monument, Mosca, CO 81146	●	●	●		●		●	●		●	●																		●	●	●
Hovenweep Natl. Monument (Colo., Utah), c/o Mesa Verde Natl. Park, Mesa Verde Natl. Park, CO 81330		●			●			●			●																		●	●	
Mesa Verde Natl. Park, Mesa Verde Natl. Park, CO 81330	●	●	●	●	●		●	●			●															●	●	●	●	●	●
Rocky Mountain Natl. Park, Estes Park, CO 80517	●	●	●	●	●		●	●	●	●	●	●							●					●					●	●	●

GUAM

War in the Pacific Natl. Historical Park, P.O. Box FA, Agana, GU 96910

HAWAII

Haleakala Natl. Park, P.O. Box 369, Makawao, HI 96768

Hawaii Volcanoes Natl. Park, Hawaii Natl. Park, HI 96718

Pu'uhonua o Honaunau Natl. Historical Park, P.O. Box 128, Honaunau, Kona, HI 96726

Puukohola Heiau Natl. Historic Site, P.O. Box 4963, Kawaihae, HI 96743

USS *Arizona* Memorial, 1 Arizona Memorial Place, Honolulu, HI 96818

IDAHO

Craters of the Moon Natl. Monument, P.O. Box 29, Arco, ID 83213

Nez Perce Natl. Historical Park, P.O. Box 93, Spalding, ID 83551

IOWA

Effigy Mounds Natl. Monument, R.R. 1, Box 25A, Harpers Ferry, IA 52146

Herbert Hoover Natl. Historic Site, P.O. Box 607, West Branch, IA 52358

KANSAS

Fort Larned Natl. Historic Site, Rte. 3, Larned, KS 67550

Fort Scott Natl. Historic Site, Old Fort Blvd., Fort Scott, KS 66701

LOUISIANA

Jean Lafitte Natl. Historical Park and Preserve, 423 Canal St., Room 210, New Orleans, LA 70130-2341

MINNESOTA

Grand Portage Natl. Monument, P.O. Box 666, Grand Marais, MN 55604

Pipestone Natl. Monument, P.O. Box 727, Pipestone, MN 56164

Voyageurs Natl. Park, P.O. Box 50, International Falls, MN 56649

MISSOURI

George Washington Carver Natl. Monument, P.O. Box 38, Diamond, MO 64840

Harry S Truman Natl. Historic Site, 223 N. Main St., Independence, MO 64050

Handicap Access columns: Visitor Center, Restrooms, Campsites

Facility/Activity	Entrance Fee	Visitor Center	Museum/Exhibit	NPS Guided Tour	Self-guiding Tour/Trail	Guide for Hire	Picnic Area	Campground	Group Campsite	Backcountry Use Permits	Hiking	Mountain Climbing	Horseback Riding	Swimming	Bathhouse	Boating	Boat Rental	Boat Ramp	Fishing	Hunting	Off-road Vehicle Trail	Bicycle Trail	Snowmobile Route	Cross-country Ski Trail	Cabin Rental	Hotel, Motel, Lodge	Groceries, Ice	Restaurant, Snacks	Campsites (H)	Restrooms (H)	Visitor Center (H)
MISSOURI (continued)																															
Jefferson Natl. Expansion Memorial, 11 North 4th St., St. Louis, MO 63102	●	●	●	●	●																									●	●
Ozark Natl. Scenic Riverways, P.O. Box 490, Van Buren, MO 63965		●	●		●		●	●			●		●	●		●	●	●	●	●					●	●	●	●	●	●	
Wilson's Creek Natl. Battlefield, Postal Drawer C, Republic, MO 65738	●	●	●		●		●				●		●									●								●	●
MONTANA																															
Big Hole Natl. Battlefield, P.O. Box 237, Wisdom, MT 59761	●	●	●	●	●		●				●								●											●	●
Bighorn Canyon Natl. Recreation Area (Mont., Wyo.), P.O. Box 458, Fort Smith, MT 59035		●	●	●	●		●	●			●		●	●		●		●	●	●									●	●	●
Custer Battlefield Natl. Monument, P.O. Box 39, Crow Agency, MT 59022	●	●	●	●	●						●																			●	●
Glacier Natl. Park, West Glacier, MT 59936	●	●	●	●	●		●	●		●	●	●	●			●		●	●					●	●	●	●	●	●	●	●
Grant-Kohrs Ranch Natl. Historic Site, P.O. Box 790, Deer Lodge, MT 59722		●	●	●	●																									●	●
NEBRASKA																															
Agate Fossil Beds Natl. Monument, P. O. Box 427, Gering, NE 69341		●	●		●		●				●								●											●	●
Homestead Natl. Monument of America, Rt. 3, Box 47, Beatrice, NE 68310		●	●		●		●				●											●		●						●	●
Scotts Bluff Natl. Monument, P.O. Box 427, Gering, NE 69341	●	●	●		●		●				●								●		●									●	●
NEVADA																															
Great Basin Natl. Park, Baker, NV 89311		●	●	●	●		●	●	●	●	●	●	●						●	●			●						●	●	●
Lake Mead Natl. Recreational Area (Nev., Ariz.), 601 Nevada Highway, Boulder City, NV 89005-2426		●	●		●		●	●	●		●		●	●		●	●	●	●	●					●	●	●	●	●	●	●
NEW MEXICO																															
Aztec Ruins Natl. Monument, P.O. Box 640, Aztec, NM 87410	●	●	●	●	●		●			●	●																			●	●
Bandelier Natl. Monument, Los Alamos, NM 87544	●	●	●		●		●	●	●	●	●								●									●	●	●	●
Capulin Mountain Natl. Monument, Capulin, NM 88414	●	●	●		●		●				●																			●	●
Carlsbad Caverns Natl. Park, 3225 National Parks Highway, Carlsbad, NM 88220	●	●	●	●	●		●			●	●																●	●		●	●
Chaco Culture Natl. Historical Park, Star Route 4, Box 6500, Bloomfield, NM 87413	●	●	●		●		●	●	●	●	●											●							●	●	●
El Malpais Natl. Monument, c/o Southwest Regional Office, NPS, P.O. Box 728, Santa Fe, NM 87504	●																														

NEW MEXICO (continued)

Site	1	2	3	4	5	6	7	8	9	10	11	12	13	14	15	16	17	18	19	20	21	22	23	24	25
El Morro Natl. Monument, Ramah, NM 87321	•	•	•		•		•	•			•												•	•	•
Fort Union Natl. Monument, Watrous, NM 87753	•	•	•		•		•																	•	•
Gila Cliff Dwellings Natl. Monument, Rt. 11, Box 100, Silver City, NM 88061		•	•		•									•										•	•
Pecos Natl. Historical Park, P.O. Drawer 11, Pecos, NM 87552	•	•	•	•	•		•																	•	•
Salinas Pueblo Missions National Monument, P.O. Box 496, Mountainair, NM 87036	•	•	•	•	•		•																	•	•
White Sands Natl. Monument, P.O. Box 458, Alamogordo, NM 88310	•	•	•	•	•		•			•	•													•	•

NORTH DAKOTA

Site	1	2	3	4	5	6	7	8	9	10	11	12	13	14	15	16	17	18	19	20	21	22	23	24	25
Fort Union Trading Post Natl. Historic Site (N. Dak., Mont.), Buford Route, Williston, ND 55801		•	•	•	•				•					•				•						•	•
Knife River Indian Villages Natl. Historic Site, R.R. 1, Box 168, Stanton, ND 58571		•	•	•	•		•		•	•				•				•						•	•
Theodore Roosevelt Natl. Park, P.O. Box 7, Medora, ND 58645	•	•	•	•	•		•	•	•	•	•		•		•		•			•				•	•

OKLAHOMA

Site	1	2	3	4	5	6	7	8	9	10	11	12	13	14	15	16	17	18	19	20	21	22	23	24	25
Chickasaw Natl. Recreation Area, P.O. Box 201, Sulphur, OK 73086		•	•	•	•		•	•	•		•		•		•		•	•	•				•	•	•

OREGON

Site	1	2	3	4	5	6	7	8	9	10	11	12	13	14	15	16	17	18	19	20	21	22	23	24	25
Crater Lake Natl. Park, P.O. Box 7, Crater Lake, OR 97604	•	•	•	•	•		•	•			•				•	•	•	•	•	•	•	•	•	•	•
Fort Clatsop Nat. Memorial, Rt. 3, Box 604-FC, Astoria, OR 97103	•	•	•	•	•		•																	•	•
John Day Fossil Beds Natl. Monument, 420 W. Main St., John Day, OR 97845		•	•		•		•				•								•		•		•	•	•
Oregon Caves Natl. Monument, 19000 Caves Highway, Cave Junction, OR 97523			•				•												•		•		•		

SOUTH DAKOTA

Site	1	2	3	4	5	6	7	8	9	10	11	12	13	14	15	16	17	18	19	20	21	22	23	24	25
Badlands Natl. Park, P.O. Box 6, Interior, SD 57750	•	•	•	•	•		•	•	•		•							•			•				•
Jewel Cave Natl. Monument, R.R. 1, Box 60AA, Custer, SD 57730		•	•	•			•																	•	•
Mount Rushmore Natl. Memorial, P.O. Box 268, Keystone, SD 57751		•	•																		•			•	•
Wind Cave Natl. Park, Hot Springs, SD 57747		•	•	•	•		•	•	•	•	•										•	•	•	•	•

TEXAS

Site	1	2	3	4	5	6	7	8	9	10	11	12	13	14	15	16	17	18	19	20	21	22	23	24	25
Alibates Flint Quarries Natl. Monument, c/o Lake Meredith Recreation Area, P.O. Box 1438, Fritch, TX 79036		•	•																						
Amistad National Recreation Area, P.O. Box 420367, Del Rio, TX 78842-0367				•	•	•	•	•		•	•	•	•	•	•	•	•				•	•	•	•	
Big Bend Natl. Park, Big Bend Natl. Park, TX 79834	•	•	•	•	•		•	•	•	•	•		•		•		•			•	•	•		•	•

TEXAS *(continued)*

Column headers (left to right):
Entrance Fee · Visitor Center · Museum/Exhibit · NPS Guided Tour · Self-guiding Tour/Trail · Guide for Hire · Picnic Area · Campground · Group Campsite · Backcountry Use Permits · Hiking · Mountain Climbing · Horseback Riding · Swimming · Bathhouse · Boating · Boat Rental · Boat Ramp · Fishing · Hunting · Off-road Vehicle Trail · Bicycle Trail · Snowmobile Route · Cross-country Ski Trail · Cabin Rental · Hotel, Motel, Lodge · Groceries, Ice · Restaurant, Snacks · Campsites (Handicap Access) · Restrooms (Handicap Access) · Visitor Center (Handicap Access)

Park	Entr. Fee	Visitor Ctr	Museum/Exhibit	NPS Guided Tour	Self-guiding	Guide for Hire	Picnic Area	Campground	Group Campsite	Backcountry Permit	Hiking	Mtn Climbing	Horseback	Swimming	Bathhouse	Boating	Boat Rental	Boat Ramp	Fishing	Hunting	Off-road Veh.	Bicycle Trail	Snowmobile	X-C Ski	Cabin Rental	Hotel/Lodge	Groceries	Restaurant	HA Campsites	HA Restrooms	HA Visitor Ctr
Big Thicket Natl. Preserve, 3785 Milam, Beaumont, TX 77701		●	●	●	●					●	●								●	●										●	●
Chamizal Natl. Memorial, c/o Federal Building, 700 E. San Antonio, Suite D-301, El Paso, TX 79901		●	●	●	●		●																							●	●
Fort Davis Natl. Historic Site, P.O. Box 1456, Fort Davis, TX 79734	●	●	●	●	●		●				●																			●	●
Guadalupe Mountains Natl. Park, H.C. 60, Box 400, Salt Flat, TX 79847-9400		●	●		●		●	●	●	●	●		●																●	●	●
Lake Meredith National Recreation Area, P.O. Box 1438, Fritch, TX 79036		●			●		●	●						●		●	●	●	●	●	●								●	●	●
Lyndon B. Johnson Natl. Historical Park, P.O. Box 329, Johnson City, TX 78636		●	●	●	●		●							●					●							●				●	●
Padre Island Natl. Seashore, 9405 S. Padre Island Dr., Corpus Christi, TX 78418-5597	●	●	●		●		●	●						●		●		●	●		●						●	●	●	●	●
San Antonio Missions Natl. Historical Park, 2202 Roosevelt Ave., San Antonio, TX 78210-4919		●	●	●	●						●											●								●	●

UTAH

Park	Entr. Fee	Visitor Ctr	Museum/Exhibit	NPS Guided Tour	Self-guiding	Guide for Hire	Picnic Area	Campground	Group Campsite	Backcountry Permit	Hiking	Mtn Climbing	Horseback	Swimming	Bathhouse	Boating	Boat Rental	Boat Ramp	Fishing	Hunting	Off-road Veh.	Bicycle Trail	Snowmobile	X-C Ski	Cabin Rental	Hotel/Lodge	Groceries	Restaurant	HA Campsites	HA Restrooms	HA Visitor Ctr
Arches Natl. Park, P.O. Box 907, Moab, UT 84532	●	●	●	●	●		●	●	●	●	●	●										●							●	●	●
Bryce Canyon Natl. Park, Bryce Canyon, UT 84717	●	●	●	●	●		●	●	●	●	●		●										●	●		●	●	●	●	●	●
Canyonlands Natl. Park, 125 West 200 South, Moab, UT 84532	●	●	●	●	●		●	●	●	●	●	●				●					●	●								●	●
Capitol Reef Natl. Park, Torrey, UT 84775	●	●	●	●	●		●	●	●	●	●	●	●						●											●	●
Cedar Breaks Natl. Monument, P.O. Box 749, Cedar City, UT 84720	●	●	●	●	●		●	●			●											●	●							●	●
Glen Canyon Natl. Recreation Area (Utah, Ariz.), P.O. Box 1507, Page, AZ 86040	●	●	●	●	●		●	●	●	●	●		●	●	●	●	●	●	●						●	●	●	●	●	●	●
Golden Spike Natl. Historic Site, P.O. Box W, Brigham City, UT 84302	●	●	●	●	●		●				●																			●	●
Natural Bridges Natl. Monument, Box 1, Lake Powell, UT 84533	●	●	●		●		●	●			●											●								●	●
Rainbow Bridge Natl. Monument, c/o Glen Canyon Natl. Recreation Area, P.O. Box 1507, Page, AZ 86040					●						●					●		●													
Timpanogos Cave Natl. Monument, R.R. 3, Box 200, American Fork, UT 84003	●	●	●	●	●		●				●																			●	●
Zion Natl. Park, Springdale, UT 84767-1099	●	●	●	●	●		●	●	●	●	●	●	●						●			●				●	●	●	●	●	●

WASHINGTON

Park	Entr. Fee	Visitor Ctr	Museum/Exhibit	NPS Guided Tour	Self-guiding	Guide for Hire	Picnic Area	Campground	Group Campsite	Backcountry Permit	Hiking	Mtn Climbing	Horseback	Swimming	Bathhouse	Boating	Boat Rental	Boat Ramp	Fishing	Hunting	Off-road Veh.	Bicycle Trail	Snowmobile	X-C Ski	Cabin Rental	Hotel/Lodge	Groceries	Restaurant	HA Campsites	HA Restrooms	HA Visitor Ctr
Coulee Dam Natl. Recreation Area, P.O. Box 37, Coulee Dam, WA 99116		●	●	●	●		●	●			●			●		●	●	●	●								●	●	●	●	●
Ebey's Landing Natl. Historical Reserve, P.O. Box 774, 23 Front St., Coupeville, WA 98239											●			●		●		●	●			●	●	●		●	●	●	●	●	●

WASHINGTON (continued)

Site	1	2	3	4	5	6	7	8	9	10	11	12	13	14	15	16	17	18	19	20	21	22	23	24	25	26	27	28	29	30
Fort Vancouver Natl. Historic Site, 612 E. Reserve St., Vancouver, WA 98661-3897	•	•	•	•			•																						•	•
Klondike Gold Rush Natl. Historical Park, 117 S. Main St., Seattle, WA 98104 (See also Alaska)		•	•																										•	•
Lake Chelan Natl. Recreation Area, 2105 Highway 20, Sedro Woolley, WA 98284		•		•	•		•	•	•	•	•	•	•			•	•		•	•				•	•	•	•		•	•
Mount Rainier Natl. Park, Tahoma Woods, Star Route, Ashford, WA 98304	•	•	•	•	•	•	•	•	•	•					•			•	•		•	•		•	•	•			•	•
North Cascades Natl. Park, 2105 Highway 20, Sedro Woolley, WA 98284							•	•	•	•	•				•															
Olympic Natl. Park, 600 E. Park Ave., Port Angeles, WA 98362	•	•	•	•	•	•	•	•	•	•	•	•	•	•	•	•	•	•				•	•	•	•	•	•	•	•	•
Ross Lake Natl. Recreation Area, 2105 Highway 20, Sedro Woolley, WA 98284			•	•		•	•	•	•	•	•			•	•	•	•		•		•			•	•	•	•		•	
San Juan Island Natl. Historical Park, P.O. Box 429, Friday Harbor, WA 98250		•	•	•	•		•			•																			•	•
Whitman Mission Natl. Historic Site, Rt. 2, Box 247, Walla Walla, WA 99362	•	•	•			•		•																					•	•

WYOMING

Site	1	2	3	4	5	6	7	8	9	10	11	12	13	14	15	16	17	18	19	20	21	22	23	24	25	26	27	28	29	30
Devils Tower Natl. Monument, Devils Tower, WY 82714	•	•	•	•	•		•	•	•		•	•				•													•	•
Fort Laramie Natl. Historic Site, Fort Laramie, WY 82212	•	•	•	•	•		•									•													•	•
Fossil Butte Natl. Monument, P.O. Box 527, Kemmerer, WY 83101		•	•	•	•				•		•																			
Grand Teton Natl. Park, P.O. Drawer 170, Moose, WY 83012	•	•	•	•	•	•	•	•	•	•	•	•	•	•		•	•	•	•			•	•	•	•	•	•	•	•	•
John D. Rockefeller, Jr., Memorial Parkway, c/o Grand Teton Natl. Park, P.O. Drawer 170, Moose, WY 83012			•	•	•		•		•	•		•		•		•	•				•	•	•	•	•	•	•		•	•
Yellowstone Natl. Park (Wyo., Idaho, Mont.), P.O. Box 168, Yellowstone Natl. Park, WY 82190	•	•	•	•	•	•	•	•	•	•	•		•		•	•	•	•	•			•	•	•	•	•	•	•	•	•